Vegetable Gardening in the Midwest

C.E. Voigt   J.S. Vandemark

Cooperative Extension Service
College of Agriculture
University of Illinois at Urbana-Champaign
Circular 1331

This publication updates and expands C1150 Vegetable Gardening for Illinois, 1978, by J.S. Vandemark and J.W. Courter, with contributing authors B.J. Jacobsen and Roscoe Randell; C1150 art by Paula Wheeler and Krista Molter.

Issued in furtherance of Cooperative Extension Work, Acts of May 8 and June 30, 1914, in cooperation with the U.S. Department of Agriculture. Donald L. Uchtmann, Director, Cooperative Extension Service, University of Illinois at Urbana-Champaign. The Cooperative Extension Service provides equal opportunities in programs and employment.

The information provided in this publication is for educational purposes only. References to commercial products or trade names do not constitute an endorsement by the University of Illinois and do not imply discrimination against other similar products. Nomenclature is based on *Hortus Third: A Concise Dictionary of Plants Cultivated in the United States,* revised and expanded by the staff of the Liberty Hyde Bailey Hortorium, Cornell University; New York: Macmillan Publishing Company, 1976.

Credits: Mary H. Overmier, editor, and Linda Brown, designer. Cover photo by David Riecks; pages 15, 23, 33, 49, 131, and 147, David Riecks; pages 1 and 43, Stephen Hunts; other, file photos, Information Services, Office of Agricultural Communications and Education. Additional drawings for the 1995 edition: pages 22 and 124, Tim Stiles; maps, page 26, Steven E. Hollinger, State Water Survey; other, Linda Brown. Printed by UIUC Office of Printing Services.

ISBN 1-883097-05-3 (casebound)   500-87239-mo-3/95

ISBN 1-883097-06-1 (softcover)   10M-8723-mo-3/95

Contents

Preface   v

Planning the Garden   1

Choosing the Best Location   4
Raised Beds   5
Container Gardens   9
Selecting Vegetables   11
Seeds, Plants, Equipment, and Supplies   12

Preparing the Garden   15

Improving Soil Tilth   17
Fertilizing the Soil   19
Plowing and Preparing the Seedbed   21

Planting the Garden   23

When to Plant   25
How to Plant   27
Floating Row Covers   32

Caring for the Garden   33

Cultivation   35
Mulching   35
Watering   37
Controlling Garden Pests   38

Starting Plants at Home   43

Growing Media   45
Pasteurizing the Soil   45
Sowing Seeds   45
Temperature   45
Watering and Fertilizing   46
Light   46
Growing Time   47

Major Vegetables   49

Asparagus   51
Bean   53
Beet   56
Broccoli   57

Brussels Sprouts   59
Cabbage   60
Carrot   63
Cauliflower   64
Celery   66
Chard   67
Chinese Cabbage   68
Collard   69
Corn, Sweet   70
Cucumber   75
Eggplant   77
Endive-Escarole   79
Jerusalem Artichoke   80
Kale   81
Kohlrabi   82
Leek   83
Lettuce   84
Muskmelon   86
Mustard   88
Okra   88
Onion   89
Parsley   93
Parsnip   94
Pea   95
Pepper   97
Potato   101
Pumpkin   103
Radish   107
Rhubarb   108
Salsify   110
Spinach   110
Squash, Summer   112
Squash, Winter   116
Sweet Potato   118
Tomato   120
Turnip-Rutabaga   127
Watermelon   129

Minor Vegetables   131

Amaranth Greens   133
Arugula   133
Bean   133

Burdock 135
Celeriac 136
Chicory 136
Dandelion 137
Garden Cress 137
Garden Huckleberry 137
Gourd 138
Horseradish 139
Husk Tomato 139
Peanut 140
Popcorn 140
Radicchio 142
Shallot 142
Southern Pea 143
Spaghetti Squash 143
Sunflower 144
Vine Crops 144

Herbs 147

Angelica 150
Anise 150
Anise Hyssop 150
Basil 151
Bay Laurel 151
Bergamot 152
Borage 152
Caraway 152
Catnip 152
Chamomile 153
Chervil 153
Chives 153
Cilantro and Coriander 154
Dill 154
Fennel 155
Garlic 155
Geranium, Scented 156
Horehound 156
Hyssop 156
Lavender 157
Lemon Balm 157
Lemon Verbena 157

Lovage 157
Mint 158
Oregano 158
Rosemary 159
Rue 159
Sage 159
Salad Burnet 160
Savory, Summer 160
Savory, Winter 160
Sorrel, French 161
Sweet Cicely 161
Sweet Marjoram 161
Sweet Woodruff 162
Tarragon 162
Thyme 163
Drying Herbs 163

Additional Information 165

Appendix A: Storing Vegetables 167
Appendix B: Sprouting Seeds 169
Appendix C: Days from Flowering to Harvest 169
for Selected Vegetables
List of Publications 170
Index of Common Names 173

Preface

This gardening book was prepared in response to the need for a complete and accurate guide to growing vegetables and herbs successfully under midwestern conditions. Although written primarily for the home gardener, this book may be equally useful to teachers, students, market gardeners, and residents of areas outside the Midwest.

The first section of the book deals with various aspects of planning, preparing, planting, and caring for the garden and with starting plants at home. The remainder contains detailed information about major vegetables (recommended varieties, when and how to plant, care, harvesting, disease and insect problems, and answers to the most commonly asked questions), minor vegetables, and herbs.

Because chemical measures for controlling pests in the home garden are continually being developed and are subject to change, no specific recommendations are included in this book. Regularly updated publications that offer this information are listed on page 170. The English system of weights and measures (such as inches, pounds, quarts, bushels, and Fahrenheit temperatures) is used throughout the book because most home gardeners have not yet adopted the metric system. The authors appreciate the suggestions and contributions of Dr. J.W. Courter, professor emeritus of the University of Illinois Department of Horticulture, who co-authored the 1978 edition with Dr. Vandemark.

C.E. Voigt
J.S. Vandemark

Planning the Garden

Planning the Garden

Home gardening is an interesting and rewarding hobby in which the entire family can become involved. Produce grown in the home garden is fresher, may have better nutrient content, and offers a wider variety of types than is commonly available on the market. Gardening also provides healthful outdoor exercise, offers productive activity for retired or partially disabled people, and is an excellent teaching tool.

Gardens range in size from a single potted plant, to small plantings around the doorway or patio, to mini-gardens (20 to 200 square feet), to large family gardens (750 square feet or more). The type of garden that you grow depends upon the space available, the kind and quantity of vegetables you need or desire, and the amount of time you want to spend working in the garden. Make your garden large enough so that it produces what is needed, but not so large that it demands an overwhelming amount of work.

Planning your garden can be an enjoyable task by the warmth of a fire on cold winter evenings. Color catalogs arrive in the cold, dead days of winter, spurring this creative urge. A well-planned garden is easier to plant and care for and is probably more productive than one that is not well planned.

Take full advantage of garden references—seed catalogs, books, magazines, demonstration gardens, garden columns, and extension publications—as you select your vegetables and make your plan. It pays to plan ahead. Be realistic about your ability to care for a garden. Do not plant a large garden in the enthusiasm of springtime and then leave on an extended summer vacation with expectations of a bountiful harvest when you return. Maintenance of a fairly large space need not become drudgery but must be performed with timeliness and regularity to be effective.

The table on page 4 shows the approximate yields of fresh vegetables per 30 feet of row, and the amounts of fresh vegetables needed for canning or freezing. From this table, you can determine how much to plant for satisfying your family's needs for fresh, canned, or frozen vegetables. You may find it necessary to make several successive plantings of certain vegetables to assure a continuous supply.

Growing seasons and growth characteristics are important aspects to consider in grouping the various vegetables in your garden. Perennial crops, such as asparagus, rhubarb, and berries, that are to be in the same location for more than one season should be planted at the side of your garden. Group early or quickly maturing vegetables together so that, after harvesting, the space may be used effectively for later plantings of vegetables. To avoid shading, plant taller crops to the north of shorter crops.

Correct spacing between rows is important to allow for proper growth of plants, ease of cultivation, and efficient use of space. If you have farm equipment available to use and space is ample, make your rows long enough and far enough apart so that you can till your garden mechanically.

Successive plantings are desirable if you wish to have a continuous fresh supply of certain vegetables. Two or three small plantings of leaf lettuce and radishes may be made a week to 10 days apart in the early spring, with additional plantings in the fall. Onion sets for green onions may be planted every 2 weeks until you have used all your sets. When space permits, there should be at least two plantings of beans, beets, broccoli, cabbage, and carrots—one as early in the spring as conditions allow, for summer use; another in the summer, for fall use and storage. If space allows, make several plantings of sweet corn and beans from late spring through early summer.

Certain later-season crops can be planted in the same location in the garden from which earlier ones have been harvested. Any early harvested crops (such as leaf lettuce, spinach, radishes, green onions, or peas) can be followed by beans, beets, carrots, cabbage, sweet corn, late spinach, late leaf lettuce, chinese cabbage, or turnips.

Intercropping (planting early maturing crops between the widely spaced rows of later- or long-season crops) is a good way to intensify production in a small garden. For example, beans, radishes, green onions, spinach, or lettuce may be planted between rows where tomatoes, peppers, cabbage, or corn are to be grown. Squash and pumpkins have traditionally been interplanted with corn, covering the ground and thus modifying soil moisture and temperature, as well as suppressing weed growth.

Rotating crops from year to year helps to control diseases that overwinter in the soil. Do not grow the same vegetable or related vegetables in or near the same location more often than once in 3 years. Rotate crops

Vegetable	Approximate pounds of yield per 30 feet of row	Pounds of fresh vegetable needed for 1 quart	
		Canned	Frozen
Asparagus	20	4	2–3
Bean, lima (pod)	10	4–5	4–5
Bean, snap	30	1½–2	1½–2
Beet	30	2½–3	2½–3
Broccoli	25	—	—
Cabbage	60	—	—
Carrot	30	2½–3	2½–3
Chard	50	—	—
Corn, sweet	30 (ears)	4–5	4–5
Cucumber, pickling	30	—	—
Cucumber, slicing	50	—	—
Eggplant	80	—	—
Lettuce, leaf	40	—	—
Muskmelon	75	—	—
Onion	50	—	—
Parsnip	40	—	—
Peas, pod	25	—	—
Pea, shelled	15	4–5	4–5
Pepper	35	—	1½
Pepper, pimento	25	4–5	—
Potato, irish (early)	30	—	—
Potato, irish (late)	45	—	—
Potato, sweet	50	2½–3	2–3
Pumpkin	125	—	—
Radish	30 (bunches)	—	—
Rhubarb	25	1	1½
Spinach	25	2–3	2–3
Squash, summer	75	2½–3	2–3
Squash, winter	125	2	3
Tomato	200	3	—
Turnip	50	—	—
Watermelon	125	—	—

from one side of the garden to the other. If your garden is on a slope, plant the rows across the slope rather than up and down. This practice decreases loss of soil from erosion of gulleys during rainstorms.

After reading pages 3 to 32 of this book, draw a sketch of your garden area showing the location of each vegetable, the spacing between rows, and the approximate dates for each planting. (See the sample sketch on page 31.) Make notations of the amount of seed and the number of plants needed. The sample plan for a small, intensive garden (30 feet long by 25 feet wide) shown on page 7 may help you plan your own garden.

Choosing the Best Location

The success of your garden depends to a great extent upon the site. Even though you are probably limited in your choice of location, you should keep the following points in mind.

Good soil. A loose, fertile, well-drained soil is the most desirable for a garden. Modern suburban developments are infamous for the poor quality of the "soil" that remains after mass construction. Given a choice, choose a house with good, native topsoil still in place. If possible, avoid heavy clays and extremely sandy soils unless adequate organic material is added. If poor soil cannot be avoided, you may need to amend and enrich the soil by adding lime, fertilizer, compost, or other organic materials and by installing proper drainage if you are to have any hope of successful vegetable production.

Raised beds may be the best solution for a garden with poor drainage. You can elevate and improve your garden soil by adding good field topsoil, potting soil, peat, or organic compost and incorporating these materials into the soil. Soil amendments are added to only the bed area, saving on the quantity applied. Double digging helps thoroughly mix in soil additives and gives maximal aeration. (See double digging, page 22.)

Do not, however, add lime unless a soil test tells you it is needed in your soil. It is not a cure-all for the ills of garden soil.

Adequate sunlight. Sunlight is absolutely necessary to produce vigorously growing vegetables. Vegetables grow best and give the best yields in full sunlight, with a minimum of 8 to 10 hours of direct sun each day. Leafy vegetables usually produce acceptable yields with less sunlight than plants that must produce fruit or enlarged storage tissues.

Clearance from trees and shrubs. If at all possible, plant your garden away from trees and shrubs. Trees and shrubs compete with garden crops for sunlight, plant food, and moisture. Trenching between small trees or shrubs and the garden temporarily alleviates this problem by severing invasive roots. Walnut trees especially should be avoided because they produce a toxin that harms vegetables.

Proximity to a water supply. Whenever possible, locate your garden close to a water source. Water is needed particularly when you are starting seeds or transplanting crops and during the development of the edible portion of the plant. A good garden hose delivers water 100 feet or more from an existing water hydrant.

Proximity to your house. By locating your garden near your house, you can have the daily pleasure of watching the vegetables grow. You will also be able to take timely action to control weeds, insects, and diseases. It is easier to see what needs doing when plants are near at hand. A few minutes spent at the proper time saves hours that it would take you to do the same job later. In some cases, disaster can be avoided by noticing a developing problem at an early stage.

Suitability to the landscape design. When planning your garden, consider its relation to the trees, shrubs, and flowers around your home. The garden should fit in well with the overall design of your landscape.

Many vegetables and herbs are colorful and attractive and can add ornamental value to garden plantings, as well as to the vegetable garden itself. Try to break the mind-set that says vegetables should be in one place, flowers in another. Some very pleasing and effective combinations of the two can be devised. The following vegetables have attractive forms and colorful flowers, leaves, or fruit. There may be several varieties of one vegetable (peppers, for example) that offer different colors and shapes of fruit.

Asparagus—fernlike foliage after spring harvest.

Beans—purple-pod or wax varieties; brightly colored pods of Horticultural varieties; dual-purpose climbers like Scarlet Runner.

Cabbage—red or savoy varieties; red, green, and pink "flowering cabbage."

Chard—red, white, or yellow leafstalk varieties.

Corn—purple husk; ears of indian corn, pod corn; strawberry, calico, and black popcorn.

Gourds—brightly colored ornamental, dipper, spoon, warted, birdhouse, sponge, and large-fruited types.

Herbs—chives, dill, purple basil, and most others.

Kale—regular or "flowering" types.

Midget or dwarf—varieties of plants such as tomatoes, melons, sweet corn, cabbage, cucumbers, and carrots, grown more for novelty than for their food value.

Okra—attractive hibiscuslike flowers; green or red pods.

Parsley—curled or flat-leaf varieties.

Pepper—yellow, red, purple, orange, or ornamental varieties.

Squash—summer: Patty Pan, Yellow Prolific types; winter: Turk's Turban, Cinderella (bush type).

Tomato—several training systems for dwarf, compact, and cherry varieties for hanging baskets, containers, and minigardens.

Raised Beds

Home garden magazines have been singing the praises of double-dug raised beds for many years. By alleviating compaction and guaranteeing aeration, this technique increases the productive potential of the soil. Raised beds, along with intensive planting, give startlingly high yields from very small spaces. Organic materials such as peat, well-rotted manure, or compost may be dug into the bed soil to further modify drainage and nutrient-holding capacity. Mulching to improve water retention also can add to the benefits of raised beds. Even raising the planting surface 6 inches makes harvest much

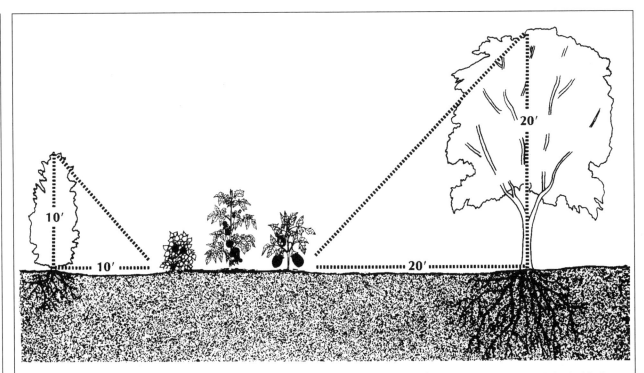

If possible, plant your garden a distance from trees and shrubs at least equal to their height. The leaves of trees and shrubs block sunlight, and the roots rob the soil of moisture and plant nutrients that are needed for proper growth of vegetables.

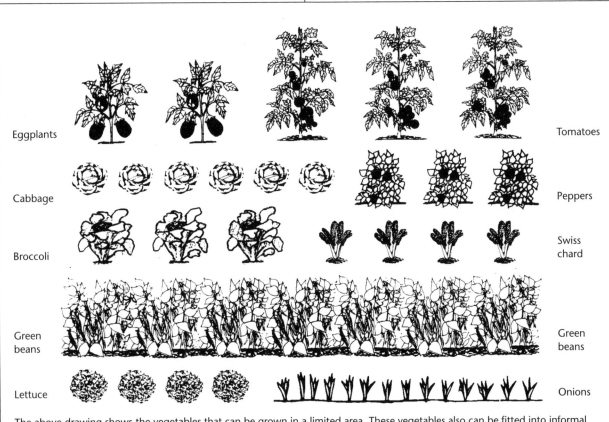

The above drawing shows the vegetables that can be grown in a limited area. These vegetables also can be fitted into informal arrangements around the patio or in the home landscape.

Row number	Inches between rows	First planting	Successive plantings
1	18	Early peas	Snap beans
2	18	Second early peas (later varities)	Lettuce, kohlrabi, snap beans
3	18	Spinach	Late broccoli, cauliflower, brussels sprouts
4	12	Leaf lettuce and radishes	Beets, carrots
5	12	Onion sets or plants	Radishes, late leaf lettuce
6	12	Onions (direct-seeded)	Radishes, late spinach

Row number	Inches between rows	Second planting	Successive plantings
7	24	Early cabbage or broccoli, cauliflower	Snap beans, lettuce, radishes
8	24	Early beets, carrots, or swiss chard	Turnips
9	24	Early snap beans	Late cabbage

Row number	Inches between rows	Third planting	Successive plantings
10	18	New Zealand spinach or peppers	None
11	30	Tomatoes or peppers	None
12	24	Lima beans	None
13	48	Choice of eggplant, summer squash, cucumbers, or bush forms of squash and pumpkins	None

Plan for a small, intensive garden (30 feet long by 25 feet wide).

easier on the backs of pickers. It requires much extra effort initially; but once the beds are established, much less annual soil preparation should be necessary.

The tops of the raised beds dry and warm faster in the spring, allowing earlier starts. Some "housecleaning" activities are performed annually, but the beds may be left more or less undisturbed, except for incorporating fertilizer and organic soil amendments. No traffic occurs on the beds, so compaction is confined to the area between them.

The addition of amendments and air to these beds greatly raises the surface level. In some soil types, these beds may be fairly stable; but in others it may be necessary to use landscape timbers, weathered railroad ties, or some other retaining walls to keep the bed in place. Use of plastic or organic mulches may help considerably to stabilize the soil surface in the beds, too.

Beds should be laid out so that the centers can be reached without stepping on the bed surface. Depending on the size of the gardener, and whether or not the bed can be reached from both sides, this distance may be 3 to 6 feet. Once digging and construction of beds is complete, all traffic should be avoided on the beds, as compaction drastically reduces the effect of increased soil aeration.

Plastic mulches of the appropriate width and trickle irrigation systems may also be applied on the beds. While spacing between beds may be greater than normal row spacings, this is usually more than offset by using double or even triple rows on the beds themselves. Uniform spacing on the beds, rather than conventional rows, may also raise plant populations and total production. Studies have shown that these high populations may result in even more marketable fruit per unit of surface area, with no significant change in fruit size or quality.

Experiments at Dixon Springs Agricultural Center in Simpson, Illinois, have shown that a combination of raised beds, black plastic mulch, and trickle irrigation increased early yield of bell peppers by 31 percent and total yield by 57 percent over control plantings. This interaction of earlier-warming beds and heat-collecting plastic clearly offers an opportunity to increase early yields. That trickle irrigation improves water relations to near-optimal conditions is well-documented. It is not surprising, therefore, that, when combined with the heat and aeration advantages of raised beds and black plastic, results are impressive.

The combination of better soil drainage and improved aeration associated with raised beds reduces the incidence of diseases that proliferate when free water

Types and Sizes of Growing Containers

	DIAMETER	HEIGHT	APPROXIMATE VOLUME
Pot	4"	3$\frac{1}{2}$"	1 pint
Pot	6"	5$\frac{1}{2}$"	3 pints
No. 10 can	6"	7"	3 quarts
Planter	8"	8"	1$\frac{1}{2}$ gallons
Planter	10"	9"	2$\frac{1}{2}$ gallons
$\frac{1}{2}$–bushel basket	13"	9$\frac{1}{2}$"	4 gallons
5–gallon can	11"	12$\frac{1}{2}$"	5 gallons
1–bushel basket	17$\frac{1}{2}$"	11$\frac{1}{2}$"	8 gallons

lingers at the soil surface or when air drainage stagnates. Getting beds raised by as little as 6 inches also improves light infiltration into the plant canopy, more quickly evaporating moisture and thus discouraging disease.

Fertilizer rates per surface area can be cut by applying fertilizer to only the beds. Fertilizer applied under plastic in raised beds gives the same or better response as larger amounts broadcast over the whole garden area. Denitrification (a problem in wet, cool soils) should be reduced with increased aeration and earlier soil warming in raised beds.

Raised beds have some clear advantages over flat-row culture. These include improved soil aeration and drainage, earlier warming of soils, better air drainage, better light infiltration, fewer disease problems, and easier weeding and harvest. While this system has some higher time and labor requirements associated with installation, the earlier yields, closer spacings on the beds, and less soil preparation in subsequent years can overcome the initial expenses in many situations. Individual gardeners need to evaluate this system in terms of their needs and, perhaps, give it a try.

Container Gardens

Growing vegetables in containers is popular with gardeners who have little or no ground space, as well as with those who also have conventional gardens. Containers may be located almost anywhere—the kitchen, patio, terrace, balcony, rooftop, or strategic locations around the yard—but they must have fertilizer, water, good drainage, light, and fresh air to grow and produce normally.

Often the vegetables grown in containers serve a dual purpose—they may be both decorative and harvestable. Popular choices for container gardens include attractive pots of kitchen herbs, hanging baskets of ripe red tomatoes, and window boxes of bright leaf lettuce or fresh radishes.

All vegetables, or even varieties of the same vegetable, are not equally suitable for growing in containers (see the table, page 11). Vegetables that grow in a limited space and produce continuous growth and yield (such as tomatoes, peppers, parsley, cucumbers, or chard) are good choices. You may also use more than one container for the same vegetable and plant at intervals. This technique establishes different growth stages for vegetables such as radishes that tend to mature their harvest at one time.

Some other characteristics that are important in selecting varieties for container gardens are (1) compact, bush, or dwarf growing habits; (2) colorful foliage or fruits; and (3) varieties that supplement your other garden harvests or the local supply.

Containers of all kinds, shapes, and sizes are used, including pots, tubs, baskets, planters, and wooden boxes. Commercial growing containers almost always have bottom holes for drainage. Homemade containers and those originally meant for some other purpose also should be provided with drainage holes. Place stones, crushed rock, or broken pot chips over the holes to retain the potting soil, prevent plugging of the holes, and ensure free drainage of excess water.

Restricting the soil volume and the root system of a vegetable plant limits the plant's supply of fertility and water to that furnished within the container. Often the container is placed in a location determined by "eye appeal" rather than one best suited for growth and development of the plant. As a result, the plant may be unduly exposed to wind and weather, and it may not receive proper care.

Use a fertile soil or growing mix. Because most soils are usually too heavy to use alone in containers, the light weight of container growing mixes may be an advantage. Slow-release fertilizers should also be incorporated into the mix.

Make sure that the volume of the rooting medium is large enough that the vegetables can grow and develop properly. Peppers, chard, and dwarf tomatoes need soil volumes of at least 1 to 2 gallons per plant. Full-sized tomato plants, cucumbers, and eggplants should have volumes of 4 to 5 gallons each. Lettuce, radishes, onions, and beets require containers with 6- to 10-inch diameters; and most herb plants, including parsley and chives, need containers with 4- to 6-inch diameters.

Volume depends upon the diameter, height, and amount of taper of the container. The rooting volume is less than the actual volume because the container is not filled to the top with the growing medium. The volumes shown in the chart on page 8 are minimums. In general, larger containers provide improved growing conditions, require less watering, and give better results than smaller containers. However, containers too large and hard to move around may become impossible to use effectively.

Because the plants remain in the containers for extended periods with a limited volume of soil for the roots to explore, you should add fertilizer regularly (at least once a week) with irrigation water. Use the fertilizers and rates suggested under "Starting Plants at Home," pages 45 to 48.

Sample Seed Packet

Front

Weight of contents. The weight also may be given in grams. The number of seeds may be indicated.

Lot number. For identification by seller.

Trade or brand name.

Seed catalog number. Name of hybrid, resistance to verticillium and fusarium wilts, nematodes, and tobacco mosaic virus.

Description of seed treatment. Fungicide, insecticide, or hot-water treatments for protection from certain insects and diseases.

Season that seeds were packaged for sale.

Date of germination test.

Percent of seeds germinated under specific laboratory conditions.

Name and address of seller.

Back

Packet produces about 40 plants

Germination procedure

When to plant

How to plant

Where to plant

Conditions of sale

General planting and growing instructions.

Warranty. Limits the liability of the seller to the purchase price of the seeds. The seller guarantees the seeds in this packet to be exactly as described, true to name, and free from insects and diseases.

Most vegetables in containers need daily watering to prevent wilting and injury. The larger the plants become, the greater their water needs. Judge water needs by water use. Changes in wind speed and direction, sunlight intensity, and temperature can vary water use greatly from day to day. Overwatering can be just as permanently damaging to plants as underwatering, but it is usually harder to overwater outdoors than indoors.

Many vegetables (tomato, cucumber, and eggplant, for example) also require support, depending upon the variety and kind of container. The plant or vines may be tied to stakes or to a trellis. Remember—plants still need direct sunlight for best growth.

Selecting Vegetables

Choose vegetables that you and your family enjoy and that can be grown successfully in your area. Some vegetables make better use of space than others and can be produced more efficiently in a small garden.

Another consideration in selecting vegetables is whether or not they taste noticeably better when they are fresh from the garden. Sweet corn is an outstanding example. Although corn requires more space than almost any other common garden vegetable, it is often grown because its quality is much higher when harvested fresh from the garden. Other highly perishable crops that taste best immediately after harvest are peas, pea pods, asparagus, fresh herbs, muskmelons, lettuce, green beans, spinach, summer squash, green onions, and vine-ripened tomatoes. These and many other fresh vegetables may not be available locally, and they bring special enjoyment when grown at home.

The table on this page (see note on sweet potatoes) shows the suitability of growing various vegetables in containers, minigardens, and full-sized gardens. The vegetables are grouped in descending order of popularity. For example, the five vegetables in group 1 are the most popular.

Hybrids and Varieties

The job of choosing the proper varieties for your garden is very important. By careful selection, you can grow vegetables that are resistant to diseases as well as yield high-quality, nutritious produce. You should decide well in advance of the garden season which varieties to grow so that you have ample time to obtain seeds or to grow your own plants. If you can determine what varieties are usually available in your area, you will know which ones you must start yourself.

Vegetables grouped according to popularity	SUITABLE FOR		
	Container garden	Mini-garden	Full-sized garden
Group 1			
Bean, snap		X	X
Lettuce	X	X	X
Onion	X (green)	X	X
Radish	X	X	X
Tomato	X	X	X
Group 2			
Beet		X	X
Broccoli		X	X
Cabbage		X	X
Carrot		X	X
Cucumber	X	X	X
Pea		X	X
Pepper	X	X	X
Squash, summer	X	X	X
Group 3			
Asparagus		X	X
Corn, sweet			X
Greens		X	X
Herbs	X	X	X
Kohlrabi		X	X
Parsley	X	X	X
Rhubarb		X	X
Group 4			
Cauliflower		X	X
Chard	X	X	X
Eggplant	X	X	X
Leek	X	X	X
Muskmelon			X
Potato, irish			X
Potato, sweet		X*	X
Pumpkin		X(bush type)	X
Squash, winter		X(bush type)	X
Turnip		X	X
Watermelon			X

*Requires frequent watering and treated as an ornamental

An increasing number of vegetables offered today in seed catalogs and at garden centers are *hybrids*. A hybrid, by definition, results from crossing (breeding) two parental lines that differ in at least one important characteristic.

Hybrids are often superior to older varieties because they combine desirable characteristics like uniformity of plant and fruit type, uniform maturity, disease resistance, improved quality, and vigor. Hybrid seed is usually more expensive than other seed and does not reproduce itself true to type in succeeding generations. You cannot save seeds of hybrids but must buy them from the hybridizer each year. Carefully consider resistance to disease and insects, along with other elements influencing yield, when selecting a new variety or hybrid to plant in your garden.

The performance of a particular variety may be influenced by any one or more of the following: (1) climate (temperature, rainfall, humidity, and light intensity); (2) soil (type, fertility, and drainage); (3) season (spring, summer, or fall cropping); (4) culture (planting distances, training methods, mulch, and fertilizer treatment); (5) method of harvest; and (6) intended use (fresh, storage, processing, or marketing).

The following suggestions can help you to compare new varieties and hybrids with favorites in your own garden.

(1) Limit the number of new varieties and hybrids that you try in any year.

(2) Select a test location with uniform soil quality and drainage, where all the plants can receive the same spray and cultural treatments. Avoid the edges or outside rows of a garden, where the results may be influenced by factors like trampling the plants, lack of competition, or damage from mowing or dogs.

(3) Plant all the varieties on the same day and in the same way. Be careful not to mix seeds or plants.

(4) Label each row and variety carefully. Draw a map showing where you planted the new varieties in case the stakes are lost, moved, or destroyed.

(5) Record observations of plant growth, yield, disease, and fruit characteristics. These records can help you make variety decisions for future gardens.

Vegetable Trials

University trials. Many states and field stations throughout the country test vegetable varieties at various locations, studying adaptability, performance, and disease resistance. Most of the varieties in this book are recommended as the result of these trials and those at commercial test plots throughout the country. There are a number of other organizations that sponsor trial gardens, such as botanic gardens, the Seed Savers Exchange, and other heirloom gardens. In addition, commercial seed suppliers often have excellent test areas and demonstration gardens that may be close to your home.

All-America Selections. All-America vegetables are those that have been tested and have been scored uniformly superior in performance under a variety of conditions in selected trial gardens throughout the United States. The winners are designated by All-America Selection (AAS) or All-America Award in seed catalogs. The title is given by All-America Selections, a nonprofit organization of seed dealers who develop and promote new varieties of both flowers and vegetables.

A vegetable that wins an All-America Award (gold, silver, or bronze medal) has demonstrated wide adaptability to soil and climatic conditions. Many of these varieties are well suited for most of the country. Not all new vegetable varieties are submitted for testing by All-America Selections, however, and many varieties that are not entered in the program may be equally suitable for a garden in your area.

Seeds, Plants, Equipment, and Supplies

Seeds

It is advisable to buy fresh seeds each year, though seeds of some plants can be used successfully for 2 years or longer when stored properly. The seeds should be clean, viable, and disease free. Most seeds from reliable seed companies meet these specifications.

Seeds should be treated to control seedborne disease organisms and to prevent decay and damping-off. Usually, the seeds that you buy are already treated. Information about the kind of treatment that the seeds have received appears on the seed package. Some companies offer seed for growers who wish to avoid pesticides, but you must specify "untreated seed" on your order.

Many new varieties and hybrids may not be available from local sources. For this reason, it is wise to purchase your seeds well in advance. Then, if you must order from a particular seed house, you have ample time to do so.

Seeds are alive, and proper storage conditions are important for their survival, for good germination, and for vigorous seedling growth. The best storage conditions are cool temperatures and a dry atmosphere. Some seed companies use special moistureproof foil envelopes to package seeds that are in peak storage condition. High temperatures and moisture (including high humidity) are very bad for stored seeds. It is usually preferable to use seeds that are no more than 1 year old. If you use older seeds, check germination before the growing season or sow more thickly than usual to ensure a good stand of plants; then you can thin if necessary.

You may store most leftover vegetable seeds *except onion, parsley, and parsnip* for planting the following year. If you decide to store your own seeds, place them in jars or tin cans that are tightly sealed against moisture, insects, and rodents. Store in a cool place—an unheated garage or outbuilding—or in your refrigerator.

The vegetable seeds that may be kept for planting the next year and seeds that may be stored for more than 1 year are listed below. Again, you must buy fresh onion, parsley, and parsnip seeds each year for good results.

Seeds may be kept for planting the next year	Seeds may be stored for 2 years
Asparagus	Beet
Bean	Cabbage
Broccoli	Cauliflower
Carrot	Celeriac
Corn, sweet	Chard
Herbs (most)	Cucumber
Kohlrabi	Eggplant
Leek	Endive
Lettuce	Kale
New Zealand spinach	Muskmelon
Okra	Pumpkin
Pea	Radish
Pepper	Squash
Salsify	Tomato
Southern pea	Turnip-Rutabaga
Spinach	Watermelon

Do not save seeds from the hybrid vegetables that you harvest. These seeds usually produce plants that are of lesser quality than the original hybrid. It also usually does not pay to save seeds from varieties unless you have a variety that is not available from any other source.

Plants

Some vegetables do best when they are transplanted into the garden. The plants may be grown at home, or they may be purchased from greenhouses, southern plant growers, and garden stores. Using plants started before outdoor conditions allow planting, rather than waiting until conditions allow seeds to be direct-seeded, decreases the time before harvest and gets your crop off to the best possible start. The plants should be healthy, stocky, of medium size, and free of disease and insects. Avoid plants that are tender, yellow, spindly, potbound, or too large. Do not buy plants with spots on the leaves, brown lesions on the stems, or knots on the roots.

Equipment

Trowel

Hoe

Spade

Rake

Spading fork

Sprinkler can

Stakes and string

Wheelbarrow

Growing your own plants at home has certain advantages. You can use varieties that are not ordinarily obtainable, have plants when you want them for spring and summer planting, have greater control over disease infection; and derive satisfaction from starting the plants.

Growing vegetable transplants requires special attention to details of media, temperature, light, watering, and seeding depth and spacing. Usually, temperatures too low for proper germination and light insufficient for healthy growth are the chief problems in growing plants at home. The results are poor germination, damping-off, and weak, spindly plants that stretch toward the light. (For specific instructions on starting your own plants, see pages 45 to 48).

Equipment

Have all your equipment and tools ready before you begin to work the soil. A hoe, spade, garden rake, trowel, measuring stick, and planting line are essential for all gardens. A wheel hoe or hand cultivator is a practical necessity for larger gardens. A seed drill is also desirable for larger gardens. Keep all tools clean and well sharpened. Each time you use your tools, clean them thoroughly and rub them with an oily rag before putting them away.

Every gardener needs a good sprayer or duster to control garden pests. Whether you use a sprayer or a duster is a matter of choice; either is effective if used properly. Inexpensive pressure sprayers, plunger-type dusters, hose-end sprayers, and hand-held plastic spray bottles are the most practical applicators for small gardens. Crank-type dusters can be used satisfactorily in both small and large gardens.

Hand-pump, compressed-air sprayers, which usually are made of plastic or galvanized steel and range in capacity from 1 to 5 gallons, are the most satisfactory for larger gardens. New, less expensive, smaller models are practical for gardens of almost any size. Empty and rinse the sprayer with clean water after each use, and hang it up to drain and dry. Do not use the same sprayer for applying both pesticides and weed killers.

Supplies

Obtain fertilizers, insecticides, and fungicides in the spring so that you have them when they are needed. Other supplies you may need include mulching material, stakes, plant protectors, and pots. The following checklist can help you in selecting your equipment and supplies.

EQUIPMENT	SUPPLIES
Small garden (necessary)	
Hoe	Dry garden fertilizer
Rake	Marking labels
Spading fork or shovel	Measuring stick or tape
Sprayer or duster	Seeds and plants
Sprinkler can	Sprays or dusts
Trowel	Stakes
	Starter fertilizer
	String
Small garden (helpful)	
Garden hose with sprinkler	Compost, manure
Hotbed, cold frame	Plant protectors
Respirator	Plant-growing mixes
Seeder	and containers
Wheel cultivator	Plastic mulch film
Wheelbarrow	Rubber gloves
	Seed protectants
	Trellis or fencing
	Wire cages
Large garden or specialized gardening	
Compost shredder	Herbicides for chemical
Garden tractor	weeding
Home greenhouse	Plant-growing lights
Power sprayer	Seed-germinating
Power tiller	cables or mats

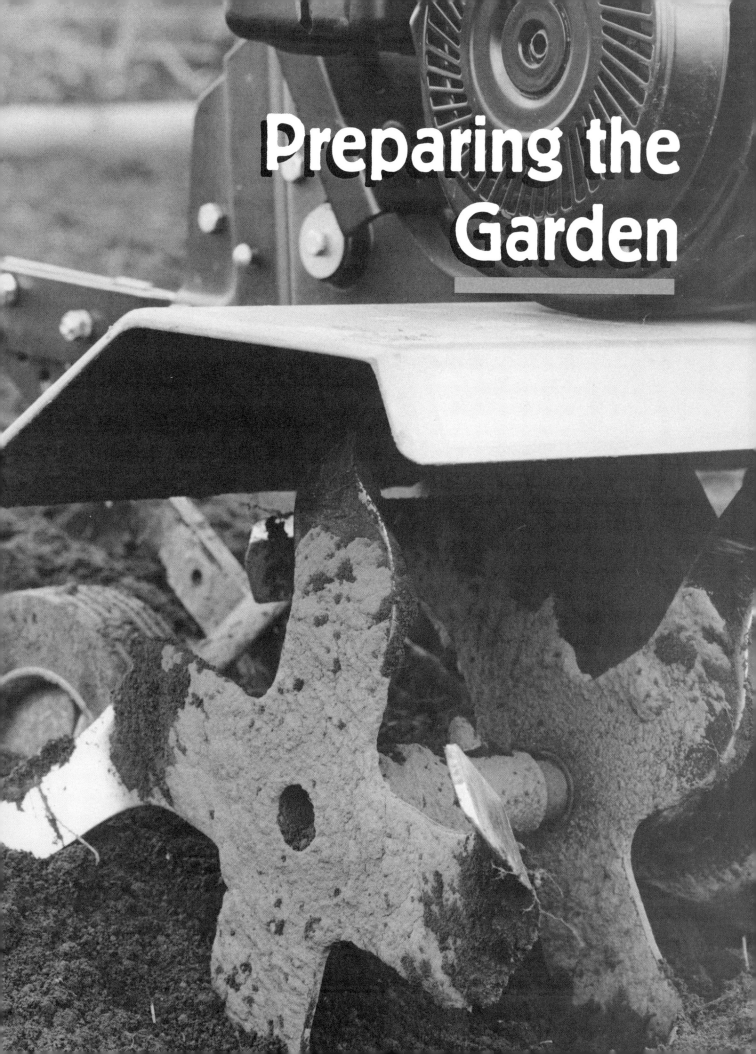

Preparing the Garden

Preparing the Garden

Improving Soil Tilth

The soil provides plant nutrients, air, water, and support. If these constituents are not available, or if the soil is in poor condition (hard and crusty when dry or sticky when wet), vegetables do not grow and develop properly. Good soil is essential for a successful garden.

A soil that is in good "tilth" (physical condition) is loose and easy to work, and it has water-holding capacity, drainage, and aeration. You can improve soil tilth by adding organic matter, manure, compost, or similar material to the soil and working it in before planting or by turning under a green manure crop.

Organic materials to be spread per 100 square feet of garden are listed in the table below. The table shows the pounds of nitrogen to be added per 100 pounds of material. Note: Corncobs, sawdust, wood chips, leaves, and straw vary considerably in nitrogen content; and you may need to apply supplemental fertilizer containing nitrogen during the growing season. Do not use lawn clippings from grass that has been treated with sprays containing fungicides, insecticides, or herbicides.

Manure is a common form of organic matter used in gardens. It also fulfills some fertilizer requirements of the soil. Because manure is low in phosphorus, you should add 1 to 1½ pounds of superphosphate to each bushel of manure. Use 500 to 1,000 pounds of horse or cattle manure per 1,000 square feet. Sheep and goat manures should be used at one-half this rate. (See the table on page 19 for the fertilizer composition of other organic materials.)

Compost can be made from leaves, straw, grass clippings, manure, and any other disease-free waste vegetable matter. To make compost, pile these materials in layers as they accumulate during the season. Add about 1 pound of a mixture of lime (or wood ashes) and fertilizer to each 10 pounds of green material. The mix can be made from 5 pounds of 10-10-10 fertilizer and 2 pounds of fine limestone. If your soil already has a high pH (is alkaline), leave out the lime or wood ashes and use the 10-10-10 fertilizer with your compost ingredients.

This fertilizer treatment hastens decay and improves the fertility of the compost. It should also moderate any nutrient deficiencies within the pile and help speed the decomposition process. Spread soil over the material to

Organic material	Material per 100 square feet	Nitrogen to be added per 100 pounds of material*
Corncobs	50 pounds (2 bushels)	1–1½ pounds
Sawdust	50 pounds (2 bushels)	1¼–1½ pounds
Woodchips	50 pounds (2 bushels)	1¼–1½ pounds
Leaves	75 pounds (3–4 bushels)	½–1 pound
Straw	60 pounds (1 bale)	½–1 pound
Hay	60 pounds (1 bale)	None
Peat moss	6–10 cubic feet	None
Compost	10–20 cubic feet	None
Lawn clippings	4 bushels	None

*1 pound of nitrogen = 10 pounds of 10-10-10 fertilizer or 3 pounds of ammonium nitrate (33.5-0-0).

Previous fertilizer treatment	Fertilizer	Pounds to apply per 1,000 sq ft	Pounds of nutrients per 1,000 sq ft		
			N	P_2O_5	K_2O
Little or none	3-12-12	50	1.5	6.0	6.0
	or 5-20-20	30	1.5	6.0	6.0
Some	5-10-10	30	1.5	3.0	3.0
Heavy (established	10-10-10	15	1.5	1.5	1.5
gardens that have	13-13-13	12	1.5	1.5	1.5
produced well)	15-15-15	10	1.5	1.5	1.5

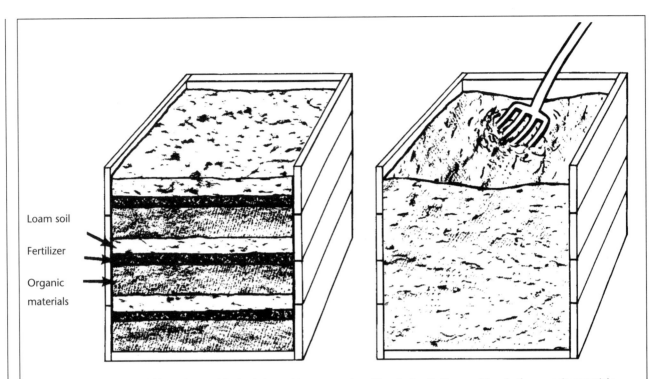

Loam soil

Fertilizer

Organic
materials

A simple wooden frame (left) can be used for both for making compost and for storing it. Thoroughly mix the organic materials, soil, and fertilizer with a spading fork or other suitable tool (right). Keep the compost pile moist, and leave a depression at the top to catch rainwater.

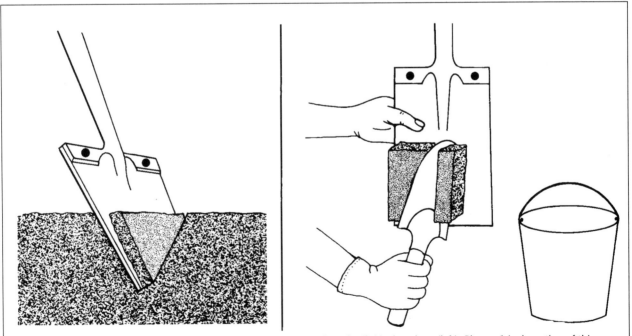

Taking a soil sample for testing. Use a spade or trowel to remove a slice of soil 6 inches deep (left). Place a 1-inch section of this slice in a pail (right). Obtain similar sections from other random locations in your garden. Mix the soil thoroughly in the pail. Remove about $1/2$ pint of the well-mixed soil, dry at room temperature, and place in a container. Do not take samples where fertilizer has been spilled or manure has been piled. Do not include debris (such as leaves, sticks, or large stones) in your sample.

hold it in place. Water the pile to keep it damp, and occasionally turn and mix the soil and decaying material. Properly constructed and balanced piles heat up to fairly high temperatures soon after they are made. The pile is ready to spread over garden soil in 6 to 12 months, or much sooner if all the materials are shredded finely to speed the composting process.

Green manure or cover crops, such as rye or oats, improve the soil tilth when they are plowed under in the spring or fall. The seed can be broadcast over prepared soil areas and between rows of late vegetables. Incorporate the seed into the soil with a rake, hand cultivator, or harrow.

The amounts of rye, ryegrass, and oat seed that should be sown per 1,000 square feet of garden, the best planting dates, and the times when the cover should be plowed under are as follow:

Rye: 3 pounds of seed; plant September 1 to 30; plow under in early spring.

Ryegrass: 1/2 pound of seed; plant September 1 to 15; plow under in early spring.

Oats: 1 to 1 1/2 pounds of seed; plant late August to early September; plow under or incorporate into the soil in early spring.

Fertilizing the Soil

Testing the soil. To find out the amounts and availability of nutrients in your garden, have the soil tested. Gather small amounts of soil from seven or eight well-scattered locations in your garden, mix the soil together, dry at room temperature, and wrap in a sturdy 1/2-pint container. Write "For Vegetable Garden" on the container, along with your name and address, and send it to the nearest soil-testing laboratory. In a few weeks, you will receive the results of the test, as well as fertilizer and lime recommendations for your garden.

If you have any questions about a soil test, call your local cooperative extension office. The telephone number should be listed in the directory under the Cooperative Extension Service.

Fertilizer elements. The principal elements applied via fertilizers are nitrogen for top growth, phosphorus for root establishment and fruit formation, and potassium for root development and disease resistance. These substances usually are referred to as nitrogen (N), phosphoric acid (P_2O_5), and potash (K_2O). A fertilizer marked 10-10-10 contains 10 percent nitrogen, 10 percent phosphoric acid, and 10 percent potash. *Do not use* fertilizers

Material	Nitrogen (N)	PERCENT OF Phosphoric acid (P_2O_5)	Potash (K_2O)
Chemical fertilizers			
Ammonium nitrate	33.5	—	—
Ammonium sulfate	20.5	—	—
Muriate of potash	—	—	48.0–62.0
Nitrate of soda	16.0	—	—
Superphosphate	—	16.0–20.0	—
Triple superphosphate	—	46.0	—
Urea	42.0–46.0	—	—
Ureaform	30.0–40.0	—	—
Organic fertilizers			
Bonemeal (steamed)	2.0	22.0	—
Cottonseed meal	2.0	3.0	1.0
Garbage tankage	1.5	2.0	.7
Manure, cattle (dried)	1.3	.9	.8
Manure, cattle (fresh)	.5	.2	.5
Manure, hen (dried with litter)	2.8	2.8	1.5
Manure, hen (fresh)	1.1	.9	.5
Manure, horse (fresh)	.6	.3	.5
Tankage (animal)	9.0	6.0	—
Tankage (processed)	7.0	1.0	.1
Wood ashes (may be a problem in gardens with higher pH soils, due to alkalinity)	—	.8	5.0

that contain either herbicides or insecticides. These fertilizers are for lawns and are not approved for use in vegetable gardens. If your soil has not been tested, use the general fertilizer recommendations that follow.

Organic materials. Organic materials benefit the soil in many ways, but they should be supplemented with other fertilizers. Some of the materials used for fertilizers are listed in the table on page 19. One or more of these materials can supply part or all of the nutrients needed in your garden, but it is usually easier and cheaper to use the chemical fertilizers.

When and how to fertilize. Fertilizer can be applied to the soil just before spading or plowing in the spring or fall; or it can be spread over the garden area and disked or raked into the top 4 to 6 inches of soil before planting. Nitrogen fertilizer is best applied as close to planting time as possible because it can be lost from the soil fairly quickly under certain conditions.

When transplanting, use starter fertilizer in addition to other soil-fertilizer treatments to give your plants a faster start. Starter fertilizer is a water-soluble fertilizer that is high in phosphorus—for example, 10-52-17 or 10-50-10. Dilute the fertilizer with water (about 1 tablespoon per gallon of water) before applying. When you transplant, pour 1 cup of the dilute solution around the roots of each plant.

If a regular starter solution is not available, you can mix 1 cup of steamed bonemeal in 1 gallon of water. Use 1 cup of the mixture for each plant (frequent stirring is necessary).

Later in the season, garden vegetables often need larger amounts of fertilizer elements, especially nitrogen, than the soil can supply. Side-dress fertilizer (apply in a band along one side of the row 6 to 12 inches from the plants) when the plants of leafy vegetables, sweet corn, and root vegetables are half grown; and when tomatoes, peppers, beans, cucumbers, and other vine crops have begun to set fruit.

Use 15 pounds of 10-10-10 or 12 pounds of 13-13-13 fertilizer per 1,000 square feet of garden area. This rate is about equal to 1½ pounds of 10-10-10 spread along a 25- to 30-foot row. Ammonium nitrate or urea fertilizer may be used at about one-third of this rate. Keep dry fertilizer off plant leaves: It may injure them. Hoe or cultivate the

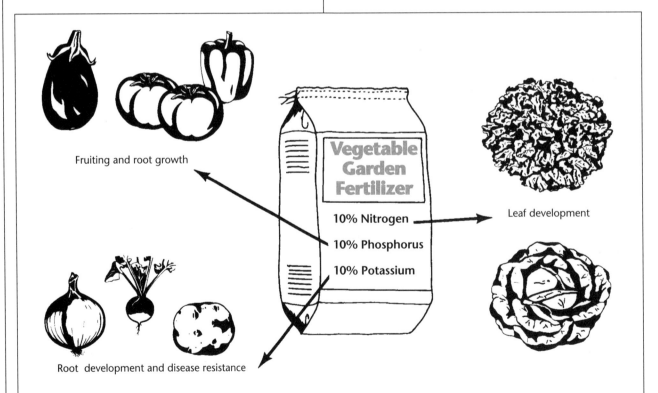

Fruiting and root growth

Leaf development

Vegetable Garden Fertilizer

10% Nitrogen

10% Phosphorus

10% Potassium

Root development and disease resistance

Vegetable garden fertilizer is a "complete" fertilizer containing nitrogen (N), phosphorus (P), and potassium (K). For most vegetable gardens, the fertilizer analysis should be equal parts of N, P, and K. The numbers on the bag indicate the percent (by weight) of each of these nutrients. For example, a 50-pound bag of 10-10-10 garden fertilizer contains 5 pounds of nitrogen, 5 pounds of phosphate, and 5 pounds of potassium oxide. These nutrients are required for root growth and development, leaf growth, fruiting, and disease resistance.

POUNDS OF LIMESTONE TO RAISE pH TO DESIRABLE LEVEL, PER 1,000 SQ FT			
Soil pH	Sandy soil	Loamy soil	Clayey soil
5.8 to 6.1	80	120	120
5.4 to 5.7	120	160	200
4.8 to 5.3	160	240	280
POUNDS OF SULFER TO LOWER pH TO DESIRABLE LEVEL, PER 1,000 SQ FT			
Soil pH	Sandy soil	Loamy soil	Clayey soil
8.5	40	50	60
7.5	10	15	20

fertilizer into the soil. In dry weather, water the soil to make the fertilizer more quickly available to the plant roots.

Soil pH. A soil that is slightly acidic to neutral (pH of 6.1 to 7.0) is best for growing most vegetables. If the soil test shows your soil is more acidic than it should be (pH below 6.1), apply the recommended amount of limestone. Add lime only if it is needed. Avoid overliming.

When soils are too alkaline (pH above 7.5), they can be corrected by adding sulfur. Work the lime or sulfur into the soil at the same time that you apply fertilizer. Changes in pH do not occur immediately because of delay in the reaction time of the soil. A single application of lime or sulfur is usually adequate for 4 to 5 years. After that period, the soil should be retested before making additional applications.

The table above shows the number of pounds of limestone or sulfur to be added per 1,000 square feet of garden area to adjust soil pH to desirable levels.

Plowing and Preparing the Seedbed

The garden can be plowed, tilled, or spaded in spring or fall. With fall preparation, the soil can be worked and planted earlier in the spring. Preparing soil in the spring is desirable when cover crops or plant residues may be necessary over the winter to control severe soil erosion problems. Do not work the soil when it is too wet. A good test is to squeeze a handful of soil. It should not be sticky and should form a ball that crumbles easily.

You may apply fertilizer before plowing or preparing the seedbed. Turn the ground over to a depth of about 6 to 8 inches. If fertilizer is added to the soil after plowing, rake or till the plowed area to work the fertilizer into the soil to a depth of 2 to 4 inches. Just before planting, prepare the seedbed by working the soil with a rake or

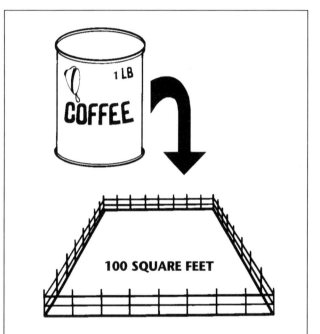

To maintain fertility in an established garden that has produced well, apply 15 pounds of 10-10-10 fertilizer per 1,000 square feet of garden area. An easy method for measuring the correct amount of fertilizer is to fill a 1-pound coffee can (holds 1½ pounds of fertilizer) with 10-10-10 fertilizer. Spread the fertilizer uniformly over an area 10 feet by 10 feet (100 square feet).

harrow. A freshly prepared seedbed prevents weeds from coming up before the vegetables.

For small-seeded crops, a smooth and finely pulverized surface ensures easier planting, better germination, and a more uniform stand. Heavy soils low in organic matter should not be worked to a fine consistency because they tend to become hard and crusty, preventing emergence of seedlings. Overworking any garden soils except sands and sandy loams damages the soil structure.

Double-digging refers to the process of aerating both the topsoil and some of the subsoil by digging out the topsoil to the depth of a shovel, in a trench one-shovel wide, across one end of the bed (see illustration). This soil is set aside in a wheelbarrow or other cart. The next shovel depth (usually subsoil) is then turned, broken up, and aerated. Any soil amendments to be added may also be incorporated at this time. The topsoil in the next shovelwide band is turned, broken, and pulverized onto the surface of the completed subsoil band. Again, any amendments may be incorporated during this operation. These steps are repeated down the length of the bed, alternating so that the topsoil can be turned over onto the most recently worked subsoil section. When the far end of the bed is reached, the soil in the wheelbarrow or cart can be moved to that end and deposited over the last section of subsoil worked, thus completing the double-digging for that bed.

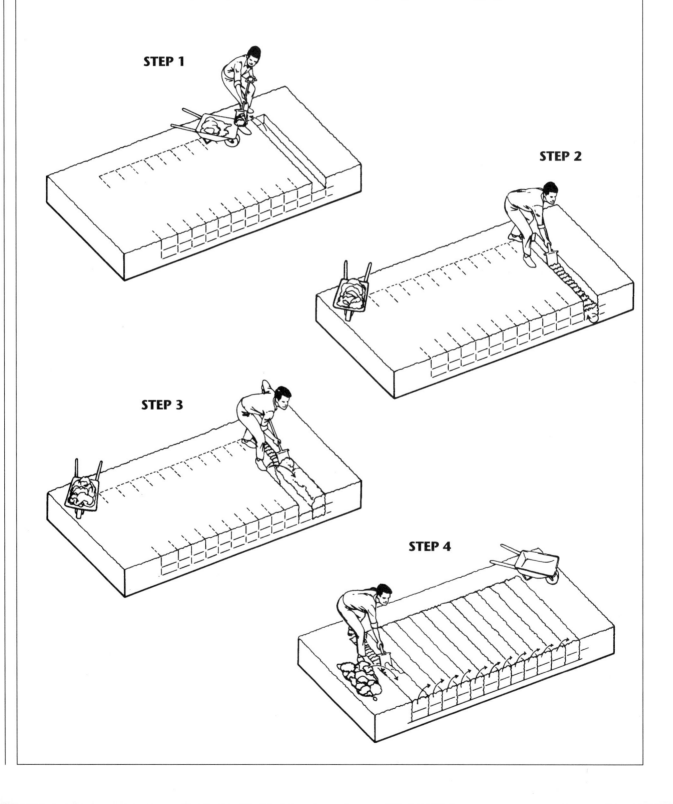

STEP 1

STEP 2

STEP 3

STEP 4

Planting the Garden

Planting the Garden

When to Plant

How early you can plant depends upon the hardiness of the vegetables and the climate in your area. Certain vegetables can withstand frost, while others cannot. Vegetables are classified as very hardy, frost-tolerant, tender, and warm-loving, according to their ability to withstand freezes, cold temperatures, or heat.

Very hardy vegetables withstand freezing temperatures and hard frosts without injury. They can be planted as soon as the ground can be prepared. Spinach and lettuce seeds even may be planted in the fall or broadcast on late snows over soil prepared in the fall. These plantings begin to develop well before the soil can be worked in the spring.

Frost-tolerant (semi-hardy) vegetables can withstand light frosts. Their seeds germinate in cool soil temperatures, but not as readily as seeds of the very hardy group. They can be planted as early as 2 or 3 weeks before the average date of the last 32°F freeze in the spring.

The very hardy and frost-tolerant vegetables are known as "cool-season vegetables." Their seeds germinate in cool soil, the plants withstand frost, and they grow and develop best in the cooler weather of early spring or fall.

Tender (not cold-hardy) vegetables are injured or killed by frost, and their seeds do not germinate well in cold soil. They are usually planted around the average frost-free date in the spring.

Warm-loving (heat-hardy) vegetables are intolerant of frost and cold, and they require warm soil and air temperatures for germination and good growth. Most are tolerant of high summer temperatures and thrive when there is ample soil moisture. The tender and warm-loving vegetables are called "warm-season vegetables."

Cool-season and warm-season vegetables are listed in the next column according to whether they are best started from seeds or transplants.

The dates of the last 32°F freeze in the spring and the first 32°F freeze in the fall can help you to determine safe planting times in your area. (See the maps on page 26.) The frost-free growing season varies greatly even within fairly localized areas. In more northern areas, late plantings are limited to very hardy and frost-tolerant vegetables. In central and southern regions, where the growing

Cool-Season Vegetables for Early Spring Planting

VERY HARDY
(Plant 4–6 weeks before average frost-free date.)

Seed	Transplants
Kale	Asparagus (crown)
Kohlrabi	Broccoli
Leaf lettuce	Brussels sprouts
Onion	Cabbage
Pea	Horseradish (root)
Rutabaga	Onion (set or plant)
Salsify	Parsley
Spinach	Potato, irish (tuber)
Turnip	Rhubarb (root)

FROST-TOLERANT
(Plant 2–3 weeks before average frost-free date.)

Seed	Transplants
Beet	Cauliflower
Carrot	Chinese cabbage
Chard	
Mustard	
Parsnip	
Radish	

Warm-Season Vegetables for Late-Spring Planting

TENDER
(Plant on average frost-free date.)

Seed	Transplants
Bean, snap	Tomato
Corn, sweet	
New Zealand spinach	
Squash, summer	

WARM-LOVING
(Plant 1–2 weeks after average frost-free date.)

Seed	Transplants
Bean, lima	Eggplant
Cucumber	Pepper
Muskmelon	Potato, sweet
Okra	
Pumpkin	
Squash, winter	
Watermelon	

Frost-Free Growing Season

The legend at the side of the maps gives the frost dates in both calendar dates (such as April 5), and chronological day numbers (counting from January 1). The average length of the frost-free growing season for your area can be determined by subtracting the day number of the last spring frost from the day number of the first fall frost. For example, if the first fall frost is day 275 (Oct. 2) and the last spring frost is day 125 (May 5), then the average frost-free growing season is 150 days (275 – 125).

AVERAGE DATE OF THE LAST SPRING FROST

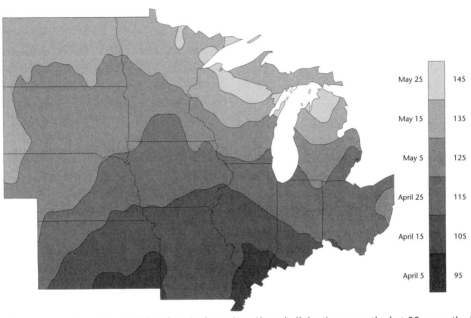

May 25	145
May 15	135
May 5	125
April 25	115
April 15	105
April 5	95

This map shows the average date of the last killing frost in the spring. About half the time, over the last 30 years, the last spring frost has occurred by this date for a given location. The actual date for a given year may vary from the average by as much as 2 weeks or more in either direction.

AVERAGE DATE OF THE FIRST FALL FROST

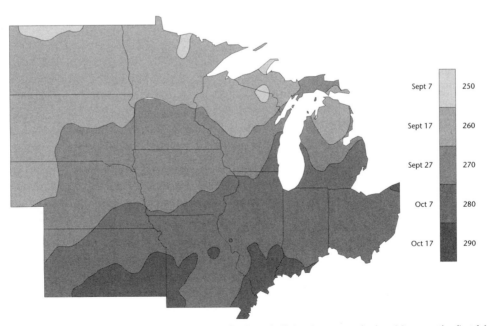

Sept 7	250
Sept 17	260
Sept 27	270
Oct 7	280
Oct 17	290

This map shows the average date of the first killing frost in the fall. About half the time, over the last 30 years, the first fall frost has occurred by this date for a given location. The actual date for any given year may vary from the average by as much as 2 weeks or more in either direction.

season is longer, many tender vegetables also can be planted for harvesting in the fall.

A fall garden not only extends your supply of fresh vegetables but also provides vegetables for winter storage. Unfortunately, a successful fall garden demands additional work and planning at a time when you are busiest with your summer garden. Irrigation is usually necessary during the late summer and early fall months. Weeds grow quickly at this time, and the garden must be kept free of weeds through shallow cultivation. Insects and diseases also thrive during warm, humid weather; and the vegetables need almost daily care. But the pleasure you can derive from a fall garden far outweighs the extra effort involved in planning and planting it.

The planting dates shown on page 28 can help you decide when to plant your vegetables.

How to Plant

Starting Seeds

In starting seeds in the garden, follow these directions:

Use disease-free seed.

Mark straight rows. Straight rows add to the attractiveness of your garden, and make cultivation, insect control, and harvesting easier. To mark a row, drive two stakes into the ground at either edge of the garden, and draw a string taut between them. Shallow furrows, suitable for small seed, can be made by drawing a hoe handle along the line indicated by the string. For deeper furrows, use a wheel hoe or the corner of the hoe blade. There is a pointed hoe designed specifically for making furrows. Use correct spacing between rows and between the plants in a row (see the table on page 30).

Hill or drill the seed. Planting in "hills" means placing several seeds in one spot at intervals in the row. Sweet corn, squash, melons, and cucumbers are often planted this way. Vegetables planted in hills allow easier control of weeds between plants. Plants in hills also tend to offer support to each other, standing better than drilled plants. "Drilling," which is the way most seeds are sown, is spacing the seeds more or less evenly down the row, either by hand or with a mechanical planter.

Space the seeds uniformly in the row. Small seeds can sometimes be handled better if they are thoroughly mixed with a small amount of dry, pulverized soil and then sown. (See the table on page 30 for the number of seeds to sow per foot or hill.)

Plant at proper depth. A good general rule is to place the seed at a depth about four times the diameter of the seed. Cover small seeds, such as carrots and lettuce, with about ¼ to ½ inch of soil. Place large seeds, such as corn, beans, and peas, 1 to 2 inches deep. In extremely wet conditions, cover more shallowly; and, under very dry conditions, plant slightly deeper.

Cover the seeds, and firm the soil. Lightly pack soil around the seeds by gently tamping the soil with your hands, an upright hoe, or a rake. Firming prevents rain-

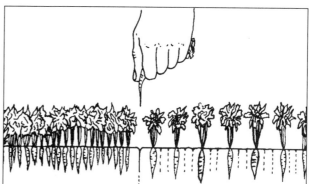

Many gardeners tend to sow small-seeded vegetables too thickly. The plants must be thinned to allow space for proper growth and development. Thin plants carefully while they are small.

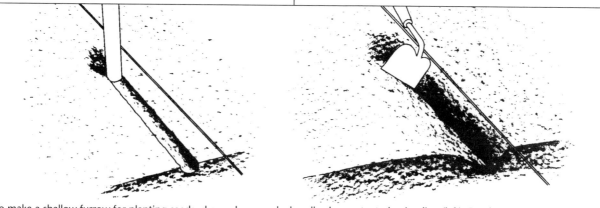

To make a shallow furrow for planting seeds, draw a hoe or rake handle along a taut planting line (left). For deeper furrows, use the edge of a hoe blade (right).

Planting Dates for Midwest Gardens
(See zone map inside back cover.)

SUMMER GARDENS
Zone 6: March 10–25
Zone 5b: March 25–April 10
Zone 4, 5a: April 10–25

Very Hardy Vegetables
Asparagus, crowns
Cabbage, seed
Collard
Kohlrabi
Leek, seed
Lettuce, leaf
Mustard greens
Onion, perennial
Onion, seed
Onion, sets
Pea
Potato, irish
Radish
Rhubarb, plants
Spinach
Turnip

Zone 6: March 25–April 10
Zone 5b: April 10–April 25
Zone 4, 5a: April 25–May 10

Frost-Tolerant Vegetables
Beet
Broccoli, plants
Brussels sprouts, plants
Cabbage, plants
Carrot
Cauliflower, plants
Chard, swiss
Chinese cabbage, plants
Leek, plants
Lettuce, head, plants
Onion, plants
Parsley
Parsnip
Radish
Salsify

Successive Plantings
Kohlrabi
Lettuce, leaf
Radish

Zone 6: April 10–25
Zone 5b: April 25–May 10
Zone 4, 5a: May 10–25

Tender Vegetables
Bean, snap
Corn, sweet
New Zealand spinach
Tomato, plants

Successive Plantings
Lettuce, leaf
Mustard greens
Radish

Zone 6: April 25–June 1
Zone 5b: May 10–June 1
Zone 4, 5a: May 25–June1

Warm-Loving Vegetables
Bean, lima
Cucumber
Eggplant, plants
Muskmelon
Okra
Pepper, plants
Potato, sweet, slips
Pumpkin
Squash, summer
Squash, winter
Watermelon

Successive Plantings
Bean, snap
Beet
Carrot
Corn, sweet

FALL GARDENS
Zone 6: June 1–July 15
Zone 5b: June 1–June 15
Zone 4, 5a: June 1–June 5

Brussels sprouts
Cabbage, direct-seeded
Collard
Kale
Kohlrabi
Pepper
Potato, irish
Squash, summer
Tomato

Successive Plantings
Early Summer
Bean, snap
Corn, sweet
Cucumber
Midsummer
Bean, snap
Beet
Broccoli, plants
Cabbage, plants
Carrot
Cauliflower, plants
Chinese cabbage, plants
Endive
Okra
Rutabaga
Late Summer
Chinese cabbage
Kohlrabi
Lettuce, Cos
Lettuce, leaf
Mustard greens
Radish, winter
Turnip
Early Fall
Lettuce, leaf
Mustard greens
Radish, spring
Spinach

water from washing away the seeds and the soil from drying rapidly, and it also assures good seed-soil contact.

Thin the plants while they are young. Carefully remove the weakest plants. If you wait too long before thinning, the plants may be injured or stunted from crowding. (See the table on page 30 for the proper distances between plants after they have been thinned or transplanted.)

Setting Plants

Some vegetables, such as broccoli, cabbage, cauliflower, eggplant, pepper, sweet potato, and tomato, are usually started in the garden by means of *transplants*. You can buy plants or grow them yourself indoors, in a cold frame, or in a greenhouse. Follow these directions when setting plants into the garden:

Transplant on a cloudy day or in the evening.

Handle plants with care. About an hour before transplanting, thoroughly water the soil in the containers (such as pots, bands, and flats) holding the plants. The roots of plants in flats should be blocked out with a knife to get as much soil as possible with each root. Carefully remove plants without disturbing the roots. Keep a ball of soil around the roots. Plants grown in cell packs already have individual soil compartments and usually pop out with their entire root system.

Dig a hole large enough so that the plant may be set slightly deeper than it grew in the container or seedbed. If you must use tall, spindly plants, plant them deeply, setting them on an angle.

Use starter-fertilizer solution to get plants off to a fast start.

Cover the roots with soil, and firm the soil around the plant. Some plant-growing containers are carefully removed before transplanting. Other containers are planted "roots and all," and the roots should be able to penetrate the container. The following containers should be carefully removed when transplanting: clay pots, plastic pots, plastic packs and trays, fiber pots and trays, and homemade containers (such as egg or milk cartons). Roots penetrate the following containers, and the containers should be buried, roots and all, below the soil line: Jiffy-7 (pellets), Jiffy-9 (pellets), peat pots, fertile cubes, and soil blocks.

Protect plants from heat, wind, or cold if necessary. Plant protectors (sometimes called "hot caps") made of paper or plastic are available to lessen trouble from frost in the spring. Homemade devices can be constructed from baskets, boxes, or jars. Do not leave the protector over the plants longer than necessary. If the weather gets warm during the day, remove the protector or open it so that the plants receive ventilation. Wire cages placed over early tomatoes (see page 125) provide a framework that can be covered with plastic or heavy paper to protect against late frosts.

To protect newly set plants from pests like cutworms, collars may be placed around each plant. Metal or cardboard cans with both ends removed work well. The worms are thwarted, and the top is open, allowing the plant to breathe. Once the plant outgrows the collar, it may be carefully removed.

Early season plantings of many crops can benefit from the soil-warming qualities of black plastic mulch. Floating row covers have been developed that are put over plants in the garden, allowing the plants to grow, but offering some insect and cold protection.

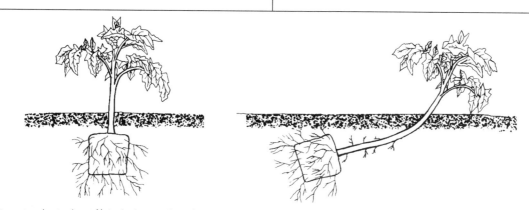

Plant tomato plants about ¹/₂ inch deeper than they were grown previously (left). If only tall tomato plants are available, plant them in a shallow furrow rather than a deep hole (right). The surface soil is warmer, and the roots will reestablish themselves along the stem.

Vegetable	Seeds to sow per foot or hill	Inches between plants when thinned or transplanted	Inches between rows
Asparagus	—	10	36–60
Bean, bush, lima	3–4	Do not thin.	18–30
Bean, bush, snap	6	Do not thin.	18–24
Beet	10	2–3	12–18
Broccoli	—	18–24	30–36
Cabbage	—	12–18	18–30
Carrot	15–20	1–2	12–18
Cauliflower	—	18–24	24–36
Celery	—	6–8	24–36
Chard, swiss	8–10	4–6	18–24
Chinese cabbage	4–6	12–15	24
Corn, sweet	1–2 in row	9–12, single plants; 36, hills (3 plants per hill)	24–48
Cucumber	3 in row	12, single plants; 36, hills (3 plants per hill)	48–72
Eggplant	—	18–24	30–36
Endive	4–6	9–12	18–24
Garlic (from cloves)	—	3–5	12–18
Horseradish (from sets)	—	24	30–36
Kale	4–6	8–12	18–24
Kohlrabi	6–8	2–5	18–24
Leek	10–15	4	12–18
Lettuce, leaf	10	4	12–18
Muskmelon	3 in row, 4–5 per hill	18–24, single plants; 36, hills (3 plants per hill)	48–72
Mustard	20	2–4	12–18
New Zealand spinach	4–6	12	24–30
Okra	3	12–24	36
Onion (from seed)	10–15	1–2	12–18
Onion (from plant or set)	—	2–5	12–18
Parsley	10–15	6	12–18
Parsnip	15–20	2–4	18–24
Pea	10–12	Do not thin.	18–24
Pepper	—	18–24	18–24
Potato, irish	1	Do not thin.	24–36
Potato, sweet	—	12–18	36–48
Pumpkin	1–2 in row, 4–5 per hill	24–36, single plants; 72, hills (3 plants per hill)	84–120
Radish, spring	10–15	1/2–1	12–18
Radish, winter	10–15	2–4	12–18
Rhubarb	—	36–48	36–48
Rutabaga	4–6	6	18–24
Salsify	10–12	2–4	18–24
Soybean, edible	8–10	Do not thin.	24–30
Spinach	12–15	2–4	12–18
Squash, summer	2–3 in row, 4–5 per hill	24–36, single plants; 48, hills (3 plants per hill)	36–48
Squash, winter	1–2 in row, 4–5 per hill	24–36, single plants; 72, hills (3 plants per hill)	84–120
Tomato	6–8	18–36	36–60
Turnip	15–18 (greens)	2–4	12–18
Watermelon	1–2 in row, 4–5 per hill	24–36, single plants; 72, hills (3 plants per hill)	84–120

Sample Sketch of a Vegetable Garden (10' x 20')

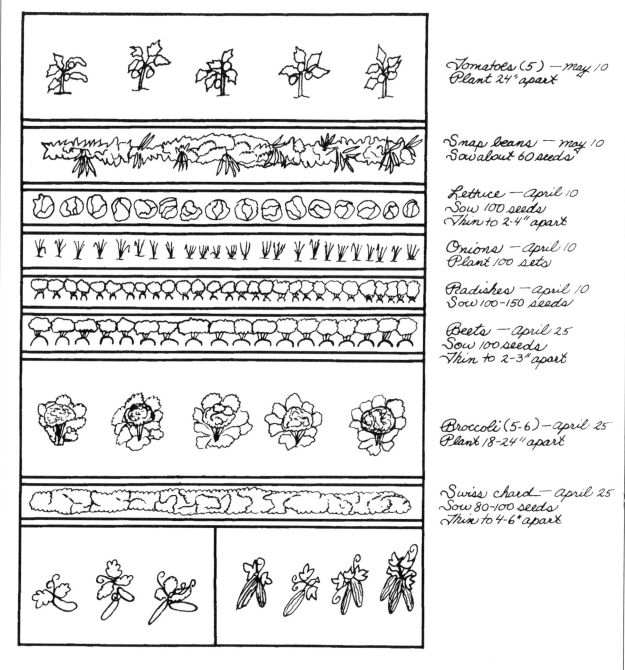

Tomatoes (5) — may 10
Plant 24" apart

Snap beans — may 10
Sow about 60 seeds

Lettuce — april 10
Sow 100 seeds
Thin to 2-4" apart

Onions — april 10
Plant 100 sets

Radishes — april 10
Sow 100-150 seeds

Beets — april 25
Sow 100 seeds
Thin to 2-3" apart

Broccoli (5-6) — april 25
Plant 18-24" apart

Swiss chard — april 25
Sow 80-100 seeds
Thin to 4-6" apart

Zucchini (2-3) — may 10
Plant hills 24" apart
Thin to best single plant

Cucumbers — may 10
Plant 10-15 seeds
Thin to best 4 plants about 12" apart

Floating Row Covers

A fairly recent innovation in early season vegetable production is the floating row cover. These covers are made of white, ultraviolet-light-stable, spun-bonded polypropylene plastic. They are extremely light in weight, self-ventilating, and they allow greater than 80 percent light transmission. Under normal conditions, their light weight allows them to be used without hoops or supports, merely "floating" on the crops as they grow. In very windy locations, they may require some sort of hoop or other support to keep the whipping action of the wind from damaging the young crop plants beneath the cover.

Floating row covers promote better growing conditions in early spring for warm-loving and frost-sensitive crops like tomatoes, peppers, melons, cucumbers, and squash. When used with black plastic mulches, the differences in energy capture and crop earliness can be astounding. In spring, covers are applied immediately after seeding or transplanting and can remain in place until crops outgrow the space under the cover or when plants begin to flower and require pollination. They can be relatively easily removed and even reapplied if necessary.

Spun-bonded row covers increase the temperature and provide some frost protection, which in cool springs can mean much earlier crops and in short-season areas may make the difference between harvesting a mature crop of a long-season vegetable and crop failure. These covers can also be used to extend the season in the fall. The protection provided may amount to a 4°F difference in temperature on frosty nights.

During daylight hours, when sunlight falls on the covers, additional heat is trapped and stored in the soil beneath the plants, increasing both top and root growth of the crop. This increased growth contributes to earlier harvest and higher early yields. It also protects against most airborne insects.

Spun-bonded row covers can be a real asset in speeding early season fresh produce to harvest, especially in short-season areas or those with undependable spring warmth. Most covers can be reused and are not prohibitively expensive in the home garden.

SOIL TEMPERATURES FOR GERMINATION OF VEGETABLE SEEDS

Vegetable	Best soil temperature range for seedling development	Days to germination
Bean, lima	75°–80°F	7–8
Bean, snap	65°–80°F	7–10
Beets	50°–80°F	7–14
Cabbage	50°–80°F	6–12
Carrot	50°–85°F	6–10
Chard	50°–80°F	7–14
Cucumber	60°–85°F	4–8
Lettuce	45°–70°F	3–8
Muskmelon	65°–85°F	4–8
Okra	75°–85°F	7–12
Onion	45°–75°F	5–15
Parsley	60°–85°F	10–15
Parsnip	60°–75°F	10–15
Pea, pod or english	50°–80°F	6–8
Pea, southern	65°–85°F	6–8
Pumpkin	70°–85°F	4–5
Radish	50°–70°F	4–7
Spinach	45°–65°F	7–15
Squash	70°–85°F	4–5
Sweet corn	55°–80°F	5–10
Turnip	70°–85°F	2–3
Watermelon	65°–85°F	5–8

Caring for the Garden

Caring for the Garden

Cultivation

Although the main purpose of cultivation is to control weeds, some soils may need cultivation, especially early in the season, to break the soil crust and aerate the soil. Weeds compete with vegetables for water, fertilizer nutrients, and light; and they may harbor insects and diseases. If weeds are allowed to become large, they shade the vegetables and result in a poor crop.

Begin cultivation as soon as weeds begin to sprout, and repeat whenever they reappear, especially as the soil dries after irrigation or rain. Do not work the soil if it is too wet. The roots of many vegetables are near the soil surface and are damaged easily by a hoe or cultivator. Cultivate or hoe shallowly near plants and carefully later in the season. Remember—the garden hoe can be your most important tool if you use it properly.

Chemical weed control is not usually recommended for the home garden. Vegetables have varying tolerances for herbicides. Herbicides must be applied accurately and uniformly at the proper stage of development of both the vegetable plant and the weed. Because your garden has many different kinds of vegetables in different stages of growth, safe, effective herbicide application is nearly impossible in a vegetable garden. Either do not apply herbicides in the yard, or exercise extreme caution near your garden because weed-spray drift can damage the vegetable plants. Farm and market gardens can benefit from herbicides when the operator has the equipment and experience to apply these chemicals correctly.

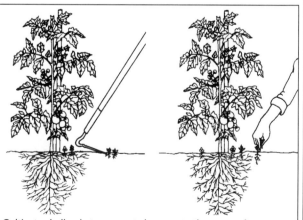

Cultivate shallowly to prevent damage to the roots of vegetable plants (left). Pull weeds by hand when they are close to the plants (right).

Mulching

Mulching is covering the soil around vegetable plants with natural or synthetic materials to control weeds, moderate soil moisture and temperature, improve plant growth and yield, improve soil structure, and keep vegetables clean. Depending on the type, a mulch may have a cooling or warming effect on the soil, and soil temperature and moisture remain more uniform.

Vegetable plants usually grow better when mulched because an extensive root system develops undisturbed under the protective soil covering. The mulch prevents root pruning and injury when cultivation or hoeing is too close or too deep. Although mulches help conserve moisture in the soil, they do not eliminate the need for water or irrigation. Mulches should be used in combination with other cultural practices such as stakes, cages, trellises, and irrigation. Light-colored organic mulches may retard early season growth of heat-loving vegetables by keeping soil temperatures cool. Pull back mulches, allowing soil to warm thoroughly in the early season.

Organic Mulches

Commonly used organic mulches include plant residues (straw, hay, leaves, grass clippings, crushed corncobs, peanut hulls, and compost); peat; wood byproducts (sawdust, wood chips, and shavings); and animal manures.

Many gardeners prefer to use organic mulches when they are available. Organic mulches improve garden tilth as they decompose, returning organic matter and plant nutrients to the soil. They encourage earthworm activity, which improves soil structure and makes nutrients more available. They keep soil moisture and temperature uniform, and usually have a cooling effect on the soil.

Organic mulches should be spread evenly over the soil between the rows and around the plants. Apply to a depth of 3 or 4 inches to keep down weeds. If weeds remain a problem, a thicker application of mulch may be needed. You still may need to remove a few weeds by hand.

Properly applied, organic mulches benefit most garden vegetables. Because organic mulches slow the soil from warming in the spring, they should be placed on the soil after the plants have begun to grow and are well established. As the season progresses (and especially for late-summer plantings), the cooling effect of organic mulches can be quite beneficial for many vegetables.

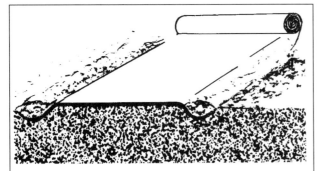

Black plastic film keeps down weeds, warms the soil, and conserves moisture and fertility. Anchor the film against the wind by covering the edge as well as the ends with 4 to 6 inches of soil. The soil should be well prepared, properly fertilized, and moist when the plastic is applied.

Vegetable	Critical period of water needs
Bean, lima	Pollination and pod development
Bean, snap	Pod enlargement
Broccoli	Head development
Cabbage	Head development
Carrot	Root enlargement
Cauliflower	Head development
Corn, sweet	Silking, tasseling, and ear development
Cucumber	Flowering and fruit development
Eggplant	Uniform supply from flowering through harvest
Melon	Fruit set and early development
Onion, dry	Bulb enlargement
Pea	Flowering and seed enlargement
Pepper	Uniform supply from flowering through harvest
Potato	Tuber set and tuber enlargement
Radish	Root enlargement
Squash, summer	Bud development and flowering
Tomato	Uniform supply from flowering through harvest
Turnip	Root enlargement

Unfortunately, organic mulches also have certain disadvantages—they are bulky, are difficult to handle, and (if low in nitrogen) may require side-dressings of nitrogen fertilizer. (Light green or yellowish leaves indicate that the vegetable plant needs nitrogen.) Wood products like sawdust are the worst in this regard. Do not use organic mulches on poorly drained soils or soils where water is standing.

Synthetic Mulches

Black plastic (polyethylene) film blocks sunlight from the soil, and weeds do not grow beneath it. It warms the soil by 5° to 10°F, benefiting early spring plantings and, especially, warm-loving vegetables. As the mulched area is shaded by foliage, the soil temperature becomes about the same as that in the unmulched areas that are also shaded by foliage. This keeps plant roots under black plastic from cooking in midsummer sunshine. Rolls of black plastic film 1½ mils thick and 3 to 4 feet wide may be used for cucumbers, eggplant, muskmelons, peppers, pumpkins, summer squash, sweet potatoes, tomatoes, watermelons, and winter squash. The film also can be used advantageously in northern areas for early planted sweet corn, broccoli, and cabbage.

Clear plastic film raises the soil temperature by at least 10° to 20°F at the surface. Clear plastic is preferable to black plastic for unusually cool seasons because the extra warming speeds up seed germination and growth in cold soil. Clear plastic film 1½ mils thick and 1½ to 3 feet wide may be used to cover rows of early planted peas, radishes, lettuce, sweet corn, beans, and potatoes.

The main problem with clear plastic is that weeds grow under the plastic. If weeds become a problem, the plastic should be removed after the vegetable seedlings have emerged. For potato plants, the film may be kept in place and covered with organic mulch to smother weeds growing underneath. Cut slits in the film so that the potato plants can penetrate. Sweet corn plants that germinate under plastic may be left folded under the plastic for up to 3 weeks in early spring, but watch for high-temperature buildup—it can burn off the plants.

Seeds can be planted through plastic mulches by cutting slits in the film with a sharp knife. An old-fashioned corn jabber (hand planter) can be used to cut slits and plant seeds in one operation. Simply push the jabber through the film, and operate it in the usual way. Flower-bulb planters with the bottom edge sharpened can be used to cut a hole in film mulch and remove a plug of soil in preparation for transplanting through the mulch.

Black and clear plastic film can readily be obtained from garden centers, hardware stores, and mail-order houses or through seed catalogs. Other synthetic mulching materials include paper, paper-plastic combinations, foil, and foil-paper combinations. New colors and color combinations in plastic mulches are being tested and may soon be available for home vegetable production.

Watering

Adequate water is essential for producing high-quality crops. There are usually dry periods during the growing season when you must water your garden to start seeds, to keep vegetables growing vigorously, to encourage continuous fruiting, and to keep the quality of harvested produce high.

When to water. Water vegetables once a week during dry periods (usually when less than 1 inch of rain falls during a week). Watering early enough in the day so that moisture on the plants dries before sunset helps to keep down many diseases. (The critical periods of water needs for various vegetables are shown on page 36.) Not watering during the intense heat of midday helps to minimize water lost to evaporation.

How to water. It is better to soak the soil thoroughly to a depth of at least 6 inches once a week than to sprinkle the garden lightly at frequent intervals. To be effective, the water should get down into the root zone of the plant. About 1 inch of water a week, including rainfall, is desirable for most vegetables during the growing season. To measure the amount applied by overhead sprinkling methods, place four or five straight-sided cans in the area being irrigated. These cans collect about the same amount of water as the soil, and the depth easily can be measured.

Trickle Tubes

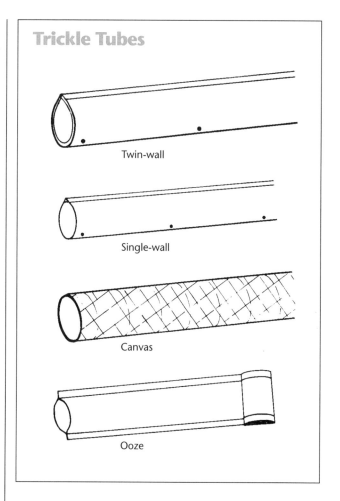

Twin-wall

Single-wall

Canvas

Ooze

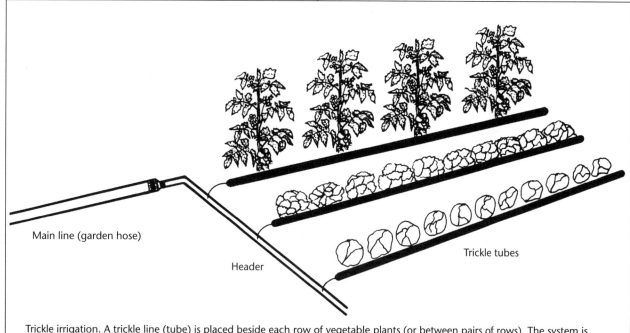

Main line (garden hose)

Header

Trickle tubes

Trickle irrigation. A trickle line (tube) is placed beside each row of vegetable plants (or between pairs of rows). The system is supplied by a clean water source from a main line (such as a garden hose or plastic pipe) to a header. Some of the new trickle irrigation systems require low water pressure, and the installation instructions vary according to the manufacturer.

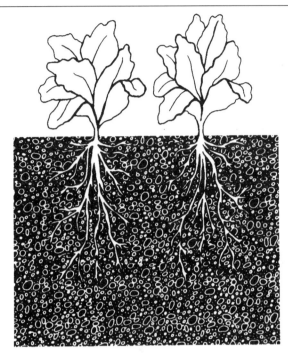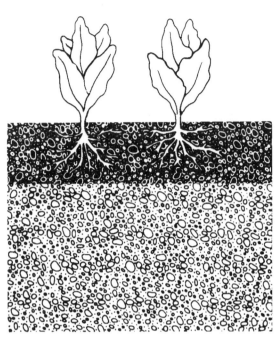

To encourage deep rooting, thoroughly water the upper 6 to 8 inches of soil (left). Shallow watering (right) promotes shallow development of roots, resulting in poor growth and increased risk of injury under severe weather conditions.

Trickle or drip irrigation is a method of watering vegetable plants analogous to side-dressing fertilizer. Water is applied directly on the row by a special tube or hose, usually at low pressure and volume. In addition to the traditional porous canvas tube, there are now many kinds of plastic tubes that pass water through their walls at a slow rate or use emitters to deliver water.

A trickle line (tube) may be placed at the side of a row of vegetable plants or between companion rows to water the soil directly beneath the plants rather than the space between the rows. Some tubes may be buried 1 to 2 inches deep in the soil. Trickle irrigation uses less water, delivers it exactly where it is needed, and provides a more uniform supply of water than other watering systems; but it can be costly to install. Some new systems are relatively uncomplicated and inexpensive.

Watering the seedbed. Summer and fall gardens often require water to establish the crop because the soil dries more quickly during the summer months. If the soil is dry when you are ready to plant, apply ½ to 1 inch of water uniformly to the area to be planted. After the water has moved uniformly through the topsoil and the surface has again begun to dry, lightly work the surface by raking or cultivating very shallowly. This operation often requires as little as one day.

Seed the vegetables, but do not apply additional water for 1 or 2 days. If it does not rain for 2 days, apply about ½ inch of water every other day until the seed germinates. This treatment is particularly important for green, wax, and lima beans. Heavy watering just after planting causes these seeds to split, resulting in "bald heads" (seedlings without cotyledons), reduced yields, or complete crop failure. Some sort of shade or other protection from the baking sun of midsummer also may help seedlings emerge and become established in moist conditions.

Controlling Garden Pests

Make sure that you have identified your problem correctly. A plant's symptoms can have many different causes: diseases (fungal, bacterial, or viral); insects (foliage feeding or soilborne); chemical injury (from insecticides, fungicides, herbicides, air pollutants, or fertilizers); nematodes; mechanical damage (from hoeing and cultivating); and weather (cold, heat, wind, or lightning). Problems resulting from each of these causes require different solutions. Although it may be necessary to use chemicals for certain pests, you can prevent many garden problems by following these general control practices:

Grow disease-resistant varieties and hybrids. Use treated seed.

Inspect purchased plants carefully. Check for cankers, spotty leaves, and root swellings. The plants should stand erect and have healthy green leaves.

Fertilize your garden properly for vigorous plant growth. Remember—nitrogen (N) promotes leaf growth; phosphorus (P) is responsible for fruit set, as well as stem and root growth; and potassium (K) is necessary for root development and general disease resistance. Proper balance of all soil nutrients increases the odds of healthy plants.

Keep weeds out of the garden. Weeds can harbor both insects and diseases. Mow or weed all areas surrounding the garden.

Mulch plants. Mulching helps to keep down soil-borne diseases and moisture stress. Always use disease-free mulches.

Do not work in the garden while the plants are wet. Cultivating or harvesting under wet conditions causes plant diseases to be spread from infected to healthy plants.

Remove plant residues after each crop. Destroy plant materials that are infected with diseases or infested with insects. Plant materials that are not infected or infested may be composted or worked into the soil. Composting does not always generate enough heat to destroy diseases or insects.

Each year, rotate the vegetables in your garden to different locations. Certain related crops are susceptible to the same diseases. If possible, avoid planting any of the vegetables within each of the following groups in the same location more than once every 3 years. For example, cabbage and turnips should not be planted in the same location more than once in a season, and then not for two succeeding years. Cabbage could be followed, however, with late beans, cucumbers, or corn.

Cole crops (cabbage family): broccoli, brussels sprouts, cabbage, cauliflower, kohlrabi, mustard, radish, rutabaga, and turnip.

Cucurbits (cucumber family): cucumber, gourd, muskmelon, pumpkin, squash (summer and winter), and watermelon.

Solanaceous (tomato and potato family): eggplant, irish potato, pepper, and tomato.

Use attractant baits to get rid of slugs and snails.

If necessary, construct a fence to keep out dogs, rabbits, and other animals.

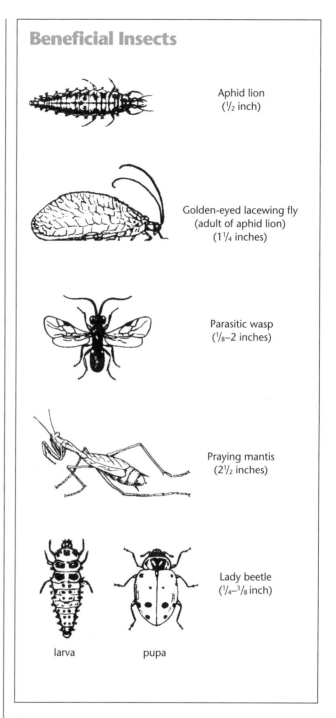

Beneficial Insects

Aphid lion
($\frac{1}{2}$ inch)

Golden-eyed lacewing fly
(adult of aphid lion)
(1$\frac{1}{4}$ inches)

Parasitic wasp
($\frac{1}{8}$–2 inches)

Praying mantis
(2$\frac{1}{2}$ inches)

Lady beetle
($\frac{1}{4}$–$\frac{3}{8}$ inch)

larva   pupa

Insects

You may find many kinds of insects in your garden. Some of these insects are destructive, others do not cause any damage, and many are actually beneficial because they feed on or disrupt destructive insects. For example, lady beetles and aphid lions feed upon aphids, and parasitic wasps feed on caterpillars and other insects. Natural populations of these beneficial insects should be encouraged, but it is questionable if it is worthwhile to purchase them for release in your garden.

Destructive Insects

Insect	Description	Crops attacked	Symptoms of damage
Aphids or plant lice	Tiny (less than $1/8$ inch long), soft-bodied, usually wingless insects. Color ranges from pale green to black. Slow-moving. Often not noticed until there are many upon a plant.	Bean, broccoli, cabbage, cucumber, irish potato, muskmelon, squash, sweet corn, tomato, watermelon.	Curled leaves; "honeydew" (clear, sticky substance on leaves and fruit given off by aphids, turns black from mold growth); many tiny, soft-bodied insects.
Blister beetles	$1/2$–$5/8$ inch long. Soft-winged black, gray, or striped beetles. Fast-moving. Usually appear in groups.	Bean, irish potato, tomato.	Blister beetles damage foliage by chewing and by secreting a toxin that causes wilting and leafburn. If unchecked, beetles can strip foliage from plants in a short time.
Cucumber beetles	$1/4$ inch long. Black-and-yellow spotted or striped beetles. Feed on foliage, flowers, stems, or fruit. Fly from one plant to another.	Cucumber, muskmelon, pumpkin, squash (summer and winter), watermelon.	Holes in foliage; chewed flowers; scarred stems and fruit surfaces. Beetles may carry bacterial wilt disease that causes plants to wilt and die.
Cutworms	Up to $1\frac{1}{2}$ inches long. Black, gray, or mottled caterpillars. Usually a single cutworm found curled up beneath soil surface at base of damaged plant.	Broccoli, brussels sprouts, cabbage, cauliflower, eggplant, kohlrabi, pepper, sweet corn, tomato.	Cut-off or wilted plants. Cutworms chew through plant stems at or just beneath soil surface. They also may feed on ripening tomato fruits, leaving small, round holes.
Flea beetles	Shiny, usually black beetles, often not observed, due to their small size ($1/16$ inch) and ability to jump quickly from plants when disturbed.	Cabbage, chinese cabbage, eggplant, radish, spinach, sweet corn, turnip.	Flea beetles scratch holes or leave white streaks in green foliage in late spring. Intense feeding results in wilting and dying of leaves and decreased yield.
Grasshoppers	Vary widely in size, up to $1\frac{1}{2}$ inches long. Color ranges from green to brown. Hop or fly. Young present in early summer, develop into large-winged adults by late summer.	Most vegetables.	Holes chewed in foliage.
Leafhoppers	Up to $3/8$ inch long. Green color. Wedge-shaped. May migrate from one area of garden to another. Hop away in large numbers when foliage is disturbed.	Bean, carrot, cucumber, irish potato, muskmelon.	Curled or crinkled foliage; "hopper burn" (cause by leafhoppers' feeding, indicated by brown edges on leaves). Leafhoppers may have migrated from damaged plants.
Maggots, root	Tiny (up to $1/8$ inch long), white, legless worms. Found in tunnels in underground parts of vegetables.	Cabbage, onion, radish, rutabaga, turnip.	Wilting or stunting of plants. Numerous brown or gray tunnels throughout underground parts of vegetables.
Slugs (snails without shells)	Range in size up to 2 inches long. Shiny, slimy, soft, legless animal. Seldom seen in daylight.	Most vegetables.	Paths of slugs marked by shiny mucous trails. Some feeding on foliage and scarring of fruit.

Destructive insects that each year attack certain vegetables (such as beans, broccoli, cabbage, cucumbers, eggplants, and muskmelons) are discussed under "Major Vegetables," pages 51 to 130.

Destructive insects that attack many garden crops are illustrated in the table on page 40. By comparing the insects with the symptoms of damage shown in the table, you can identify many common garden problems. (Because control measures are being developed continually and are subject to change, no specific recommendations for the control of insects and diseases are included in this book. Regularly updated publications that offer this information are listed on page 170.)

Diseases

Vegetables are subject to many diseases caused by plant pathogens (fungi, bacteria, viruses, and nematodes). Those diseases that are frequently found on particular vegetables are discussed under "Major Vegetables," pages 51 to 130. Diseases common to many vegetables are discussed in the following paragraphs.

Damping-off of seedlings. Damping-off is caused by several soil fungi that affect both germinating seed and tender seedlings in the garden, in the home, or in special plant-growing structures (such as cold frames, greenhouses, and hotbeds). When a seedling is attacked at ground level, it collapses. Damping-off can be prevented to a large extent by planting seeds in sterilized soil, with proper moisture content and temperature, and by good culture (for example, using correct planting depth, spacing, and watering).

Unless the fungi are controlled, they spread rapidly, and the entire seedling crop can be destroyed in a few days. Most commercially purchased seed has been treated with a fungicide by the seed processor to protect against damping-off. You also should pasteurize any soil (see page 45) that is brought into the house for growing transplants.

Fungal diseases of mature plants. Many fungal diseases attack vegetables, infecting both foliage and fruit. Early blight of tomatoes is an example of a common fungus-caused disease in gardens. Some fungal diseases (fusarium and verticillium wilts, for example) can be controlled best by planting resistant varieties.

Common blight diseases of carrots, cucumbers, irish potatoes, melons, pumpkins, squash, peppers, and eggplants can be prevented by applying a recommended fungicide. To obtain effective control of fungal diseases on these crops, you must (1) select the correct fungicide;

(2) apply it at the proper time; and (3) thoroughly cover all above-ground plant surfaces.

Fungicides may be applied as a dust or as a spray. They are most effective when used as a preventive measure—before the disease appears. Follow the directions on the label of the container.

Root-knot nematodes. All vegetables are attacked by small, wormlike animals called *nematodes*. Root-knot nematodes burrow into the roots of plants and cause small, knotlike to rounded swellings or "galls." Galls are swellings *within* the root, as contrasted with beneficial bacterial nodules, which are attached loosely on the roots of peas and beans. Plants with severe galling of the roots grow slowly; appear unthrifty; tend to wilt in dry, hot weather; never reach expected production; and may die prematurely. The only control available to home gardeners is to change the location of the garden or to fumigate the entire area with a nematicide.

If you suspect that nematodes are damaging your crops, ask your local extension office for information on how to collect and mail specimens for nematode analysis.

Bacterial and viral diseases. Many garden plants can become infected with bacterial and viral diseases. These diseases primarily are transmitted by insects carrying the disease-causing organisms or, mechanically, by rain or irrigation splashing, hoeing, cultivating, pruning, and harvesting. When weeds and perennial plants are hosts for infection, insect control is essential. For this reason, infected plants should be removed and destroyed as soon as possible.

Blossom drop. Extreme weather conditions may cause blossoms and small fruits to drop. Blossom drop results in the failure of fruits to develop on beans, peppers, and tomatoes when night temperatures fall below 55°F in the spring or when hot, drying winds occur in the summer. Insects, diseases, and herbicides sometimes also may be involved in blossom drop.

Starting Plants at Home

Starting Plants at Home

Growing Media

It is desirable to use a sterile plant-growing medium. Several kinds of soilless germinating mixes, growing mixes, potting soils, peat cubes, and compressed peat pellets may be obtained from garden centers, seed stores, and garden catalogs. These normally should be free from insects, diseases, and weeds and have enough fertilizer incorporated for the first 3 to 4 weeks of plant growth. They are easy to use, and many gardeners and commercial growers believe that their extra cost is justified.

Outdoor soils also may be used for growing plants. Unfortunately, these soils often need improvement in fertility, aeration, and drainage; and they may harbor insects or disease organisms.

If you are going to use outdoor soil, you should fertilize it and mix in rotted compost or manure the summer before you intend to use it. A good soil mixture for growing plants may be made by combining the following ingredients: 1 part fertile garden soil; 1 part shredded peat moss or well-decomposed compost; and 1 part vermiculite, perlite, or sand. Mix thoroughly and pasteurize before using.

Pasteurizing the Soil

Pasteurization (heating at 180°F) usually kills most common diseases, weeds, and insects in the soil. You can pasteurize soil at home in the oven. After making sure that the soil mixture has adequate moisture for seed germination, put the mixture in a pan or glass dish (the mixture should be no more than 3 to 4 inches deep).

Place a thermometer in the center of the mixture, cover with aluminum foil, and put the pan in the oven.

Set the oven at 250° to 275°F, and heat until the soil temperature (as indicated by the thermometer) is 180°F. Lower the oven temperature and maintain the soil temperature at 180°F for 30 minutes. Remove the soil from the oven and allow it to cool before planting. Be careful not to contaminate the mixture with unclean hands, tools, soil, or seeds.

It is equally important to clean old or used plant containers, pots, and tools with a disinfectant. You can use 1 part household bleach (5.45 percent sodium hypochlorite) mixed in 9 parts water. Thoroughly wash the container and tools outdoors, and allow them to dry completely before use.

Sowing Seeds

The traditional method of starting seeds has been to sow them in shallow boxes (flats) in rows about 2 inches apart and cover lightly with vermiculite. Soon after the seedlings come up, they can be transplanted to trays, pots, or other containers.

A simpler method of starting seeds is to sow the seeds directly into the final growing container. This method saves a step in handling the tender seedlings and avoids transplant shock. It requires additional space, however, because a larger number of containers are needed. The dates for planting various vegetable seeds indoors follow.

Temperature

The temperature of the medium is important for rapid and successful seed germination. Often the medium has a lower temperature than the surrounding air. To ensure the proper temperature for seed germination, use a thermometer with a soil probe. The tempera-

PLANTING DATES			
Vegetable	Zone 6	Zone 5b	Zone 4 & 5a
Broccoli Cabbage Cauliflower Lettuce	February 15 to March 1	March 5 to March 15	March 25 to April 5
Eggplant Herbs Pepper Tomato	March 5 to March 15	March 25 to April 5	April 1 to April 15
Cucumber Muskmelon Watermelon	April 1 to April 10	April 15 to April 25	April 25 to May 5

ture can be increased by covering the seed containers with glass or clear plastic, or by adding heat with special heating cables or mats. Heating cables or mats are especially helpful when large numbers of plants are to be grown.

The table on page 48 shows the optimal temperature ranges for germinating seeds and for growing vegetable plants. Frost-tolerant plants can be hardened out-of-doors for 1 to 2 weeks before they are transplanted into the garden. Growing times for plants may be changed significantly by temperature, moisture, and light.

Watering and Fertilizing

Next to proper temperature, uniform moisture is the most important requirement for seed germination. Some containers, such as peat pellets, dry out quickly and may need frequent watering. Water the plants as they grow in size, but do not water too much. Overwatering is at least as dangerous as underwatering at the seedling stage.

Your soil or growing medium should be fertile enough to sustain the plants for the first 3 to 4 weeks. Once seedlings are up, established, and growing, you may supplement the fertility of the soil or growing medium by adding water-soluble fertilizer. Use a soluble fertilizer (such as 10-50-10, 20-20-20, or 18-12-6) at the rate of 1 tablespoon per 1 gallon of water. Apply once a week, or

Structures for growing transplants may be homemade or purchased. The structures should be sturdy, and the lights or the plant shelf should be adjustable for height.

less often, as needed for plant growth. It is good practice to use plain water between feedings because water prevents the accumulation of fertilizer salts that can eventually injure the young plants.

Light

Vegetable plants need direct light. A window that receives sunlight only part of the day may not furnish enough light to grow high-quality plants. Many gardeners use plant-growing lamps as a primary source of light when there is no natural light or as a supplement to the natural light coming through a window.

Large lighting setups may require special electrical circuits, and the wiring and ballasts may be separate from the fixtures themselves. Light fixtures may be purchased as complete units or assembled at home. If you are not fully competent in these installations, ask an electrician for help.

Properly designed and utilized artificial light systems in a workroom, family room, kitchen, garage, or basement may be the total source of light for seedling production. Make sure that the temperature in this area is suitable for the plants you want to grow. For the best plant growth, as well as for germination, you may need to provide supplemental heat in addition to light. An accurate thermometer is essential.

Two double-tube fixtures (a total of four tubes) placed side by side are preferable to one fixture with two fluorescent tubes. The paired double-tube fixtures can provide light for a growing area 16 to 18 inches wide. Long fluorescent tubes (48, 72, or 96 inches long) produce more light than shorter ones (18, 24, or 36 inches) combined to produce the same length. The standard 40-watt, 48-inch fixture is the most popular; and replacement parts for these units are readily available.

Cool-white tubes are the most commonly used. Add one or two incandescent light bulbs with each bank of four-tube fluorescent lamps. This simple addition provides light quality for plant growth that is superior to fluorescent light alone.

There are several kinds of "plant-growth" lamps designed for indoor-light gardening. Their light does not appear as strong to the eye as light from cool-white tubes. However, the color may be objectionable in a room environment (it usually has a pinkish glow).

Seedlings and plants should be lighted for 12 to 16 hours per day. Do not light onion plants for more than 12 hours. A timer that automatically turns the lights on and off is helpful.

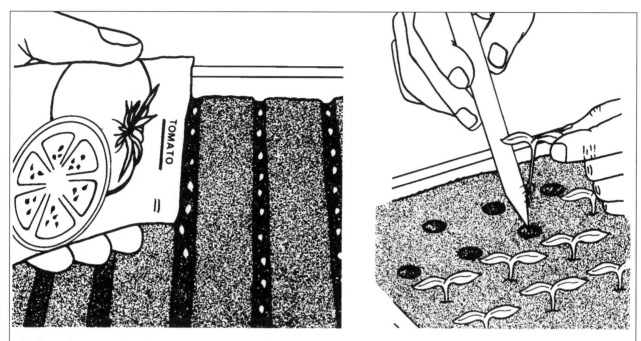

Seeds can be sown uniformly in germinating flats or containers (left) and covered lightly with soil or vermiculite. The seedlings may be left in the original containers or transplanted into flats, pots, peat pellets, or other growing containers soon after the seed leaves (cotyledons) are fully developed. Make a hole in the growing medium with a dibble (a pencil-like pointed stick). Hold the seedling carefully by the tip of the seed leaf to avoid damage to the tender stem (right). Insert the roots of the seedling in the hole and gently firm the medium. Water thoroughly.

Place the lamps close to the leaves of the plants. A distance of 6 to 12 inches is recommended. There is twice as much light (intensity) 6 inches away from a fluorescent tube as 18 inches away. Make either the light fixtures or the plant shelf moveable to permit adjustment of the distance between plant and lights as the plants grow in size. The total weight of lights, plants, and growing media can be substantial. For this reason, be sure that the lighting fixture supports and plant tables are sturdy.

Before plants grown inside under lights are transplanted outdoors, they should be hardened gradually by exposing them to outside conditions. Place the plants outdoors a few hours each day, starting in a very sheltered location, and gradually extend the exposure period as you approach planting time. Frost-tolerant vegetables

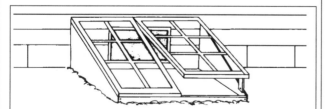

A cold frame (which depends upon solar energy for heat) or hotbed (with supplemental nighttime heat) can provide outdoor growing space for large numbers of plants and for hardening plants in preperation for planting.

can be left outdoors in cold frames for their final growth and hardening. The degree of success achieved in growing plants under lights varies with the kind of plants, the length of time that they are grown, and the combination of lights and intensities that are used.

Growing Time

The time required to grow plants to a stage suitable for transplanting to the garden varies with the kind of vegetable and the environmental conditions under which the vegetable is grown. If you cannot provide the best conditions, grow your plants for less time (3 to 6 weeks, for example) than shown in the table on page 48, and then transplant the smaller, younger plants in the garden. Even though they may not be as large as they might have been under ideal conditions, they are preferable to tall, weaker, spindly plants for starting outdoors.

You can also germinate the seed indoors until the seedlings are started, and then place them outdoors in a protected location during the day. Bring the plants inside at night to protect them against cold temperatures. A hotbed or cold frame is helpful if many plants are grown.

Growing plants out of season in a home greenhouse can be a rewarding hobby. The best plants are usually grown in greenhouses because light, temperature, ventilation, and moisture are controlled more easily.

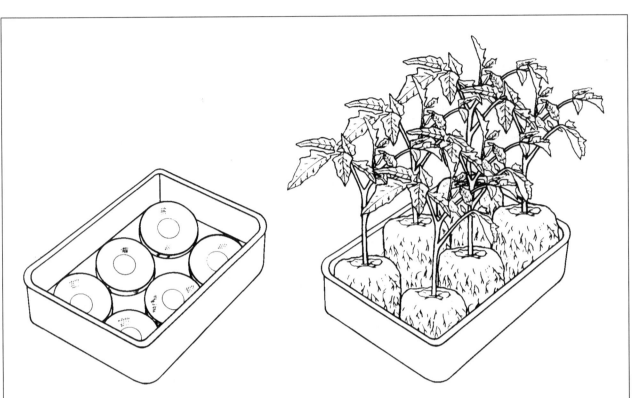

Peat pellets for growing plants at home readily can be obtained through catalogs or from garden centers. The pellets, which are dry and compressed, can be purchased in a special plastic tray for easy handling (left). When you are ready to plant, expand the pellets by submerging them in water. Use warm water for best results. Seeds may be planted or seedlings may be transplanted into the expanded pellets (right). Use a dibble (pencil-like stick) to make a hole in the top of each pellet. Gently firm the peat mixture over the seeds or around the roots of the seedlings.

| | **SEED GERMINATION** | | | **GROWING PLANTS** | | |
Vegetable	Optimal soil temperature, degrees F	Days for seedlings to emerge	Optimal air temperature, degrees F	Spacing for best transplants, inches	Weeks before transplanting	Frost susceptibilty
Broccoli	70–80	5	60–70	3 X 3	5–7	Tolerant
Brussels sprouts	70–80	5	60–70	3 X 3	5–7	Tolerant
Cabbage	70–80	4–5	60–70	3 X 3	5–7	Tolerant
Cauliflower	70–80	5–6	60–70	3 X 3	5–7	Tolerant
Cucumber	70–95	2–5	70–80	3 X 3	3–4	Very susceptible
Eggplant	75–85	6–8	70–80	4 X 4	6–8	Very susceptible
Herbs	70–80	6–15	70–75	2 X 2	4–8	Varies
Lettuce	60–75	2–3	55–75	2 X 2	5–7	Moderately tolerant
Muskmelon	75–95	3–4	70–80	3 X 3	3–4	Very susceptible
Onion	65–80	4–5	60–70	—	8–10	Very tolerant
Pepper	75–85	7–8	65–80	3 X 3	6–8	Susceptible
Tomato	75–80	6	60–75	3 X 3	4–7	Susceptible
Watermelon, regular	75–95	4–5	70–80	3 X 3	4–6	Susceptible
Watermelon, seedless	85–95	5–6	70–80	3 X 3	4–6	Susceptible

Major Vegetables

Asparagus

Asparagus, *Asparagus officinalis* (sometimes called "grass"), is a hardy perennial. It is the only common vegetable that grows wild along roadsides and railroad tracks over a large part of the country. Although establishing a good asparagus bed requires considerable work, your efforts will be rewarded. A well-planned bed can last from 20 to 30 years. For this reason, asparagus should be planted at the side or end of the garden, where it will not be disturbed by normal garden cultivation. Asparagus is one of the first vegetables ready to harvest in the spring.

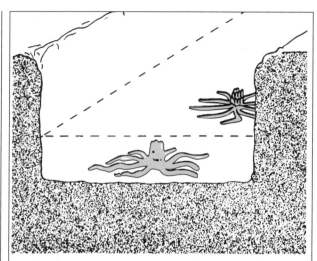

Set asparagus plants 9 to 12 inches apart in a trench 6 inches deep and 12 to 18 inches wide. Cover them with 2 inches of soil (dotted line in drawing), and gradually fill in the trench with soil during the first season.

Varieties

The list of commonly available varieties has significantly changed in recent years. Standard varieties like Mary Washington, Martha Washington, and Waltham Washington are still being offered; but a number of new varieties that are either predominantly or all male recently have been introduced into common usage. Asparagus plants are naturally either male or female. The females bear seeds, which take considerable energy from the plant, and sprout new seedlings, which cause overcrowding in the bed. Male plants produce thicker, larger spears because they put no energy into seeds and have no weedy seedling problem. A line that produces only male plants was discovered and has been incorporated into some truly amazing varieties. Jersey Giant, Jersey Knight, Jersey Prince, Syn 53, Syn 4-362, UC 157, and Viking KBC are new hybrids with larger yields. It is advisable to plant the best variety available, as an asparagus bed should remain productive for at least 15 to 20 years. If you are starting a new bed, you may never get to choose a variety again if your bed produces that long. All the newer varieties are cold tolerant and are resistant to rust and fusarium.

When to Plant

Asparagus should be planted as soon as the ground can be worked in the spring. One-year-old crowns or plants are preferred. Seeds are sown in a production bed and allowed to grow for a year. These plants are then dug, the soil removed, and the plants offered for sale.

They may be purchased from a garden store or nursery or through a seed catalog. The young plants have compact buds in the center (crown), with numerous dangling, pencil-sized roots. Adventurous gardeners can start their own plants from seed. Although this adds a year to the process of establishing the bed, it does ensure fresh plants and the widest possible variety selection.

Spacing of Plants and Depth of Planting

Place the plants in a trench 12 to 18 inches wide and a full 6 inches deep. The crowns should be spaced 9 to 12 inches apart. Spread the roots out uniformly, with the crown bud side up, in an upright, centered position, slightly higher than the roots.

Cover the crown with 2 inches of soil. Gradually fill the remaining portion of the trench during the first summer as the plants grow taller. Asparagus has a tendency to "rise" as the plants mature, the crowns gradually growing closer to the soil surface. Many gardeners apply an additional 1 to 2 inches of soil from between the rows in later years.

Care

As asparagus plants grow, they produce a mat of roots that spreads horizontally rather than vertically. In the first year, the top growth is spindly. As the plants become older, the stems become larger in diameter.

As noted, asparagus plants are dioecious (either solely male or solely female). The female plants develop more spears or stems than the male plants, but the stems are smaller in diameter. With normal open-pollinated vari-

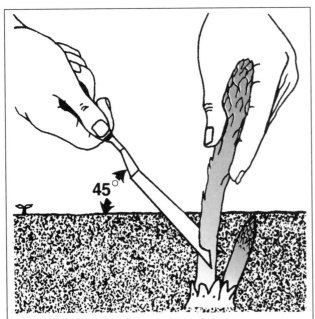

Cutting asparagus spears. Place the knife under the soil line next to the spear to be cut. Do not cut beyond the spear. You may damage other spears that have not yet emerged from the soil.

Harvesting

Asparagus can be harvested the third year after planting crowns, but for no more than 1 month the first season. The plant is still expanding its root storage system, and excessive removal of spears weakens the plants. During the fourth year and thereafter, the spears may be harvested from their first appearance in the spring through May or June (as long as 8 to 10 weeks).

Harvest spears 5 to 8 inches in length by cutting or snapping. To cut a spear, run a knife into the soil at the base of the spear and carefully sever it. Because the spear is cut below the point where fiber develops, it becomes necessary to remove the fibrous base from the tender stalk. Cutting may damage some spear tips that have not yet emerged from the ground. To snap a spear, grasp it near the base and bend it toward the ground. The spear breaks at the lowest point where it is free of fiber.

Either method is acceptable. Cutting is often preferred by commercial growers, and snapping by home gardeners. Asparagus deteriorates rapidly after harvest. If it is not eaten immediately, it should be processed or refrigerated.

Asparagus beetle
(¼ inch)

Common Problems

Asparagus beetles are commonly found in home plantings. If numerous, they may be controlled by a suggested insecticide or by handpicking.

Questions and Answers

Q. What causes my asparagus spears to have loose heads? *A. When the weather turns hot, the growing point expands rapidly, and the bracts (modified green leaves) are spread by the early development of the stems and ferns. The asparagus is safe to eat because only the appearance is affected.*

Seed (4X)*

Seedling   Spear tip

*X = times actual size (length and width). For example, 4X indicates that the seed is shown approximately four times the actual size.

eties, gardeners plant both male and female plants in an approximate ratio of 1:1. After the first year, small red berries form on the female plants in late summer. These then fall to the ground, sprouting plants that essentially become perennial weeds in the asparagus bed.

Following freezing weather in the fall, the asparagus tops should be removed to decrease the chances of rust disease overwintering on the foliage.

Because asparagus remains in place for years, advance soil preparation helps future production greatly. Working green manure crops, compost, manure, or other organic materials into the proposed bed well in advance of planting is a good approach. Asparagus should be fertilized in the same way as the rest of the garden the first 3 years. In the spring, apply 10-10-10, 12-12-12, or 15-15-15 fertilizer at the rate of 20 to 25 pounds per 1,000 square feet of area, and incorporate with soil tillage. Starting in the fourth year, apply the same amount of fertilizer, but delay application until June or July (immediately after the final harvest). This approach encourages vigorous growth of the "fern," which produces and stores nutrients in the roots for next year's production season.

Weeds and grasses are the worst problems with asparagus. They compete with the developing spears, make an unsightly area in the garden, and significantly decrease yield and quality. Start frequent, light, shallow cultivation early in the spring in both young plantings and mature patches that are being harvested.

Q. Early spring freezes caused the asparagus spears in my garden to turn brown and wither. Are they safe to eat? *A. Frozen tips should be picked and thrown away. These spears, although not poisonous, are off-flavor.*

Q. Can I start asparagus from seed? *A. Yes. You can grow your own plants by planting seeds ¹/₂ inch deep and 2 inches apart in the row. Start the seeds in the spring when the soil temperatures have reached 60°F. Dig the plants the following spring, before growth begins, and transplant them to the permanent bed as soon as the garden can be worked. Growing your own plants delays establishment of your bed an additional year, but it ensures that you are starting with freshly dug crowns that have not lost vigor by being dug, stored, and shipped. Also, variety selection is usually much greater when shopping for seeds rather than crowns.*

Bean

Bean is a tender, warm-season vegetable that ranks second to tomato in popularity in home gardens. Beans may be classified by (1) growth habit (bush or pole beans); (2) use (as immature pods, shellouts, or dry beans); and (3) type (green, yellow, purple, snap, romano, or lima beans).

Bush beans, *Phaseolus vulgaris* var. *humilis,* stand erect without support. They are the most popular type because they yield well and require the least amount of work. Green bush beans were formerly called "string beans" because fiber developed along the seams of the pods. Plant breeders have reduced these fibers through selection, and green beans are now referred to as "snap beans." Bush beans are available in green, yellow, purple, romano, runner, and lima varieties.

Pole beans, *Phaseolus vulgaris,* climb supports and are easily harvested. They are also available in green, yellow, purple, romano, runner, and lima varieties.

Varieties

Green Bush (snap bean): Blue Lake 274 (58 days to harvest; plump, tender pods; slow-developing seeds; resistant to bean mosaic); Bush Kentucky Wonder (57 days; familiar long, flattened pods); Contender (50 days; long, oval, attractive green pods; resistant to bean mosaic); Derby (57 days; 1990 AAS winner; slim, tender, prolific, excellent pods); Jade (53 days; extra-long, straight, slender pods); Provider (50 days; long, round,

fleshy, medium green pods; yields well in adverse weather; resistant to bean mosaic); Strike (55 days; attractive, straight, smooth, tender pods; high yield); Tendercrop (55 days; long, super-smooth pods, held high off the ground; resistant to bean mosaic); Tendergreen Improved (54 days; long, straight, round green pods; resistant to bean mosaic); Topcrop (50 days; round, smooth, meaty, tender medium green pods); and White Half-Runner (60 days; plants run up to 3 feet but need no support; slim green pods).

Wax Bush (yellow): Cherokee Wax (50 days; smooth, straight, oval, clear light yellow pods; resistant to bean mosaic); Goldcrop Wax (54 days; AAS winner; upright, vigorous plant; straight, shiny yellow pods, held well off the ground); Golden Wax (50 days; flat, broad stringless pod); Goldkist (56 days; tender, attractive, rust resistant); Pencilpod Wax (58 days; 6-inch, round, straight golden yellow pods); and Slender Wax (55 days; early coloring, medium-sized, round, straight golden yellow pods).

Purple Bush (snap bean): Royal Burgundy (51 days; round, tender, flavorful, stringless pods; seed germinates well in cooler soils) and Royalty (55 days; original purple-pod bush bean; 5-inch, curved, bright purple pods).

Green Pole (snap bean): Blue Lake (65 days; oval, straight, stringless, juicy, and tender pods; resistant to bean mosaic); Kentucky Blue (65 days; AAS winner; round, extra-straight, 7-inch pods); and Kentucky Wonder (65 days, fine flavor, 9-inch pods in clusters).

Wax Pole (snap bean): Kentucky Wonder Wax (68 days; fine flavor; oval, 7- to 8-inch yellow-gold pods).

Purple Pole (snap bean): Purple Pod (65 days, heavy producer) and Trionfo Purple Pod (62 days; 7-inch, slender, oval-round pods with solid texture, rich taste).

Romano Bush (italian): Bush Romano (56 days; delicious, broad, flat pods); Jumbo (55 days; giant italian-style green bean; extra-long, dark green pods with rich flavor; Roma II (53 days; flat, broad pods with distinctive flavor); and Wax Romano (59 days; wide, flat, medium yellow pods; highly flavored).

Romano Pole (italian): Romano (60 days; long, flat, broad pods).

Lima Bush (large-seeded): Burpee Improved Bush (75 days; large flat-oval beans, easy to shell; resistant to bean mosaic) and Fordhook 242 (75 days; AAS winner; heat-resistant plants; heavy yielder; resistant to bean mosaic).

Lima Bush (baby): Baby Fordhook (70 days; small, dark green beans on 14-inch plant); Eastland (70 days; dependable, heavy yielder); Henderson (65 days; flat,

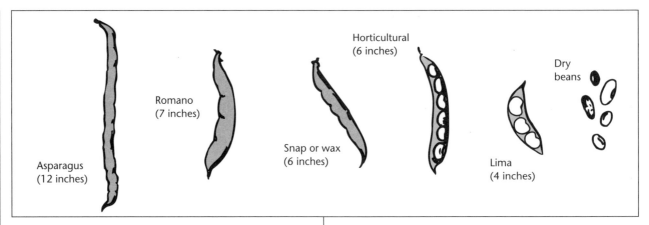

Asparagus (12 inches) · Romano (7 inches) · Snap or wax (6 inches) · Horticultural (6 inches) · Lima (4 inches) · Dry beans

pale green beans); Jackson Wonder (65 days; light green when immature, purple and pinkish splashed when ripe; heavy, dependable yield); Speckled Dixie Butterpea (76 days; oval seeds, round in cross-section; pale green when immature); and Thorogreen (66 days; 20-inch plants; pale green beans).

Lima Pole, *Phaseolus limensis:* King of the Garden (88 days; large, tasty, handsome beans); Prizetaker (90 days; largest beans; 6-inch pods with 3 to 5 giant seeds); and Sieva (72 days; pole-type baby lima; small, flat seeds).

Horticultural: Dwarf Horticultural (62 days; bush; used mostly as green shellout bean) and French Horticultural (75 days; bush; bright red splashed on yellow pods; half-runner plant; large cream-colored shell beans).

Dry (bush): Dark Red Kidney (95 days; bush; standard soup and chili bean); Great Northern (90 days; large, half-runner; white bean, excellent for soup; resistant to bean mosaic); Pinto (90 days; half-runner; standard for Mexican cuisine; resistant to bean mosaic); White Kidney (90 days; bush; kidney-shaped white bean); and White Marrowfat (100 days; large, egg-shaped white bean).

Scarlet Runner, *Phaseolus coccineus:* Dwarf Bees (65 days; 15-inch, dwarf runner bean; large scarlet flower clusters borne above the foliage); Red Knight (70 days; pole; choice, 10- to 12-inch, smooth, stringless pods); and Scarlet Runner (70 days; pole; scarlet flowers, beans tasty when young).

When to Plant

Beans are sensitive to cold temperatures and frost, and they should be planted after all danger of frost is past in the spring. (See the maps, page 26.) If the soil has warmed before the average last-frost date, an early planting may be made a week to 10 days before this date. The beans do not germinate until after the frost date has passed. You can assure yourself a continuous supply of snap beans by planting every 2 to 4 weeks until early August.

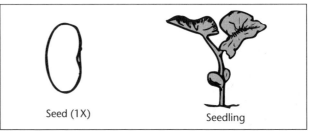

Seed (1X) · Seedling

Spacing of Plants and Depth of Planting

Plant seeds of all varieties 1 inch deep. Plant seeds of bush beans 2 to 4 inches apart in rows at least 18 to 24 inches apart. Plant seeds of pole beans 4 to 6 inches apart in rows 30 to 36 inches apart; or in hills (four to six seeds per hill) 30 inches apart, with 30 inches between rows.

Care

Seeds of most varieties tend to crack and germinate poorly if the soil's moisture content is too high. For this reason, never soak bean seed before planting, water just after planting, or plant right before a heavy rain.

Beans have shallow roots, and frequent shallow cultivation and hoeing are necessary to control small weeds and grasses. Because bean plants have fairly weak root systems, deep, close cultivation injures the plant roots, delays harvest, and reduces yields.

Harvesting

Snap beans. Harvest when the pods are firm, crisp, and fully elongated, but before the seed within the pod has developed significantly. Pick beans after the dew is off the plants and they are thoroughly dry. Picking beans from wet plants can spread bean bacterial blight, a disease that seriously damages the plants. Be careful not to break the stems or branches, which are brittle on most bean varieties. The bean plant continues to form new flowers and produce more beans if pods are continually removed before the seeds mature.

Lima beans. Harvest lima beans when the pods are plump and firm and the seeds are fully developed, but still green and tender. The pods of different varieties vary greatly in external appearance as the beans are developing. Test pick a few pods to be sure that the beans are at a desirable stage of maturity. Lima beans are of best quality when young. They become mealy and tough-skinned if allowed to remain on the plant beyond peak maturity. In areas where the season is long enough, ripe lima seeds may be harvested as dry beans. Bush-type lima beans are usually harvested in two or three pickings. The pole varieties continue to yield until frost if the old pods are removed as the beans mature. Northern short-season areas should rely on the "baby" limas, which mature much earlier than larger "potato" limas.

Horticultural beans. Harvest horticultural beans when the pods start changing from green to yellow. At that time, the beans (often referred to as "shellouts") are fully formed. They can be stored for a few days under refrigeration. Shellouts are usually served as a buttered vegetable or with pork.

Dry beans. Dry beans are planted less often in home gardens because they are generally available in food markets at moderate prices. They may be grown much as snap beans and produce good yields. Pull the vines when the leaves of the plants have turned yellow and begin to fall naturally. Dry the plants in the garden or on a clean floor. When the plants are dry, the pods start to split and the seed is easily removed. Store thoroughly dry bean seeds in jars or cans in a cool, dry location (see pages 167 and 168).

Bean leaf beetle
(¹/₄ inch)

Common Problems

The **bean mosaic diseases** cause plants to turn a yellowish green and produce few or no pods. The leaves on infected plants are a mottled yellow and are usually irregularly shaped. The only satisfactory control for these diseases is to use mosaic-resistant bean varieties.

Bright yellow or brown spots on the leaves or water-soaked spots on the pods are signs of **bacterial bean blight.** Bacterial blight is best controlled by planting disease-free seed grown in the irrigated, dry areas of the western states; avoiding working among wet bean plants; and removing all bean debris from the garden.

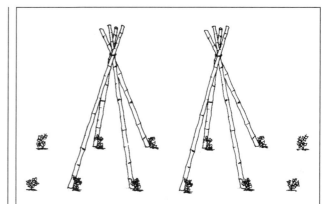

Pole beans may be supported by placing poles at the bases of two plants from each of two adjoining rows. The four poles, which form a "teepee," are tied firmly with heavy twine to hold them in place. When the bean plants begin to elongate, they should be started up the supports.

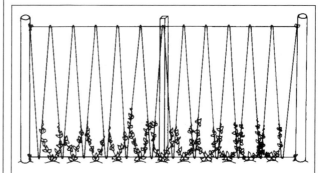

Pole beans (as well as asparagus beans, cucumbers, gourds, and other vining vegetables) also may be supported by twine laced between two 9- to 12-gauge wires. The wires are fastened to 7- to 8-foot posts located at the ends of each row. Stakes or poles between the posts prevent sagging or breaking caused by wind or the weight of the bean plants. Beans may be harvested easily from both sides of the row.

Bean leaf beetles feed on bean plants, causing holes in the leaves. These beetles can cause serious damage, especially when the plants are young. Use a suggested insecticide for control.

Questions and Answers

Q. My beans appear healthy, but not very many beans have formed. Why not? *A. The blossoms drop and fail to form pods during periods of hot, dry winds.*

Q. Is it a good practice to plant pole beans at the base of corn plants for double cropping? *A. No. Neither crop can reach its maximal potential. Weed control becomes difficult, and cornstalks offer weak support when the beans are maturing.*

Q. Is it necessary to plant beans in a different area of the garden each year? *A. Yes. Beans are subject to diseases that may carry over in the soil to reinfect the following bean crop.*

Q. Will bean varieties cross in my garden? *A. Because the flowers are largely self-pollinated, bean varieties usually do not cross. These crosses show up only when seed is saved from cross-pollinated flowers. In any event, you should obtain new seeds each year to avoid seedborne diseases.*

Q. Can I use beans from my garden that have matured past the green, edible stage? *A. Yes. Snap beans (pole or bush) may be harvested for shellouts and for dry beans; and lima beans may be harvested for butter beans.*

Q. Why do some snap bean varieties have white seeds? *A. Most bean varieties are developed for the canning and freezing industry. When varieties with colored seeds are used, the cooking water is slightly off-color. White seed is preferred because it does not discolor the cooking water.*

Q. What are the fuzzy, bright yellow insects on my bean plants? *A. These are larvae of the Mexican bean beetle. The adult resembles a large ladybug. The larvae do the most damage. They are generally not a serious problem, but they occasionally reach damaging numbers, particularly early in the season. Use a suggested insecticide for control.*

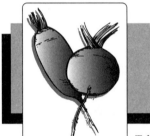 

Table beet, *Beta vulgaris*, (also known as garden beet, blood turnip, or red beet) is a popular garden vegetable throughout the United States. Beet tops are an excellent source of vitamin A, and the roots are a good source of vitamin C. The tops are cooked or served fresh as greens, and the roots may be pickled for salads or cooked whole, then sliced or diced. Beet juice is a basic ingredient of Russian borscht. The garden beet is closely related to swiss chard, sugar beet, and mangel. Mangels (also known as stock beets) are considered too coarse for human consumption but are grown for stock feed.

Varieties

Garden (open-pollinated): Some commonly available open-pollinated varieties include Crosby's Egyptian (56 days to harvest; uniform, sweet, dark red roots; semi-globe to heart shaped; glossy, bright green tops, excellent for greens); Detroit Dark Red (58 days; tender, round, dark red roots); Early Wonder (52 days; flattened globe shape; dark red, sweet, and tender); Lutz Green Leaf (70 days; an heirloom winter-keeper type; purplish red exterior, deep red interior; large, glossy green tops, excellent

for greens; roots stay tender even when large; stores extremely well); Ruby Queen (60 days; AAS winner; excellent quality; early; round, tender, sweet, fine-grained, attractive, uniform roots); Sangria (56 days; ideal globe shape, even in crowded rows; deep red; good greens when young); and Sweetheart (58 days; extra-sweet, round, tasty roots; tops good for greens).

Garden (hybrid): Avenger (57 days; uniform, vigorous; smooth, medium, globe-shaped red roots; glossy tops, good for greens); Big Red (55 days, best late-season producer, excellent flavor and yield); Gladiator (48 days; juicy, fine-grained flesh, deep red throughout; holds color without fading when cooked; uniform shape, size, and flavor; excellent for canning); Pacemaker (50 days; early; short tops, excellent-quality roots); Red Ace (53 days; early; sweet, red roots; resists zoning in hot weather; vigorous grower); and Warrior (57 days; highly uniform, globe shape; develops quickly, holds quality as roots grow large; dark red color inside and out; tops fringed with red).

Mini: Little Ball (50 days; very uniform, small size; good shape; very tender; grows quickly to form smooth roots) and Little Mini Ball (54 days; roots the size of a silver dollar at maturity; round; canned whole; short tops good for greens).

Specialty: Cylindra (60 days; long, cylindrical; all slices of equal diameter); di Chioggia (50 days; Italian heirloom; rounded, candy-red exterior; raw interior banded red and white; sweet, mellow flavor; bright green tops, mild and tasty; germinates strongly and matures quickly; does not get woody with age); Golden (55 days; buttery color, sweet mild flavor); and Green Top Bunching (65 days; round, bright red roots, good internal color in cool weather; tops superior for greens).

When to Plant

Beets are fairly frost hardy and can be planted in the garden 30 days before the frost-free date for your area. (See the maps, page 26.) Although beets grow well during warm weather, the seedlings are established more easily under cool, moist conditions. Start successive plantings at 3- to 4-week intervals until midsummer for a continuous supply of fresh, tender, young beets. Irrigation assures germination and establishment of the later plantings.

Spacing of Plants and Depth of Planting

The beet "seed" is actually a cluster of seeds in a dried fruit. Several seedlings may grow from each fruit. Some seed companies are now singulating the seed for preci-

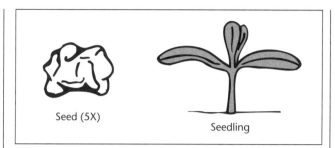

Seed (5X)

Seedling

sion planting, by dividing the fruit. Plant seeds about ½ inch deep and 1 inch apart. Allow 12 to 18 inches between rows. Poor stands are often the result of planting too deeply or the soil's crusting after a heavy rain. The seedlings may emerge over a relatively long period of time, making a stand of different sizes and ages of seedlings. Some gardeners find that placing a board over the row after planting preserves the soil moisture and eliminates crusting from hard rains. The board must be removed as soon as the first seedling starts to emerge.

Hand thinning is almost always necessary. The seedlings should be thinned to 1 to 3 inches apart. If thinning is delayed until the plants are 3 inches tall, those removed may be cooked as greens, similar to spinach. Some cooks leave the small root (usually about the size of a marble) attached to the greens.

Though it is seldom done, beets actually may be transplanted. Some care must be taken to get the roots oriented vertically so that the beets can develop properly.

Care

Frequent shallow cultivation is important because beets compete poorly with weeds, especially when small. Because beets have extremely shallow roots, hand weeding and early, frequent, and shallow cultivation are the most effective methods of controlling weeds in the rows. Deep cultivation after the weeds are large damages the beet roots. Like most root crops, beets need a fertile soil (especially high in potassium) for vigorous growth. Keep your beet plants uniformly supplied with moisture for best performance.

Harvesting

Beets can be harvested whenever they grow to the desired size. About 60 days are required for beets to reach 1½ inches in diameter, the size often used for cooking, pickling, or canning as whole beets. Beets enlarge rapidly to 3 inches with adequate moisture and space. With most varieties, beets larger than 3 inches may become tough and fibrous. Beets may be stored in a polyethylene bag in a refrigerator for several weeks. Beets also may be stored

in outdoor pits if the beets are dug before the ground freezes in the fall. Cut off the tops of the beets 1 inch above the roots. Beets store best at 32°F and 95 percent humidity. Do not allow them to freeze.

Questions and Answers

Q. What causes the beets in my garden to develop tops but no roots? *A. The most frequent cause for beet plants' failing to develop roots is overcrowding from improper thinning.*

Q. What causes my beet roots to have internal black spots and many of the bottom leaves to die? *A. Beets are a relatively heavy feeder of the element boron. Applying 1 tablespoon of household borax (dissolved in a 12-quart pail of water) along 100 feet of row may help to alleviate this condition. Do not apply excess boron, as the difference between a shortage of this element and a toxic amount is relatively small. If the soil is acidic, it should be limed according to a soil test. Never apply lime without a soil test to verify a low soil pH (acidity).*

Q. What varieties should I grow for beet greens? *A. A special vigorously growing variety, Green Top Bunching, is excellent for producing greens. Crosby Egyptian and Early Wonder also can be used for greens. Planting the seeds ½ inch apart without thinning produces an abundance of greens. Swiss chard is a heavy producer of greens very similar to beet greens.*

Broccoli, *Brassica oleracea* var. *botrytis* (also known as italian broccoli, sprouting broccoli, and calabrese), is a hardy vegetable of the cabbage family that is high in vitamins A and D. It develops best during cool seasons of the year. Broccoli has become popular for both small and large gardens, and it now is eaten much more frequently than in past years. Recent discoveries of health benefits associated with eating broccoli have helped to popularize this vegetable. Improvements in varieties, growing techniques, packing, and handling methods have greatly improved the quality of the fresh product available on the market. Talented cooks have also become more adept at preparing this tasty, healthful vegetable.

When broccoli plants of most varieties are properly grown and harvested, they can yield over an extended period. Side heads develop after the large, central head is removed. Two crops per year (spring and fall) may be grown in most parts of the country. New heat-tolerant varieties allow broccoli to be produced in all but the hottest parts of the season. Transplants are recommended to give the best start for spring planting because transplanting gets the plants established more quickly, so that they can bear their crop with minimal interference from the extreme heat of early summer. Fall crops may be direct-seeded in the garden if space allows or may be started in flats to replace early crops as their harvest ends.

Varieties

Hybrid: Cruiser (58 days to harvest; uniform, high yield; tolerant of dry conditions); Emerald City (58 days, deep blue, good for fall); Everest (55 days; tolerant to downy mildew, brown head, and head rot); Green Comet (55 days; early; heat tolerant); Green Goliath (55 days; huge, 10- to 12-inch heads); Green Valiant (60 days; spring, summer, or fall; tolerant of extremes); Legend (60 days; for summer or fall; extremely uniform); Pinnacle (62 days, very reliable producer); Premium Crop (65 days, highly tolerant to downy mildew); Packman (55 days; uniform; for summer or fall); and Southern Star (50 days; early; heat tolerant).

Open-Pollinated: Broccoli Raab, *Brassica rapa* var. *ruvo*, (60 days, specialty type with tender greens, many small heads); DeCicco (60 days, small head, nonuniform maturity); Purple Sprouting (85 days, purple heads, extremely tender texture); Romanesco (75 days; peaked, spiraling, pale green heads; unique); and Waltham 29 (75 days, late variety for fall production).

When to Plant

Transplant young, vigorously growing plants in early spring. (See the maps, page 26.) Plants that remain too long in seed flats may produce "button" heads soon after planting. For fall crops, buy or grow your own transplants or plant seeds directly in the garden. For fall planting, start seedlings in midsummer for transplanting into the garden in late summer. To determine the best time for setting your fall transplants, count backward from the first fall frost in your area and add about 10 to the days

to harvest from transplants. Remember that time from seed to transplant is not included in this figure.

Spacing of Plants and Depth of Planting

Plant seeds ¼ to ½ inch deep, or set transplants slightly deeper than they were grown originally. Plant or thin seedlings 18 to 24 inches apart in the row, and allow 36 inches between rows. Broccoli plants grow upright, often reaching a height of 2½ feet. Space plants 2 feet apart in all directions in beds.

Care

Use starter fertilizer for transplants, and side-dress nitrogen fertilizer when the plants are half grown (see page 20). Provide ample soil moisture, especially as the heads develop.

Harvesting

The edible parts of broccoli are compact clusters of unopened flower buds and the attached portion of stem. The green buds develop first in one large central head and later in several smaller side shoots. Cut the central head with 5 to 6 inches of stem, after the head is fully developed, but before it begins to loosen and separate and the individual flowers start to open (show bright yellow). Removing the central head stimulates the side shoots to develop for later pickings. These side shoots grow from the axils of the lower leaves. You usually can continue to harvest broccoli for several weeks.

Common Problems

Aphids (see page 40); **cabbage worms** (page 62); and **diseases** (page 61).

Questions and Answers

Q. How large should the central head of broccoli grow before cutting? A. Harvest the central head when the individual florets begin to enlarge and develop, and before flowering begins. Size varies with variety, growing conditions, and season of growth; but central heads should grow to be 4 to 6 inches in diameter, or even larger. Late side shoots may reach only 1 to 2 inches in diameter.

Q. What causes small plants, poor heading, and early flowering? A. Yellow flowers may appear before the heads are ready to harvest during periods of high temperatures. Planting too late in the spring or failing to give the plants a good start contributes to this condition. Premature flower development also may be caused by interrupted growth resulting from extended chilling of young plants, extremely early planting, holding plants in a garden center until they are too old or too dry, and severe drought conditions. Small heads that form soon after plants are

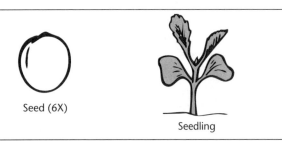

Seed (6X)

Seedling

set in the garden are called "buttons" and usually result from mistreated seedlings' being held too long or improperly before sale or planting. Applying a starter fertilizer at transplanting gets the plants off to a good start but cannot correct all the difficulties mentioned.

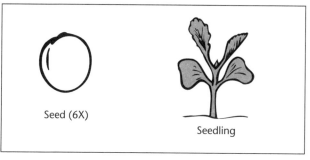

Seed (6X)

Seedling

Brussels Sprouts

Brussels sprouts, *Brassica oleracea* var. *gemmifera* (named after Brussels, Belgium, where the vegetable was first popular), is a hardy, slow-growing, long-season vegetable belonging to the cabbage family. In the proper season of the year, it can be grown with fair success in most areas of the country. In mild areas, or where there is deep snow cover, the sprouts may overwinter.

The "sprouts" (small heads that resemble miniature cabbages) are produced in the leaf axils, starting at the base of the stem and working upward. Sprouts improve in quality and grow best during cool or even lightly frosty weather. Brussels sprouts require a long growing period, though newer hybrids have greatly reduced this requirement. In all but the most northern states, summers are usually too warm for completely satisfactory production from spring plantings. Plants set out in late spring to early summer grow satisfactorily and mature high-quality sprouts when the fall weather begins to cool.

Varieties

Hybrid: Bubbles (82 days to harvest, dependable, tolerates warm weather, resistant to rust); Jade Cross (90 days, resistant to yellows); Jade Cross E (90 days; sprouts larger, easier to remove from stalk than with original strain); Oliver (85 days; early; easy-to-pick, attractive sprouts); Prince Marvel (90 days; tight, sweet sprouts); Royal Marvel (85 days; tolerant to bottom rot and tipburn; tight sprouts; very productive); and Valiant (90 days; smooth, uniform sprouts).

Open-Pollinated: Long Island Improved (90 days; variable, harder to produce heavy, uniform crop with this variety) and Rubine (105 days; red plants and sprouts; novel, but very late maturing, not nearly as productive as recommended hybrid green types).

When to Plant

Transplant in early summer to midsummer about the same time that you would plant late, long-season cabbage. The seed should be sown in a protected location in seed flats, 4 to 5 weeks before transplanting. Transplant the seedlings to the permanent garden location when space and time allow, but at least 90 to 100 days before the first-frost date for your area. (See the maps, page 26.) For summer harvest, you must plant transplants of an early, heat-resistant variety in very early spring. Sprouts maturing in hot weather or under dry conditions are more likely to develop bitterness. Fall production is the most practical and rewarding in most parts of the country.

Spacing of Plants and Depth of Planting

Space plants 24 to 36 inches apart in the row, or 24 inches in all directions in beds. Cover seeds ¼ to ½ inch deep, and transplant the seedlings when they are about 3 inches tall. Do not allow transplants to become stunted in the flats before transplanting.

Care

Brussels sprouts are grown much like the related cole crops, cabbage and broccoli. Apply one side-dress application of nitrogen fertilizer (see page 20) when the plants are 12 inches tall, and water to keep the crop growing vigorously during the heat of summer. Without ample soil moisture, the crop fails. Insect control is also very important at this stage to keep the plants growing vigorously. Cultivate shallowly around the plants to prevent root damage. The sprouts form in the axils of the leaves (the space between the base of the leaf and the stem above it).

Commercial gardeners remove the leaves to accelerate harvest, but this practice is not essential in the home garden. Some gardeners believe that the sprouts develop better if the lowermost six to eight leaves are removed from the sides of the stalk as the sprouts develop. Two or three additional leaves can be removed each week, but several of the largest, healthiest, fully expanded upper leaves should always be left intact on top to continue feeding the plant. About 3 weeks before harvest, the plants may be topped (the growing point removed) to speed the completion of sprout development on the lower-stem area.

Harvesting

The small sprouts or buds form heads 1 to 2 inches in diameter. They may be picked (or cut) off the stem when they are firm and about 1 inch in size. The lower sprouts mature first. The lowermost leaves, if they have not been removed already, should be removed when the sprouts are harvested. Harvest sprouts before the leaves yellow.

Common Problems

Aphids (see page 40); **cabbage worms** (page 62); and **diseases** (page 61).

Questions and Answers

Q. Why do my sprouts remain loose tufts of leaves instead of developing into firm heads? *A. When the sprouts develop in hot weather (after spring seeding or during a warm fall), they often do not form compact heads. Use transplants for early plantings, and maintain ample soil moisture. You also can cut off the top growing point when the plant reaches 24 to 36 inches in height. This practice stops leaf growth and directs the plant's energy to the developing sprouts. In addition, check the variety you have planted. The newer, faster-maturing varieties are generally more suitable for getting dependable yields.*

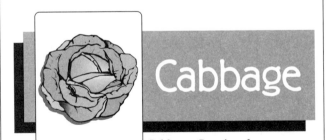

Cabbage, *Brassica oleracea* var. *capitata,* is a hardy vegetable that grows especially well in fertile soils. There are various shades of green available, as well as red or purple types. Head shape varies from the standard round to flattened or pointed. Most varieties have smooth leaves, but the savoy types have crinkly textured leaves. Cabbage is easy to grow if you select suitable varieties and practice proper culture and insect management. Always regarded as a good source of vitamins, cabbage recently has been shown to have disease-preventive properties as well.

Cabbage thrives during both spring and fall seasons, tolerating frost but not extreme heat. Cabbage is used in slaw, salads, sauerkraut, soups, and other cooked dishes.

Varieties

Green cabbage is grown more often than the red or savoy types, but red cabbage has become increasingly popular for color in salads and cooked dishes. The savoy varieties are grown for slaw and salads. Varieties that mature later usually grow larger heads and are more suitable for making sauerkraut than the early varieties. All the varieties listed here are resistant to fusarium wilt ("yellows") unless otherwise indicated. All are hybrid varieties unless marked OP, for open-pollinated variety.

Green: Charmant (64 days to harvest; 3 to 4 pounds; early; dark green); Cheers (75 days, solid round heads, tolerant to black rot and thrips); Early Jersey Wakefield (OP–63 days; pointed heads; stands well, resists splitting); Fortuna (82 days; 3 to 4 pounds; widely adapted; resistant to tipburn, black rot); Grand Slam (82 days; 7- to 8-inch heads; tolerant to black leaf speck, black rot, cold temperatures); Green Cup (73 days; 4 to 6 pounds; uniform, tight heads); King Cole (74 days; large, firm, extremely uniform heads); Quisto (89 days; 4 to 6 pounds; good fresh, for kraut or storage); and Stonehead (70 days; 3 to 4 pounds; solid, very dense, slow to burst).

Savoy: Savoy Ace (80 days, 3 to 4 pounds, holds well, cold resistant, not resistant to yellows); Savoy King (85 days, dark green color, very uniform); and Savoy Queen (88 days, 5 pounds, deep green color, good heat tolerance).

Red: Lasso (OP–70 days, compact plants, solid heads, resists splitting); Red Meteor (75 days, firm, good for all seasons); Rookie (68 days, 3 to 6 pounds, tolerant to black rot and tipburn); Ruby Ball (71 days, 4 pounds, slow to burst, resists both cold and heat); and Ruby Perfection (85 days, 3 pounds, slow to burst, stores well).

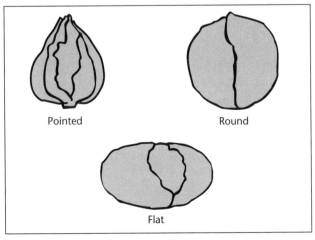

Pointed   Round   Flat

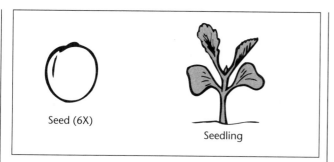

Seed (6X)

Seedling

When to Plant

Transplant early cabbage soon enough that it matures before the heat of summer. Many varieties are available, and two or three varieties of different maturities can provide harvest over a long period. Hardened plants are tolerant of frosts and can be planted among the earliest of cool-season garden vegetables. Cabbage is easily transplanted from either bare-root or cell-pack-grown plants. Late cabbage must be started during the heat of midsummer, but it develops its main head during the cooling weather of fall. It may be transplanted or seeded directly in the garden. In summer, if possible, place seed flats or seedbeds where some protection from the sun is available, either natural or artificial. Try especially hard at this season to transplant on cloudy, overcast, or rainy days for minimizing shock from the direct sun of summer.

Spacing of Plants and Depth of Planting

Space plants 12 to 24 inches apart in the row, depending upon the variety and the size of head desired. The closer the spacing, the smaller the heads. Early varieties are usually planted 12 inches apart, and later varieties are planted 18 to 24 inches apart. In beds, plant cabbage 12 to 18 inches apart in all directions. Early varieties produce 1- to 3-pound heads, and later varieties produce 4- to 8-pound heads. Sow cabbage seed ¼ to ½ inch deep. Keep the seeds moist, and thin or transplant the seedlings to the desired spacing. The plants removed may be transplanted to another row or flat.

Care

Use starter fertilizer when transplanting, and sidedress nitrogen fertilizer when the plants are half grown (see page 20). Cultivate shallowly to keep down weeds. Ample soil moisture is necessary throughout the growing season to produce good cabbage. Irrigation is especially important in fall plantings to help the young plants withstand the intense sunlight and heat of summer and to supply the developing heads with sufficient water to develop quickly.

Harvesting

Cabbage can be harvested anytime after the heads form. For highest yield, cut the cabbage heads when they are solid (firm to hand pressure) but before they crack or split. When heads are mature, a sudden heavy rain may cause heads to crack or split wide open. The exposed internal tissue soon becomes unusable. Harvest and salvage split heads as soon as possible after they are discovered.

Cabbage for storage must be firm, mature, and free from injury by insects or diseases. The late varieties usually store better than the early ones. Cabbage should be stored under cold, moist conditions (see pages 167 and 168).

In addition to harvesting the mature heads of the cabbage planted in the spring, you can harvest a later crop of small heads (cabbage sprouts). These sprouts develop on the stumps of the cut stems. Cut as close to the lower surface of the head as possible, leaving the loose outer leaves intact. Buds that grow in the axils of these leaves (the angle between the base of the leaf and the stem above it) later form sprouts. The sprouts develop to 2 to 4 inches in diameter and should be picked when firm. Continue control of cabbage worms and other pests. If this control cannot be maintained, remove and destroy or compost the stumps because they serve as a breeding ground for diseases and insect pests.

Common Problems

Yellows or fusarium wilt is a relatively common disease that causes the leaves of plants to wilt and die. The first sign of the disease is yellowing and browning of the lower leaves. The plants are stunted before wilting occurs. Grow yellows-resistant (YR) or yellows-tolerant varieties. Most modern hybrids have this tolerance or resistance bred into them.

Blackleg and black rot are two diseases that cause severe losses. The plants may be stunted, turn yellow, and die. Blackleg is named for the black cankers on the stem. The taproot often rots away. Black rot can be recognized by large, V-shaped, yellow-to-brown areas in the leaves, starting at the leaf edge. The veins turn black. Soft rot usually follows black-rot infection.

Control is essentially the same for blackleg and black rot. Both diseases are spread by seed, transplants, and insects. Buy seed that has been hot-water treated to kill the disease organisms. Do not buy transplants that are wilted, are an unhealthy shade of green, or have black spots on the stems or leaves.

When you find diseased plants in the garden, collect the leaves, stems, and tops; and burn or dispose of them. Do not put diseased plants into the compost pile. Avoid cultural practices (crowding, overwatering, planting in poorly drained soil, and inadequate insect control) that support the disease organisms of black rot and blackleg. If possible, grow black-rot-resistant varieties.

Aphids (see page 40). Apply a suggested insecticide before cabbage heads begin to form.

Flea beetles (see page 40). Apply a suggested insecticide.

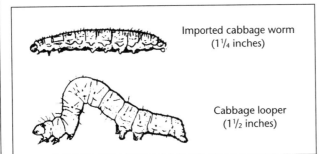

Imported cabbage worm (1¼ inches)

Cabbage looper (1½ inches)

Cabbage worms. Three species of cabbage worms (imported cabbage worms, cabbage loopers, and diamondback moth worms) commonly attack the leaves and heads of cabbage and related cole crops. Imported cabbage worms are velvety green caterpillars. The moth is white and commonly is seen during the day hovering over plants in the garden. Cabbage loopers ("measuring worms") are smooth, light green caterpillars. The cabbage looper crawls by doubling up (to form a loop) and then moving the front of its body forward. The moth is brown and is most active at night. Diamondback worms are small, pale green caterpillars that are pointed on both ends. The moth is gray, with diamond-shaped markings when the wings are closed. The damage caused by diamondback larvae looks like shot holes in the leaf.

The larval or worm stages of these insects cause damage by eating holes in the leaves and cabbage head. The adult moths or butterflies lay their eggs on the leaves but otherwise do not damage the plants. The worms are not easy to see because they are fairly small and blend with the cabbage leaves. Cabbage worms are quite destructive and can ruin the crop if not controlled. They are even worse in fall plantings than in spring gardens because the population has had several months to increase. About the time of the first frost in the fall, moth and caterpillar numbers finally begin to decline drastically. Protect your plants with suggested biological or chemical insecticides from the time that they are transplanted until harvest.

Rabbits. In many settings, rabbits can quickly devour cabbage-family transplants. Especially in early spring, the lush green plants present a delectable, irresistible morsel to these furry fiends. Usually, if plants are protected until they increase in size, the pests eat only individual leaves, not entire plants. Metal cans with both ends removed often offer some protection from rabbits as well as cutworms. Hotcaps or row covers also may deter them. Wire mesh bent in an arch and placed over the entire row also should deter suburbia's number-one protected garden pest.

Questions and Answers

Q. What can I do to prevent my cabbage heads from splitting? *A. Splitting is caused by the pressure of excessive water taken up after the heads are solid. Cutting the roots (spading on two sides of the plant) or breaking the roots (lifting and twisting the head to one side) can often reduce excessive splitting or bursting, but it also damages the plant and requires that the heads be harvested relatively soon.*

Q. What causes cabbage to develop seedstalks rather than solid heads? *A. Cabbage plants "bolt" (form premature seedstalks) when they are exposed to low temperatures (35° to 45°F) for extended periods. Such chilling may happen if plants are set out too early or if an unseasonal blast of cold assaults the garden. After the plants have stems as large as a pencil, they are subject to this "cold conditioning," which initiates the flowering response.*

Q. What is flowering cabbage? *A. Nonheading varieties of cabbage (similar to flowering kale) have been developed for ornamental uses. They have colorful white, pink, or red rosettes of leaves surrounded by green or purple outer leaves. Most colorful during cool fall weather, they should be started in early summer to midsummer and set out with fall and winter plantings of regular, heading varieties of cabbage. Flowering cabbage (and flowering kale) are edible as well as ornamental.*

Q. Why do butterflies fly around my cabbage plants? *A. Those butterflies (white or brown) are probably the moths of cabbage worms. They lay eggs on the plants. The eggs hatch into the worms that cause considerable damage unless controlled. Most control strategies are aimed at the developing larvae rather than the mature moths themselves.*

Q. What causes large, lumpy swellings of my cabbage roots? The plants also are stunted. *A. Swellings and distorted roots on stunted, wilted plants may be symptoms of clubroot disease. This disease is caused by a fungus that remains in the garden soil for many years once it becomes established. It is spread by movement of infested soil and infected transplants. Other related cole crops (like broccoli and cauliflower) also may become infected. If you suspect that you have clubroot disease in your garden, ask your local extension office for help. If, in fact, you have clubroot in a location, destroy infected plant parts (including the roots) and for at least 4 years avoid planting any member of the cabbage family there, including radishes, turnips, and ornamental relatives of cabbage.*

Carrot, *Daucus carota* var. *sativas,* is a hardy, cool-season biennial that is grown for the thickened root it produces in its first growing season. Although carrots can endure summer heat in many areas, they grow best when planted in early spring. Midsummer plantings, which mature quickly in cool fall weather, produce tender, sweet "baby" carrots that are much prized. Carrots are eaten both raw and cooked, and they can be stored for winter use. They are rich in carotene (the source of vitamin A) and high in fiber and sugar content.

Carrot

Varieties

Small, Round: Orbit (58 days to harvest, good color, few off-types, best harvested at the size of a 50-cent piece) and Thumbelina (60 days; 1992 AAS winner; round roots; good for planting in containers and in heavy, shallow, or rocky soil).

Baby: Baby Spike (52 days; 3- to 4-inch roots, ½ inch thick; excellent internal color; tender; holds small size well); Little Finger (65 days; tiny tender roots; 5-inch roots, ½ inch thick; golden orange, sweet, and crisp); Minicor (55 days; slender fingerling carrots; colors early; uniform, cylindrical, blunt tip; good flavor); and Short 'n Sweet (68 days; rich, sweet flavor; 4-inch roots, broad at shoulder, tapered to a point; good for heavy or poor soil).

Chantenay: Red-Cored Chantenay (70 days; heavy yield; good flavor; short, thick roots, broad at the shoulder, tapered to blunt tip); and Royal Chantenay (70 days; broad-shouldered, tapered roots; bright orange; good for heavy or shallow soils).

Danvers: Danvers Half-Long (75 days; very uniform, 7- to 8-inch roots tapered to very blunt end; sweet, tender) and Danvers 126 (75 days; heavier yield than Danvers; smooth roots; tops withstand heat).

Nantes: Bolero (hybrid–70 days; 7- to 8-inch roots, uniformly thick, tapered slightly to blunt tip; superior resistance to foliage disease); Ingot (hybrid–70 days; 8-inch roots, 1½ inches thick; indistinct core; deep orange color; strong tops; extremely sweet); Nantes Coreless (68 days; orange-red; small core, medium top); Scarlet Nantes (70 days; bright orange, slightly tapered, 6-inch roots; crisp, tender, and flavorful; standard for high-quality

carrots); Sweetness (hybrid–63 days; very sweet and crunchy; cylindrical, 6-inch roots, 1 inch thick); and Touchon (70 days; interior, exterior bright orange; 7-inch roots, nearly coreless).

Imperator: Avenger (hybrid–70 days; extra-fancy; slightly blunt, tapered roots, 9 to 10 inches long); Gold Pak (76 days; 8-inch roots, 1½ inches thick; sweet, tender, as coreless as any; good for juice); Imperator 58 (68 days; smooth, fine-grained, long, tapered roots; standard long, thin type); Legend (hybrid–65 days; high yield; smooth, uniform, 9- to 11-inch roots, 1½ inches at shoulder; tolerant to cracking); Orlando Gold (hybrid–78 days; uniform, long, tapered shape; excellent flavor, color; 30 percent more carotene); and Tendersweet (75 days; long, tapered roots; rich orange color; sweet, coreless).

Novelty: Belgium White (75 days; very mild flavor; long, tapered, white roots; productive, vigorous).

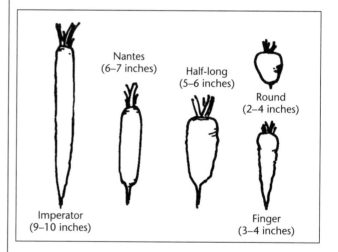

Nantes (6–7 inches)
Half-long (5–6 inches)
Round (2–4 inches)
Imperator (9–10 inches)
Finger (3–4 inches)

When to Plant

Carrots are usually planted with other frost-tolerant vegetables as soon as the soil mellows in the spring. They may be planted earlier in gardens with sandy soil. The soil should be plowed and prepared to a depth of 8 to 9 inches to allow full development of the carrot roots, and the seedbed should be worked uniformly to break up clumps and clods that prevent penetration of the roots. Varieties with extremely long roots (Imperator and Tendersweet) usually are recommended only for home gardens with deep, sandy soil. Excess organic debris worked into the soil just before planting also may affect root penetration, causing forked and twisted roots.

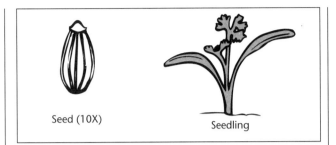

Seed (10X)   Seedling

Spacing of Plants and Depth of Planting

Plant seeds ¼ to ½ inch deep (no more than two or three seeds per inch) in early spring. Later sowings may be planted ½ to ¾ inch deep when the soil is dryer and warmer. Space rows 12 to 18 inches apart. A single radish seed planted every 6 to 12 inches can mark the row. Germination requires as long as 2 weeks, and the seedlings may not emerge uniformly. If heavy rains occur after sowing, packing the soil surface, no seedlings may emerge. Thin the seedlings, when they are about 1 inch tall, to no more than three seedlings per inch for finger carrots; one or two seedlings per inch for carrots that will be harvested young; and one seedling per 1 to 2 inches for larger varieties like Danvers and Chantenay that will be allowed to develop to full size and be harvested mature for canning or freezing.

Care

Carrots germinate best in warm, moist soil. Covering the row with clear polyethylene film (see page 36) warms the soil and conserves moisture. Remove the film immediately when seedlings appear. To assure germination of successive plantings during the late spring and summer months, it may be necessary to supply water by sprinkling. In the heat of summer, some shade may be necessary to keep the tiny seedlings from burning off at the soil line.

Young carrot seedlings are weak and grow slowly . It is essential to keep weeds under control for the first few weeks. Cultivate shallowly with a knife-blade cultivator or hoe. Deep cultivation may injure the roots.

Harvesting

Carrots can be harvested or "pulled" when the roots are at least ½ inch in diameter. Under usual conditions, carrot tops may not be strong enough to withstand actually being pulled from the ground, and digging helps to remove the roots without damage. Finger carrots are usually ready to harvest within 50 to 60 days. Other varieties should be allowed to grow until they have reached a diameter of at least ¾ inch (about 60 to 70 days after planting). They then may be harvested over a 3- to 4-week period. Summer-planted carrots may be left in the ground until a killing frost. Some gardeners place a straw mulch over the row so that carrots can be harvested until the ground freezes solid. In many areas, a heavy mulch allows harvest of carrot roots throughout the winter. For carrots to be stored, cut off the tops 1 inch above the root, and place in storage at 32°F with high humidity. Carrots may be placed in a refrigerator, buried in lightly moist sand in an underground cellar, or stored in the garden in a pit insulated with straw (see pages 167 and 168). Under proper storage conditions, carrots keep 4 to 6 months.

Questions and Answers

Q. What causes my carrots to turn green on the crown (top) of the root? *A. This condition is called "sunburning." It causes an off-flavor and dark green pieces in the cooked product. Cut away the green portion, and use the rest of the root. When the tops are healthy, sunburning can be avoided by pulling a small amount of loose soil up to the row when the roots are swelling (about 40 to 50 days after planting).*

Q. Why are my carrots misshapen, with forked and twisted roots? *A. Forking may result from attacks of root-knot nematodes (see page 41), from stones, from deep and close cultivation, or (more frequently) from planting in a soil that was poorly prepared. Twisting and intertwining result from seeding too thickly and inadequate thinning of seedlings.*

Q. What causes my carrots to have fine hairy roots, poor color, and a bitter taste? *A. These conditions are caused by a viral disease known as "aster yellows." See "Bacterial and viral diseases," page 41, for control recommendations.*

Cauliflower

Cauliflower, *Brassica oleracea* var. *botrytis*, is a cool-season vegetable that can be cooked, pickled, eaten raw with dips, or used as a salad delicacy. It is more demanding to grow well than most of its relatives in the cabbage family. Cauliflower does not tolerate as much heat or cold as cabbage or grow as well as broccoli in dry weather.

Recently, the specialty market has seen a boom in "broccoflower," which is really a form of cauliflower with green-pigmented heads. These types are easier to grow because they do not require blanching. Flavor and texture are also rated excellent.

Varieties

Open-Pollinated: Self-Blanche (71 days to harvest; 7-inch heads with excellent leaf protection; does not need tying, especially in fall crops) and Snowball Y Improved (68 days, 6-inch heads protected by heavy leaf cover).

Hybrid: Andes (68 days, most adaptable self-blanching type); Candid Charm (65 days, large head, excellent protection); Serrano (70 days; 6- to 7-inch heads; excellent leaf cover, head quality); Snow Crown (60 days; resistant to yellows; tolerant of heat, cold); Snow Grace (65 days, 8-inch head, tight curd, improved Snow Crown type); Snow King (50 days; 8- to 9-inch heads; very early; heat tolerant); and White Corona (30 days; 3- to 4-inch heads; exceptionally early; good for small gardens and short seasons).

Purple: Violet Queen Hybrid (70 days, purple head, needs no blanching, turns green when cooked).

"Broccoflower": Chartreuse Hybrid II (62 days; no tying; greenish yellow curd) and Green Goddess Hybrid (65 days, no tying; lime green, good taste, easy to grow).

When to Plant

Cauliflower is best started from transplants for both spring and fall crops. Do not transplant sooner than 2 to 3 weeks before the average frost-free date in the spring. (See the maps, page 26.) Cauliflower is more sensitive to the cold than its cabbage-family relatives. It is important to start cauliflower early enough that it matures before the heat of the summer but not so early that it is injured by the cold. In some seasons, that compromise may be almost impossible to achieve. Transplant autumn cauliflower about the same time as fall cabbage. Use starter fertilizer (see page 20) when transplanting. Start the transplants so that they grow actively until transplanting and never cease growth. Always use young, active transplants. Never buy stunted plants started in flats and held too long before transplanting; results with inferior plants are almost always disappointing.

Spacing of Plants and Depth of Planting

Space plants 18 to 24 inches apart in the row. Use the wider spacing for fall plantings.

If plants are not available, or if you wish to grow your own transplants, see "Starting Plants at Home," pages 45 to 48. For fall harvest, start seeds indoors or in a protected location 4 to 5 weeks before you need the plants (see "Planting Dates for Midwest Gardens," page 28). Plant seeds ¼ to ½ inch deep (10 seeds per inch) in a seed

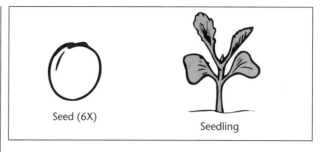

Seed (6X)   Seedling

row for later transplanting, or 1 or 2 seeds per cell in flats; and keep them watered during germination and growth of seedlings. Transplant the seedlings to the permanent location in the garden. Transplants grown in cell packs suffer much less shock when planted and usually yield superior results.

Care

Cauliflower plants should be kept growing vigorously from the seedling stage through harvest. Any interruption (extreme cold, heat, drought, or plant damage) can abort development of the edible portion. Large plants that never develop a head are extremely disappointing. Cauliflower must have a consistent and ample supply of soil moisture. Side-dress nitrogen fertilizer (see page 20) when the plants are half grown.

When the head begins to form (shows 2 to 3 inches of white curd at the growing point), it is ready to blanch. Tie the outer leaves together over the center of the plant to protect the head from sunburn and to keep it from turning green and developing an off-flavor. The variety Self-Blanche is named for its natural tendency to curl its leaves over its head. Several other varieties possess this trait, especially when maturing in the fall. Under cool conditions, these varieties blanch very well, and tying is unnecessary.

Harvesting

The cauliflower head's curd develops rapidly under proper growing conditions. It grows 6 to 8 inches in diameter and is ready to harvest within 7 to 12 days after blanching begins. The mature heads should be compact, firm, and white. Harvest the heads by cutting the main stem. Leave a few green outer leaves attached to protect the heads. Cut the heads before they become overmature and develop a coarse, "ricey" appearance. Once individual florets can be seen, quality deteriorates rapidly. Because cauliflower does not ordinarily develop side shoots, plants may be disposed of or composted after heads are harvested.

Common Problems

Cabbage worms (see page 62); **black rot** (page 61). If growth is interrupted, the heads may not develop or may develop poorly. Growth can be interrupted by plants' being held too long, causing hardening and cessation of growth before transplanting; by too much chilling before or after transplanting; or by drought.

Questions and Answers

Q. What causes leaves in the head and separation of the head into loose, smaller curds? *A. These conditions are caused when cauliflower matures during hot weather. Try to time maturity dates of cauliflower to minimize the risk of extreme heat as the heads form.*

Q. Why does my late cauliflower fail to make satisfactory heads? *A. Late plantings are sometimes difficult to grow. The young plants often do not become well established under hot, dry summer conditions. Give the plants ample water, and do not plant late cauliflower plants too close together.*

Q. Is purple cauliflower grown in the same way as regular cauliflower? *A. Purple cauliflower is actually a type of broccoli that is purple. It resembles cauliflower in overall appearance and does not require blanching. The purple head turns green when cooked.*

Q. What causes browning of the curd? *A. This condition is caused by downy mildew. Downy mildew, which is brought on by wet conditions, can be controlled through the use of a suggested fungicide. Raised-bed culture and any other cultural measures that encourage good soil and air drainage also help minimize the risk from this disease.*

Celery, *Apium graveolens* var. *dulce,* is a member of the same family as carrots, parsley, and parsnips. It was first mentioned as a food crop in 1623 France. Originally, celery was available for only a short season; but now, with specialized growing areas around the country and improved storage, it is available throughout the year. Celery is grown for the crisp, juicy, flavorful petioles that are usually formed into tight upright rosettes. A labor-, water-, and nutrient-intensive crop, it can be produced in much of the United States, preferably in a cool, moist season.

Varieties

Green: Florida 683 (100 days to harvest, bushy, medium green); Hercules (100 days; dark green, extra-heavy plant; top yields); Matador (105 days; dark green, smooth petioles; shorter plant; yellows tolerant); Picador (100 days, extra tall, semi-smooth, medium green, yellows tolerant); Starlet (110 days; tall; medium green; good taste; resistant to fusarium races 1 and 2); Utah 52-70 (98 days, dark green, uniform, compact); and Ventura (100 days; tall; long petioles; tolerant to fusarium).

Self-Blanching: Golden Plume (90 days, yellow) and Golden Self-Blanching (115 days; tender; solid, compact, sturdy plant).

Leaf: Dinant (150 days, numerous thin stalks, full flavor) and Leaf Celery.

Novelty: Pink and Red (both color up best in fall; hardier than green types; retain color when cooked).

When to Plant

Because celery has a small seed size, slow germination, and a long season of growth, plants should be started in flats and transplanted into the garden when they are about 3 inches tall. Cover seeds with 1/8 to 1/4 inch of soil, and keep moist. Allow 2 to 4 weeks for germination. For early crops, sow seed in February or March. It takes 10 to 12 weeks to get plants ready for the field, so count backward from the average latest frost to determine when to sow seeds for your area. (See the maps, page 26.)

Spacing of Plants and Depth of Planting

Space plants 12 to 18 inches apart in rows 3 feet apart, or 15 inches apart in all directions in beds. Celery may be direct-seeded, but since seed germination and seedling growth are slow, early weed control is extremely difficult.

Care

Celery requires rich soil and abundant and regular supplies of moisture and nutrients. Celery plants are not good at searching for nutrients or water. Various organic mulching materials may help maintain even soil moisture, temperature, and fertility. Celery prefers maturing

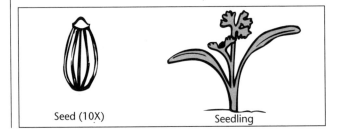

Seed (10X)   Seedling

in a cool season, so late-spring plantings that mature in autumn usually give best results except in mild areas where cool, moist winters produce the best celery. Weed control throughout the season is very important as celery is a poor competitor and is quickly affected by competing weed growth.

Harvesting

To produce celery resembling that found in food stores, the leaf stalks must be "blanched." Green, unblanched stalks are dark green and have a very strong flavor, which is wonderful for cooking but virtually inedible fresh out of hand. Blanching is accomplished by excluding light over a period while the plants continue growing. Cardboard, paper, boards, or even hilled-up soil can be used for this purpose.

In the garden, wrap paper around the plant, leaving the topmost foliage exposed. Tie the paper in place with twine, and check at intervals to see how blanching is progressing. When stalks reach a uniform light greenish yellow color, whole plants may be harvested by cutting just above the root at the base of the plant. Because plants blanched too long become very susceptible to rots, try to harvest as soon as blanching is complete.

Soil should not be used to blanch in warm seasons as it encourages rots.

Self-blanching types are naturally pale in color and tight-growing, yielding a pale central bunch without any tying and blanching. Any fully green foliage normally is very strong in flavor.

Leaf types are used green as seasonings, much like flat-leaf parsley but with the distinctive celery flavor.

Common Problems

Pink rot, early blight, and late blight are three fungal diseases that may attack celery. Good air circulation and drainage can help avoid infection. If problems occur, fungicide treatments may be necessary. Check labels for available effective products.

Fusarium or yellows is a fairly common disease that can be minimized in infested soils by using resistant or tolerant varieties.

Questions and Answers

Q. My celery plants sent up seedstalks rather than producing nice, tight bunches of leafstalks. What went wrong? *A: Plants set out too early and exposed to too-cold conditions may bolt prematurely to seed. Delay setting plants in the garden until the season has settled if bolting has been a problem in past years.*

Chard

Chard, *Beta vulgaris* var. *cicla* (also known as swiss chard), is a member of the beet family that can be grown successfully as a vegetable green in most parts of the country. It may be planted early because the seedlings are tolerant to moderate frost. Chard is essentially a beet that has been selected for leaf production at the expense of storage root formation.

Chard produces fresh greens throughout the summer, even in southern locations. The large, fleshy leafstalks may be white, yellow, or red, with broad, crisp, green leaf blades. The leaf blades are prepared like spinach, and the midribs or stalks may be cooked in the same manner as asparagus. Chard is an attractive ornamental that adds to the beauty of a garden. Many gardeners like to grow chard because it is not available in food markets, yields well, and has few production problems.

Varieties

Red Midrib: Burgundy, Rhubarb, and Ruby. **White Midrib:** Fordhook Giant, Geneva, Large White Broad-Ribbed, Lucullus, Perpetual, and Winter King. **Red, White, or Yellow Midrib (mixed):** Rainbow.

When to Plant

Chard does well on any soil where beets, lettuce, or spinach can grow. Plants may be started inside and transplanted to the garden after the danger of frost is past, but most gardeners plant seeds directly into the garden in early spring to midspring.

Spacing of Plants and Depth of Planting

For seeding outdoors, plant seeds ½ to ¾ inch deep (8 to 10 seeds per foot of row), in rows far enough apart for proper cultivation. Like beets, chard "seed" is actually a dried berry, a multiple fruit with more than one seed inside. This makes precision seeding difficult and makes thinning more often necessary for a proper stand. Thin the seedlings to 4 to 6 inches apart. An alternative method is to thin the seedlings to 2 to 3 inches apart; then, when they are large enough for greens (6 to 8 inches tall), harvest the excess plants whole, leaving a

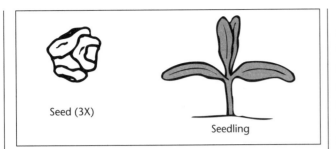

Seed (3X)

Seedling

final spacing of 9 to 12 inches between plants. Transplants should be set in the garden 9 to 12 inches apart.

Harvesting

The most common method of harvesting chard is to cut off the outer leaves 1½ inches above the ground while they are young and tender (about 8 to 12 inches long). Be careful not to damage the terminal bud, at the center of the bottom of the growing rosette of foliage.

Chinese Cabbage

Chinese cabbage, *Brassica rapa* var. *pekinensis* (also known as celery cabbage and wong bok), is an ancient oriental crop that is gaining popularity. The name "chinese cabbage" is misleading because this hardy, cool-season salad vegetable is more closely related to mustard, not cabbage. Its mild flavor may be somewhat similar to that of celery (although chinese cabbage is not related to celery), and its leaves are thinner, fuzzier, and more delicate than those of cabbage. Unfortunately, many gardeners do not consider growing chinese cabbage as a salad vegetable because spring sowings fail to form desirable heads.

Varieties

There are two more or less distinct forms: pe tsai, a heading type that resembles Cos lettuce but grows larger and denser, and pak choi (white mustard cabbage), a nonheading type that grows in loose, upright form like swiss chard. Within the pe tsai group, there are two head types: a tall, cylindrical, upright michihli type and the shorter, broader napa type. The pak choi varieties are usually more susceptible to early seedstalk formation.

Napa Pe Tsai: Blues (hybrid–65 days to harvest; early; multiple-disease resistance; slow to bolt; good for spring to early summer planting); China Express (hybrid–64 days; early; good disease resistance; good for spring, fall, or winter crop); China Flash (hybrid–55 days; extra early; sweet flavor; very slow to bolt; good for spring or fall crop); China Pride (hybrid–68 days; large, strong, uniform, broad heads; multiple-disease resistance; best for fall or winter crop); Orange Queen (hybrid–75 days; deep green heads with orange interior; very cold tolerant); Orient Express (hybrid–43 days; very early, heat resistant; small, solid oblong heads); and Two Seasons (hybrid–62 days; large, oval heads; resistant to bolting and soft rot).

Michihli Pe Tsai: Green Rocket (hybrid–65 days; holds well after picking; tall, solid heads); Jade Pagoda (hybrid–70 days; upright, 16-inch heads; cold tolerant; slow to bolt; resistant to soft rot); Michihli (75 days, dark green foliage, standard open-pollinated upright variety, best in cool seasons); and Monument (hybrid–80 days; tall, bright green heads; very disease tolerant).

Pak Choi (Bok Choy, *Brassica rapa* var. *chinensis):* Joi Choi (hybrid–45 days, white petioles, dark green leaves, slow to bolt, good for fall crops); Lei Choi (47 days; white petioles, rounded, dark green leaves; slow-bolting, compact plant); Mei Quing Choi (hybrid–45 days, medium green petioles and leaf blades; heat, cold tolerant; good for warm-season production); and Mi Choi (hybrid–45 days; long, smooth, white petioles, dark green leaves; good for warm-season production).

When to Plant

For best development, it is important that growth not be interrupted. Because chinese cabbage seedlings are more sensitive to transplanting than cabbage seedlings, the plants are best started in individual containers (like peat pellets or pots). For spring planting, transplant 2 to 3 weeks before the frost-free date and while the plants are still young (4 to 5 weeks). (See the maps, page 26.) Except in an extremely early spring, sowing seeds of heading types directly in the garden may not allow enough time for the seedlings to grow before warm summer days stim-

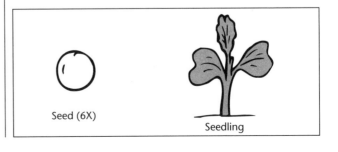

Seed (6X)

Seedling

ulate seedstalk formation and the plant becomes useless.

Chinese cabbage develops best during cool weather and is an excellent vegetable for fall gardens. Start seeds in midsummer for chinese cabbage grown as a fall crop. Varieties have been developed specifically for spring or fall crops, so choose one that matches the season in which it will be grown.

Spacing of Plants and Depth of Planting

Space plants 12 inches apart for upright varieties such as Michihli, 15 to 24 inches apart for the larger, broader heading types, and 8 to 12 inches apart for loose-leaf or bok choy types. For fall planting, sow seeds directly in the garden ¼ to ½ inch deep and 3 to 4 inches apart. Thin to the proper spacing for the variety chosen. Keep the soil moist, and thin or transplant with care.

Care

Maintain sufficient soil moisture to keep the plants growing vigorously. Side-dress nitrogen fertilizer (see page 20) when the plants are half grown.

Harvesting

The pak choi type develops long, loose, dark green leaves. The pe tsai type forms moderately firm, 2- to 5-pound heads. The blanched inner leaves are somewhere between mustard and cabbage in appearance. They are crisp, delicate in flavor, and an excellent salad substitute for lettuce or cabbage. Especially in spring, begin harvest as soon as the first heads begin to become firm. They do not hold very long in the warm days of early summer.

Common Problems

Aphids (see page 40); **cabbage worms** (page 62); and **flea beetles** (page 40).

Questions and Answers

Q. Why does my chinese cabbage fail to form a good head in the spring? Instead it sends up an early seedstalk. *A. Chinese cabbage quickly goes to seed during warm summer days. Dry weather accelerates the process. For best results, choose early varieties, start plants in individual containers, and transplant after the last hard frosts in the spring. Chinese cabbage seeded in late spring also goes to seed.*

Collard

Collard, *Brassica oleracea* var. *acephala* (also known as tree-cabbage or nonheading cabbage), is a cool-season vegetable green that is rich in vitamins and minerals. It grows better in warm weather and can tolerate more cold weather in the late fall than any other member of the cabbage family. Although collard is a popular substitute for cabbage in the Deep South, it can also be grown in northern areas because it is tolerant of frost. Hybrid varieties only very recently have been introduced, bringing hybrid uniformity and vigor to collards.

Varieties

Open-Pollinated: Champion (60 days to harvest; dark green, long-standing, compact plant; good cold tolerance); Georgia LS (75 days; wavy leaves; slow to bolt); Morris Heading (80 days, tall, savoyed-leaf type); and Vates (75 days, low-growing plant with smooth leaves).

Hybrid: Blue Max (68 days, slightly savoyed; heavy yields); Flash (73 days; early; long dark green leaves; slow to bolt); Heavi-Crop (65 days, hybrid Vates type); HiCrop (75 days; good taste, texture even in hot weather); and Top Bunch (67 days, heavy yield potential, compact plant).

When to Plant

Plant in early spring for summer harvest, and again in midsummer for fall and early winter harvest.

Spacing of Plants and Depth of Planting

Sow the seeds ¼ to ½ inch deep. Thin the seedlings to 6 inches apart, allow them to grow until they begin to touch, then harvest whole plants to give 18 inches between plants, which allows enough space for plants to mature. Thinned plants may be eaten. Allow at least 3 feet between rows because plants become large.

Care

If you maintain ample soil moisture during hot periods in the summer and control insect and disease pests, collards produce an abundant harvest.

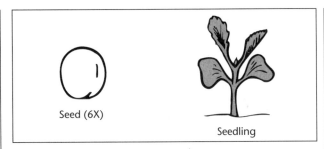

Seed (6X)

Seedling

Harvesting

All green parts of the plant are edible and may be harvested at any time during the growing season. Plants grown 6 inches apart can be cut at ground level when they reach 6 to 10 inches in height. Plants left at wider spacing should be harvested by picking the larger leaves when the plants are 10 to 12 inches tall. This harvesting method allows the younger leaves to continually develop for later use.

Some gardeners prefer the young, tender leaves and cut the inner rosette of young growth. This "loose head" may be blanched by tying the outer leaves together to keep out the sun. As with other cole crops, frost improves the flavor in the fall.

Common Problems

Aphids (see page 40); **cabbage worms** (page 62); and **diseases** (page 61).

Corn, Sweet

Sweet corn, *Zea mays* var. *rugosa*, is a warm-season vegetable that can be grown easily in any garden with sufficient light, fertility, growing season, and space. It is especially popular with home gardeners because it tastes appreciably better when it is harvested and eaten fresh from the garden. Successive plantings can yield continual harvest from early summer until frost if the weather cooperates.

Sweet corn may be divided into three distinct types according to genetic background: normal sugary (SU), sugary enhancer (SE), and supersweet (Sh$_2$).

Standard sweet corn varieties contain a "sugary (SU) gene" that is responsible for the sweetness and creamy texture of the kernels. This gene makes these original types sweeter and more tender than field corn. Sugary varieties have less initial kernel sugar than SE or Sh$_2$ varieties, and they rapidly convert their sugars to starch once ears are picked. SUs are best suited to being picked, husked, and eaten within a very short time. In the home garden, this is sometimes possible but not always practical. The old adage was "start the water boiling, run to the patch, pick and husk the corn, run back to the pot, cook the corn, and eat or process immediately."

Sugary enhancer hybrids contain the sugary enhancer (SE) gene, which significantly raises the sugar content above standard SUs while retaining the tenderness and creamy texture of standard varieties. Higher initial sugar allows them to hold sweetness longer and be better suited for short-term refrigerated storage. The taste, tenderness, and texture are outstanding. SEs are the gourmet corns of choice for home gardeners because they contain the best qualities of both SU and Sh$_2$ types. Fresh from the garden, virtually all current SE releases have eating quality that is superior to all other types. No isolation from standard SUs is necessary.

Supersweet hybrids contain the shrunken-2 gene and have a higher sugar content than the standard SU varieties. The Sh$_2$ gene greatly slows the conversion of sugar to starch. These hybrids hold their sweetness much longer than SU or SE types and are ideally suited for 2- to 3-day distance shipping. For this reason, these varieties have taken over the winter production areas of the South, where long-distance shipping is routine. The kernels of the extra-sweet varieties have a crispy, tough-skinned texture and contain low amounts of the water-soluble polysaccharides that impart the creamy texture and "corny" flavor to other sweet corn varieties. Although the lack of creamy texture is not especially noticeable in fresh corn on the cob, it affects the quality of frozen and canned corn, as does the toughness of the seed coat. Unless corn must be stored, shipped, or mechanically harvested, SEs are superior in eating quality to Sh$_2$s.

The supersweet hybrids generally require warm soil for optimal germination. Even then, they may not emerge uniformly, causing a stand of mixed-age seedlings that later do not pollinate together. Supersweets (Sh$_2$) should be isolated from any other type of corn tasseling at the same time to ensure sweetness and tenderness. Their pollen is weak and easily supplanted by other types, which causes the kernel to revert to a form with the toughness and starchiness of field corn. Because corn is wind-pollinated, this isolation distance can be 500 feet or more, especially downwind.

STANDARD (SU)

Yellow

Yellow	Harvest	Ear size	Comments
Earlivee	58 days	7"—14 rows	extra early
Golden Cross Bantam	85 days	8"—12 to 14 rows	old home-garden variety
Iochief	86 days	8"—14 to 16 rows	popular midseason variety
Jubilee	82 days	8"—16 rows	high yield; deep, narrow kernels; excellent for canning
NK-199	84 days	8"—18 to 20 rows	extremely thick, attractive ears; silks easily removed
Seneca Horizon	65 days	7"—16 to 18 rows	excellent quality
Sundance	69 days	7½"—14 rows	best cold-soil tolerance, early season vigor; handsome ears

White

White	Harvest	Ear size	Comments
Pearl White	75 days	7 to 8"—12 to 16 rows	good cool-soil and drought tolerance; easy snapping
Platinum Lady	86 days	8½"—14 rows	delicate flavor; tender kernels; slender, elegant ears
Silver Queen	92 days	8 to 9"—14 to 16 rows	dark green flag leaves, attractive ears; standard, high-quality white corn; resistant to bacterial wilt and *Helminthosporium*

Bicolor

Bicolor	Harvest	Ear size	Comments
Bi Queen	92 days	8 to 9"—16 rows	like a bicolor Silver Queen
Butter & Sugar	75 days	7"—14 rows	popular for home garden
Honey & Cream	80 days	7"—12 to 14 rows	sweet, tender; long, tight husks
Quickie	64 days	7½"—12 rows	earliest SU bicolor
Sugar & Gold	67 days	6½"—10 to 12 rows	husk green, with reddish tinge; excellent quality; prefers cooler-season areas

SUGARY EXTENDER (SE)

Yellow

Yellow	Harvest	Ear size	Comments
Bodacious	72 days	8"—16 to 18 rows	superior flavor, holding ability; ears snap easily; prefers warm soil
Champ	68 days	8"—16 to 18 rows	excellent eating quality, tip cover
Incredible	83 days	8 to 9"—18 rows	big, flavorful ears; excellent appearance, yield
Kandy Korn	89 days	8"—14 to 16 rows	purplish red-streaked ear flags, excellent quality, long shelf life
Maple Sweet	70 days	7½"—14 to 16 rows	excellent flavor, easy snapping
Merlin	84 days	9"—20 to 22 rows	superior flavor, ear size, disease tolerance; easy snapping
Miracle	84 days	9½"—16 to 18 row	good holding quality; large, tender, attractive, tasty ears
Precocious	66 days	7"—12 to 14 rows	very early; excellent eating, good tipfill
Spring Treat	67 days	7"—14 rows	easy snapping; straight rows of kernels
Sugar Buns	72 days	7½"—14 rows	excellent flavor; attractive, relatively small ears; deep kernels
Terminator	83 days	9"—20 rows	large ears, superior disease resistance
Tuxedo	75 days	7½"—16 to 20 rows	excellent early vigor; good tipfill, husk cover; excellent eating quality; tolerant to Stewart's wilt, rust, and smut

White

White	Harvest	Ear size	Comments
Alpine	79 days	8"—16 rows	widely adapted; excellent yield; cool-soil tolerance; attractive ear
Argent	86 days	8 to 9"—16 rows	good cold-soil vigor; tolerant to Stewart's wilt; like a white Incredible
Avalanche	78 days	8"—16 rows	excellent eating; good ear appearance
Cotton Candy	72 days	7 to 8"—16 to 18 rows	extended harvest; reddish green stalks
Divinity	78 days	8"—16 rows	excellent flavor, tenderness; snow white color; excellent tip cover; tolerant to drought, Stewart's wilt
Pristine	76 days	8 to 9"—16 rows	terrific eating quality, tolerant to Stewart's wilt
Seneca Starshine	71 days	7 to 8"—16 rows	blocky ears, with pure white kernels; excellent tenderness, flavor, appearance; prefers 50°F or higher soil temperature for germination
Seneca White Knight	74 days	8 to 9"—16 rows	high quality; attractive ears; great taste
Snowbelle	79 days	7 to 8"—14 to 16 rows	creamy texture; pretty, compact ears
Spring Snow	65 days	7 to 8"—12 rows	excellent husk cover; very early; attractive ears; very tender kernels; compact plant
Sugar Snow	71 days	8 to 9"—16 rows	extremely sweet, snow white kernels; good cold-soil tolerance
Telstar	79 days	8"—16 rows	vigorous; dark green flag leaves; tasty; attractive ear

SUGARY EXTENDER (SE) continued

Bicolor	Harvest	Ear size	Comments
Ambrosia	75 days	8"—16 rows	good spring vigor; fairly large, tasty ears; tolerant to Stewart's wilt
Calico Belle	79 days	8"—16 to 18 rows	high yield; attractive; delicious taste; good disease tolerance
D'Artagnan	71 days	8"—16 rows	superior quality in an early SE bicolor
Diamonds & Gold	79 days	8"—18 rows	sweet, tender; good tipfill; attractive dark green ears
Double Delight	85 days	9"—16 rows	large, tasty ears; dark green husk; like a bicolor Incredible
Double Gem	74 days	8 to 9"—16 to 18 rows	excellent eating quality; blocky ears; usually double ears on stalks
Kiss 'N Tell	68 days	7 to 8"—14 to 16 rows	two ears per stalk; good tipfill
Lancelot	80 days	8"—16 to 18 rows	vigorous, stress-tolerant plant; good yields; high-quality ears under adverse conditions
Medley	73 days	8"—16 rows	dark green flags; good tip cover; tolerant to Stewart's wilt
Peaches & Cream	83 days	8"—16 to 18 rows	tasty, popular home-garden variety; vigorous plant; good ear protection
Seneca Brave	73 days	8"—18 to 20 rows	husky, excellent-quality ears; strong plants
Seneca Dawn	69 days	7 to 8"—14 to 16 rows	excellent early bicolor; good vigor, eating quality

SUPERSWEET (SH$_2$)

Yellow

	Harvest	Ear size	Comments
Challenger	76 days	8½"—16 rows	excellent early SH$_2$, adapts to variety of growing conditions
Crisp 'N Sweet	85 days	9"—18 rows	high yield; excellent disease resistance; good germination, seedling vigor
Early Xtra Sweet	70 days	8"—16 rows	like the original, but earlier
Excel	82 days	8½"—16 rows	exceptionally high yield, easy to harvest
Illini Gold	79 days	8½"—16 rows	midseason supersweet
Illini Xtra Sweet	85 days	8"—14 to 16 rows	the original SH$_2$ supersweet hybrid
Jubilee Supersweet	83 days	9"—18 rows	excellent home-garden supersweet
Showcase	83 days	8"	large ear on short plant, outstanding eating quality

White

	Harvest	Ear size	Comments
Aspen	83 days	8 to 9"—16 rows	large, attractive ears; high eating quality
Camelot	86 days	8"—18 to 20 rows	clean, sturdy plants; excellent quality, holding traits
How Sweet It Is	85 days	8"—16 rows	AAS winner, sensitive to cold soil, holds quality well
Pegasus	85 days	8½"—18 rows	good cold-soil germination, vigor
Treasure	83 days	8½"—18 rows	good vigor, seedling emergence

Bicolor

	Harvest	Ear size	Comments
Aloha	82 days	9"—16 rows	excellent appearance
Dazzle	82 days	8"—16 to 18 rows	good-looking ear; good disease resistance; creamy texture
Honey 'N Pearl	78 days	8½"—16 rows	1988 AAS winner, stands well, excellent quality
Hudson	83 days	8"—18 rows	smooth, well-filled ears; superior eating quality, tenderness
Phenomenal	85 days	8½"—16 rows	excellent eating quality, beautiful ears
Radiance	73 days	8"—16 to 18 rows	excellent seedling emergence, plant vigor

Varieties

Most of the varieties listed here (like nearly all sweet corn sold today) are hybrids. They are arranged by genetic type and kernel color. The maturity dates are relative because the actual number of days to harvest varies from year to year and location to location.

When to Plant

Sweet corn requires warm soil for germination (above 55°F for standard sweet corn varieties and about 65°F for supersweet varieties). Early plantings of standard sweet corn should be made at, or just before, the mean frost-free date unless you use special soil-warming protection such as clear polyethylene mulch film. (See the maps, page 26.)

OPEN-POLLINATED (SU)

Yellow	Harvest	Ear size	Comments
Ashworth	69 days	6 to 7" ears, 12 rows	good cold-soil germination; good flavor for an early type
Golden Bantam	82 days	6 to 7" ears, 10 to 14 rows	rich corn flavor, sweet, tender
White			
Country Gentleman	96 days	7" ears, kernels not in rows	very tender, shoe-peg type; drought resistant
Stowell's Evergreen	100 days	9" ears, 18 to 20 rows	big, juicy, white kernels; ripens over long period
Trucker's Favorite	95 days	8 to 9" ears, 14 rows	delicious white kernels, high yields
Bicolor			
Double Standard	73 days	7" ears, 12 to 14 rows	first bicolor open-pollinated type; good cold-soil germination; good flavor, tenderness; traditional corn taste
Black			
Black Aztec	75 days	7" ears, 8 to 10 rows	vigorous, drought tolerant; sweet *white* kernels in roasting-ear stage, dark blue-black at maturity; good for blue corn meal

For a continuous supply of sweet corn throughout the summer, plant an early variety, a second early variety, and a main-crop variety in the first planting. For example, you may wish to select Sundance (69 days) for the first early variety, Tuxedo (75 days) for the second early variety, and Incredible (83 days) for the main-crop variety. Make a second planting and successive plantings of your favorite main-crop or late variety when three to four leaves have appeared on the seedlings in the previous planting. Plantings can be made as late as the first week of July.

Spacing of Plants and Depth of Planting

Plant the kernels (seeds) ½ inch deep in cool, moist soils and 1 to 1½ inches deep in warm, dry soils. Space the kernels 9 to 12 inches apart in the row. Plant two or more rows of each variety side by side to ensure good pollination and ear development. Allow 30 to 36 inches between rows.

All sweet corns should be protected from possible cross-pollination by other types of corn (field, pop, or flint). If you plant supersweet or synergistic sweet corn varieties, plan your garden arrangement and planting schedule so as to prevent cross-pollination between these varieties and with any other corn, including nonSh$_2$ sweet corns. Supersweet varieties pollinated by standard sweet corn, popcorn, or field corn do not develop a high sugar content and are starchy. Cross-pollination between yellow and white sweet corn varieties of the same type affects only the appearance of the white corn, not the eating quality.

Care

Cultivate shallowly to control weeds. Chemical herbicides are not recommended for home gardens. Although corn is a warm-weather crop, lack of water at critical periods can seriously reduce quality and yield. If rainfall is deficient, irrigate thoroughly during emergence of the tassels, silking, and maturation of the ears.

Hot, droughty conditions during pollination result in missing kernels, small ears, and poor development of the tips of the ears. Side-dress nitrogen fertilizer (see page 20) when the plants are 12 to 18 inches tall.

Some sweet corn varieties produce more side shoots or "suckers" than others. Removing these side shoots is time consuming and does not improve yields.

Harvesting

Each cornstalk should produce at least one large ear. Under good growing conditions (correct spacing; freedom from weeds, insects, and diseases; and adequate moisture and fertility), many varieties produce a second ear. This second ear is usually smaller and develops later than the first ear.

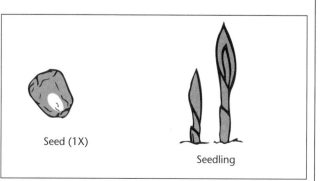

Seed (1X)

Seedling

Sweet corn ears should be picked during the "milk stage" when the kernels are fully formed but not fully mature. This stage occurs about 20 days after the appearance of the first silk strands. The kernels are smooth and plump, and the juice in the kernel appears milky when punctured with a thumbnail. Sweet corn remains in the milk stage less than a week. As harvest time approaches, check frequently to make sure that the kernels do not become too mature and doughy. Other signs that indicate when the corn is ready for harvest are drying and browning of the silks, fullness of the tip kernels, and firmness of the unhusked ears.

To harvest, snap off the ears by hand with a quick, firm, downward push, twist, and pull. The ears should be eaten, processed, or refrigerated as soon as possible. At summer temperatures, the sugar in sweet corn quickly decreases and the starch increases.

Cut or pull out the cornstalks immediately after harvest, and put them in a compost pile. Cut the stalks in 1-foot lengths or shred them to hasten decay.

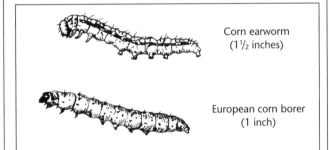

Corn earworm
(1½ inches)

European corn borer
(1 inch)

Common Problems

Corn earworms are a problem in sweet corn every year. Earlier plantings are not badly infested in areas where the pest does not overwinter, but later harvests usually have severe earworm damage unless timely control measures are followed. Corn earworms deposit eggs on the developing silks or on the leaves near the ear. The tiny caterpillars follow the silks down into the ear, where they feed on the tip. Only one corn earworm will be found per ear because the caterpillars are cannibalistic, with the largest devouring any others present. Once the worm is inside the protective husk covering, there is no effective control. A suggested insecticide must be applied before the worms enter the silk channel. For good control in heavy infestations, make several applications 2 to 3 days apart until the silks are brown. Anything that restricts the worm—such as tightening the tip of the husk with a rubber band or clothespin after the silk appears, or inserting mineral oil (½ medicine dropperful) in the silk tube—helps to decrease the damage.

Corn rootworm beetles may cause extensive silk damage, which interferes with pollination. Later plantings usually suffer the greatest damage, especially where field corn is grown. Beetles multiply in early plantings of field corn, mature, and migrate to plantings of young, tender sweet corn. Silk and the young, tender, green leaves are preferred feeding sites. If infestation is sufficient to remove silk before pollination, cobs develop without a full set of kernels. Control measures must be taken as the silk emerges and one or more times every 3 days until pollination is complete.

European corn borers damage stalks, tassels, and ears. As their name indicates, corn borers bore into the plant; and the stalks break over when damage is severe. Corn borers also may bore into the cob and be found after cooking. A suggested insecticide can be applied at 5-day intervals, beginning when eggs hatch in June. Spray applications for earworms usually give adequate control of corn borers.

Flea beetles (see page 40) often attack early in the spring as the corn plants emerge through the soil. Flea beetles can be quite damaging when numerous, and they may carry Stewart's bacterial wilt disease (see next paragraph). Suggested insecticides must be applied early to control flea beetles.

Stewart's wilt is a bacterial disease spread by the flea beetle. This disease causes yellow streaks in the leaves, stunting, and death of young plants of susceptible varieties. The disease occurs more frequently in the southern states and is not severe after cold winters or when resistant varieties are planted. If possible, plant varieties with good resistance.

Smut is caused by a fungus that invades the kernels. It develops as a swollen black pustule (gall) in the ear and sometimes infects the tassel. Some sweet corn varieties are more tolerant to smut than others. Smut occurs most frequently on white varieties and is often severe when extremely dry or hot weather occurs just before and during tasseling. Remove and destroy smut galls while they are moist and firm. Do not discard these galls in or near the garden. Place in the garbage or burn them. The smut is not poisonous, but it is unpleasant to handle. Break off the infected part of the ear. The remainder is suitable for eating.

The immature smut fungus or "maize mushroom" is highly prized in Mexican cooking. Harvest when the fungus is expanded, but before it becomes black and dried out. This time generally is about 2 to 3 days before the sweet corn reaches peak eating quality.

Questions and Answers

Q. How long does it take sweet corn to develop from the first appearance of silks to harvest? *A. About 5 days are required for complete pollination after the first silks appear. Harvest begins about 20 days after first silking.*

Q. The germination of my Illini Xtra Sweet is low. How can I get a better stand? *A. The seeds of supersweet varieties are shrunken and do not germinate readily in cold, wet soil. Do not plant too early in the spring. Wait until the soil is warm, preferably 65°F. Sow the seed more thickly, and thin if necessary. Fungicide seed treatments may also be helpful.*

Q. Why don't my sweet corn ears fill out to the tips? *A. Several conditions can cause poor kernel development at the tip of the ear: dry weather during silking and pollination; planting too close; poor fertility, especially lack of potassium; and poor natural pollination. These conditions may be overcome by watering in dry weather; planting at recommended spacing (9 to 12 inches in the row); proper fertilization; and planting short rows in blocks of two or more for more complete pollination.*

Q. What is the best way to grow early corn? *A. Choose an early maturing variety, plant early and shallowly (about ½ inch deep), and cover the row with clear polyethylene film. Use 1- or 2-mil film 3 feet wide, and cover the edges and ends to warm the soil around the seeds. The small plants can be left under the plastic for 2 to 4 weeks. Remove the film, or cut slits and carefully pull the plants through before the weather becomes too hot. It is wise to experiment with this technique on a small scale first. Unseasonable heat can quickly cook and kill young seedlings under clear plastic.*

Q. How can I keep raccoons out of my sweet corn? *A. It is virtually impossible to keep raccoons out of a garden, although many methods are employed. The most successful seems to be an electric fence made with two wires, one about 4 inches above ground level and the other at 12 inches. The fence must be operating well in advance of the time that the corn approaches maturity. Raccoons prefer to eat sweet corn in the early milk stage, just before it is ready to harvest.*

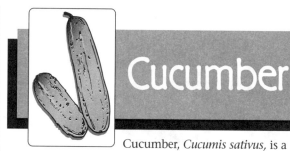

Cucumber

Cucumber, *Cucumis sativus,* is a tender, warm-season vegetable that produces well when given proper care and protection. The vines of standard varieties grow rapidly and require substantial space. Vertical training methods and new dwarf varieties now allow cucumbers to be grown for slicing, salads, and pickling, even in small garden plots.

Varieties

Long, Green, Slicing: Burpless (hybrid–62 days to harvest; the original sweet, long, chinese-type hybrid; does well on a trellis); Dasher II (hybrid–58 days; gynoecious, very productive; top quality; excellent disease resistance); Marketmore 76 (68 days; very uniform, dark green, straight fruit; multiple-disease resistance); Marketmore 86 (56 days; long, dark green, slender fruit; shorter vine; earlier than Marketmore 76); Orient Express (hybrid–64 days; high yields; delicious, crunchy "burpless" type); Slice Master (hybrid–58 days; gynoecious; fruit holds up well under poor growing conditions; uniform; good disease resistance); Straight 8 (58 days; AAS winner; long-time favorite; excellent flavor; evenly dark green fruit); Supersett (hybrid–52 days; high yield; uniform; good tolerance to disease and stress); Sweet Slice (hybrid–62 days; sweet, bitter-free fruit; 10 to 12 inches long; resistant to downy and powdery mildews, mosaic, scab); Sweet Success (hybrid–54 days; AAS winner; european-style slicing cucumber; crisp, sweet, and tender); and Turbo (hybrid–67 days; straight, dark green fruit; disease resistant; dependable).

Long, Green, Slicing (compact plant): Bush Crop (55 days; delicious, 6- to 8-inch fruit on dwarf, bushy plants); Fanfare (hybrid–63 days; AAS winner; great taste, high yield, extended harvest; disease resistant); Salad Bush (hybrid–57 days; AAS winner; uniform 8-inch fruit on compact plants; tolerant to wide variety of diseases); and Space Master (56 days; 8-inch fruit on space-saving plants; adaptable).

Pickling: Bush Pickle (48 days; compact plant; good for container growing; not for the Deep South); Calypso (hybrid–52 days; high yields; gynoecious; blocky, dark green fruits with white spines; good disease resistance);

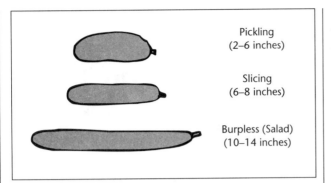

Pickling
(2–6 inches)

Slicing
(6–8 inches)

Burpless (Salad)
(10–14 inches)

Carolina (hybrid–49 days; straight, blocky fruits with white spines; medium-sized plant with good vigor, disease resistance); Lucky Strike (hybrid–52 days; straight, medium dark green fruit; seed emerges well in cooler soil); National Pickling (54 days; straight, medium green, tapered fruit with black spines); and SMR-58 (58 days; straight, blocky, medium green fruit).

Novelty: Boothby's Blond (63 days; Maine heirloom; pale yellow, pickling-shaped fruit with black spines); Gherkin (60 days; 2- to 3-inch, nearly round, spiny fruit; not the true West Indian gherkin, which is a different species altogether; see Q-and-A, page 77); Lemon (65 days; small, light yellow, lemon-sized, white-fleshed fruits; sweet, tender, easy to digest); and White Wonder (60 days; blocky fruit to 8 inches long; ivory white; crisp, firm, mild flesh).

When to Plant

Cucumbers are usually started by planting seed directly in the garden. Plant after the danger of frost has passed and the soil has warmed in the spring. (See the maps, page 26.) Warm soil is necessary for germination of seeds and proper growth of plants. With ample soil moisture, cucumbers thrive in warm summer weather. A second planting for fall harvest may be made in mid-summer to late summer.

Cucumbers may be transplanted for extra-early yields. Sow two or three seeds in peat pots, peat pellets, or other containers 3 to 4 weeks before the frost-free date. Thin to one plant per container. Plant transplants 1 to 2 feet apart in rows 5 to 6 feet apart when they have two to four true leaves. Do not allow transplants to get too large

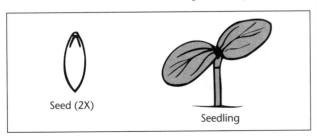

Seed (2X)

Seedling

in containers or they do not transplant well. Like other vine crops, cucumbers do not transplant successfully when pulled as bare-root plants.

Spacing of Plants and Depth of Planting

Plant seeds ½ to 1 inch deep, and thin the seedlings to one plant every 12 inches in the row or to three plants every 36 inches in the hill system. If you use transplants, plant them carefully in warm soil 12 inches apart in the row.

Care

Cucumber plants have shallow roots and require ample soil moisture at all stages of growth. When fruit begins setting and maturing, adequate moisture becomes especially critical. For best yields, incorporate compost or well-rotted manure before planting. Cucumbers respond to mulching with soil-warming plastic (see page 36) in early spring or organic materials in summer. Use of black plastic mulch warms the soil in the early season and can give significantly earlier yields, especially if combined with floating row covers.

Side-dress nitrogen fertilizer (see page 20) when the plants begin to vine. Cucumber beetles should be controlled from the time that the young seedlings emerge from the soil (see "Common Problems," page 77).

In small gardens, the vines may be trained on a trellis or fence. When the long, burpless varieties are supported, the cucumbers hang free and develop straight fruits. Winds whipping the plants can make vertical training impractical. Wire cages also can be used for supporting the plants (see "Tomato," page 125). Do not handle, harvest, or work on the plants when they are wet.

Harvesting

Pick cucumbers at any stage of development before the seeds become hard. Cucumbers usually are eaten when immature. The best size depends upon the use and variety. They may be picked when they are no more than 2 inches long for pickles, 4 to 6 inches long for dills, and 6 to 8 inches long for slicing varieties. A cucumber is of highest quality when it is uniformly green, firm, and crisp. The large, burpless cucumbers should be 1 to 1½ inches in diameter and up to 10 inches long. Some varieties can grow considerably larger. Do not allow cucumbers to turn yellow. Remove from the vine any missed fruits nearing ripeness so that the young fruits continue to develop. The cucumber fruits grow rapidly to harvest size and should be picked at least every other day.

Common Problems

Cucumber beetles (see page 40). Spotted and striped cucumber beetles attack seedlings as they emerge from the soil. The beetles may appear in large numbers and can quickly stunt or kill the small plants. The beetles also may carry bacterial wilt disease (see upcoming section). Cucumber beetles can be controlled by applying a suggested insecticide.

Aphids (see page 40). Watch for buildup of colonies of aphids on the undersides of the leaves, especially near vine tips. Use a suggested insecticide if these colonies appear.

Bacterial wilt. Plants are infected with the bacterial wilt disease by the attack of cucumber beetles. The disease organism overwinters inside the beetles' bodies. The beetles hibernate among the trash and weeds around the garden, emerging in time to feed on tender cucumber seedlings. Plants usually are infected with the disease-causing bacteria long before they show any symptoms. When the vines wilt and collapse (usually about the same time that the first cucumbers are half grown), it is too late to prevent the disease.

Questions and Answers

Q. Some of my small cucumbers are badly misshapen. Will they develop into normal cucumbers? *A. No. They should be removed from the vines. Misshapen cucumbers may result from poor pollination or low fertility. Side-dressing a complete fertilizer may help later cucumbers to develop normally.*

Q. Why do some of my plants suddenly wilt and die? Dead or dying plants are scattered all over my cucumber patch. One plant in a hill may be healthy, while another dies. *A. These are typical symptoms of the bacterial wilt disease. This disease is spread by cucumber beetles early in the season. The beetles must be controlled immediately when the plants are small.*

Q. Is there really a "burpless" cucumber? *A. Yes. Burpless cucumbers are no longer considered novelties and are offered in most garden catalogs. They are mild, sweet, and crisp when fresh. The skin is tender and free of bitterness, although many people peel it off. Most varieties are long (10 to 12 inches) and curved, unless grown on a trellis. These varieties are better eaten fresh, using conventional varieties for most pickling uses.*

Q. What cucumber variety should I buy for gherkins? *A. Buy the West Indian gherkin. It is a close relative of the garden cucumber used for pickling. The fruits are generally oval, 1 to 3 inches long, and more spiny than cucumbers. They are also called "burr cucumbers" but are usually listed in catalogs as West Indian gherkin. They are grown in the same way as cucumbers. Small-fruited, prickly varieties of cucumber are sometimes sold as "gherkins." If small, tender cucumbers are what you want to pickle and call "gherkins," then these misnamed cucumber varieties serve the purpose well.*

Q. Why do my cucumbers fail to set fruit and yield properly? *A. The first yellow flowers appearing on the plants are male flowers that provide pollen. These flowers normally drop off after blooming. The small cucumber is evident at the base of the female flower (even before it opens) and should develop into an edible fruit if properly pollinated. Anything that interferes with pollination of the female flowers reduces fruit set and yield, including cold temperatures and rainy weather that hamper bee activity, or improper use of insecticides that kill bees.*

Q. What are gynoecious hybrids? *A. Gynoecious ("female-flowering") hybrids are special hybrids of slicing and pickling cucumbers that are advertised in many garden catalogs. Because they have all female flowers, they may be earlier and higher yielding than other varieties. Usually, the seed company mixes in a small proportion of seed of a standard cucumber as a pollinator.*

Q. How far away from melons should I plant my cucumbers? I am concerned about cross-pollination. *A. Contrary to popular opinion, cucumbers do not cross-pollinate with muskmelons or watermelons and cause them to become bitter, tasteless, or off-flavor. Because cucumbers and melons require considerable space in the garden, however, plant the rows far enough apart for proper vine growth without overlapping.*

Q. What causes my cucumber plants to be stunted? The leaves are a mottled yellow, and the fruits are blotchy and taste bitter. *A. This condition is caused by the cucumber mosaic virus. Grow mosaic-resistant varieties.*

Q. What causes the white mold growth on the upper surfaces of my cucumber leaves? *A. This condition is caused by powdery mildew, a fungal disease that is most severe during late summer and fall plantings. Grow resistant varieties.*

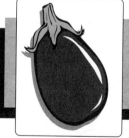

Eggplant

Eggplant, *Solanum melongena* var. *esculentum* (also known as guinea squash and aubergine), is a very cold-sensitive vegetable that requires a long warm season for best yields. The culture of eggplant is similar to that of bell pepper, with transplants being set in the garden after all danger of frost is past. Eggplants are slightly larger plants than peppers and are spaced slightly farther apart. Eggplant requires careful attention for a good harvest. Small-fruited, exotic-colored, and ornamental varieties can be grown in containers and used for decoration.

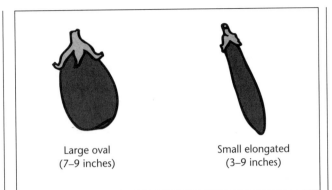

Large oval
(7–9 inches)

Small elongated
(3–9 inches)

Varieties

All varieties are hybrids unless designated OP (for open-pollinated).

Large Oval Fruit: Dusky (60 days to harvest, good size, early production); Epic (64 days, teardrop-shaped); Black Bell (68 days, round to oval, productive); Black Magic (72 days); Classic (76 days, elongated oval, high quality); Black Beauty (OP–80 days); Burpee Hybrid (80 days); and Ghostbuster (80 days; white, slightly sweeter than purple types; 6- to 7-inch oval).

Elongated Fruit: Ichiban (70 days); Slim Jim (OP–70 days; lavender, turning purple when peanut-sized; good in pots); and Little Fingers (OP–68 days; 6- to 8-inch, long, slim fruit in clusters).

Ornamental Fruit: Easter Egg (52 days; small white, egg-sized, -shaped, turning yellow at maturity; edible ornamental).

When to Plant

Eggplant is best started from transplants. Select plants in cell packs or individual containers. It is important to get the plants off to a proper start. Do not plant too early. Transplant after the soil has warmed and the danger of frost has passed. (See the maps, page 26.) Eggplants are more susceptible than tomato plants to injury from low temperatures and do not grow until temperatures warm.

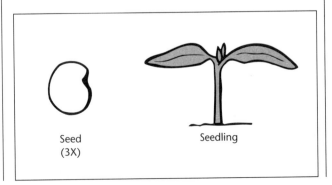

Seed
(3X)

Seedling

Spacing of Plants

Space plants 18 to 24 inches apart in the row, or even closer for small-fruited types. Three to six plants are usually sufficient for most families unless eggplant is a favorite vegetable, eaten often. Allow 30 to 36 inches between rows, or space plants 24 inches apart in all directions in raised beds.

Care

Use starter fertilizer (see page 20) for transplanting. Side-dress nitrogen fertilizer (page 20) when the plants are half grown and again immediately after harvest of the first fruits. Given sufficient moisture and fertility, eggplant thrives in the heat of summer. The plants tolerate dry weather after they are well established but should be irrigated during extended dry periods for continued peak production.

Harvesting

Harvest the fruits when they are 6 to 8 inches long and still glossy. Use a knife or pruning shears rather than breaking or twisting the stems. Many eggplant varieties have small prickly thorns on the stem and calyx, so exercise caution or wear gloves when harvesting. Leave the large (usually green) calyx attached to the fruit.

When the fruits become dull or brown, they are too mature for culinary use and should be cut off and discarded. Overmature fruits are spongy and seedy and may be bitter. Even properly harvested fruits do not store well and should be eaten soon after they are harvested. Large, vigorous plants can yield as many as four to six fruits at the peak of the season.

Common Problems

Verticillium wilt causes yellowing, wilting, and death of the plants.

Flea beetles (see page 40) cause tiny holes in the leaves. Damage can be severe, especially on young plants, if unchecked. These beetles can be controlled by applying an insecticide.

Questions and Answers

Q. I planted my eggplants early, but they did not grow very well. *A. They probably were planted while the soil was too cold. It is better to hold the plants (but keep them growing) until the soil warms. If necessary, repot into larger containers to maintain vigor. Mulching with black plastic film (page 36) can help warm the soil, especially in northern areas. Floating row covers can help with cool, early seasons as well as bar harmful insects from succulent young plants.*

Endive-Escarole

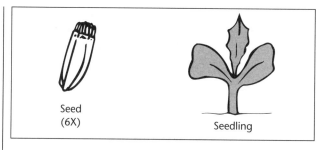

Seed
(6X)

Seedling

Endive and escarole, both *Cichorium endivia,* are closely related hardy annual vegetables that have the same growing requirements. The primary difference between them is that endive has curled, finely cut leaves, while escarole has broad, flat, slightly cupped leaves. They are cool-season plants that grow best in the spring in northern locations and better during the fall months over much of the rest of the country. (Although endive is grown in Florida, it is produced there as a winter vegetable.) Endive and escarole are delicacies when blanched and used for salads or as a garnish. Even when grown under perfect conditions, these vegetables have a hint of bitterness in the flavor, which is an acquired taste.

Varieties

All varieties of endive and escarole can be harvested within 80 to 100 days, depending on the planting season.

Endive: Frisan (good for late fall); Green Curled Ruffec (very uniform, attractive); Lorca (extremely curled, for fall); Neos (extra frilly, compact, self-blanching); Nina (small, smooth, deeply cut, for early harvest); Salad King (slow to bolt, large size, to 2 feet); Tosca (shoestring leaves, for spring or summer); and Traviata (upright, self-blanching).

Escarole: Bossa (summer or fall); Broad-Leaved Batavian (large, smooth leaves); Florida Deep Heart (broad-leaved, southern type); Full Heart (coarsely crumpled leaves); Grosse Bouclee (deep green outer leaves); Nuvol (self-blanching, least bitter); Salanca (self-blanching, for fall); and Sinco (big head, leaves curled around heart, for cool weather).

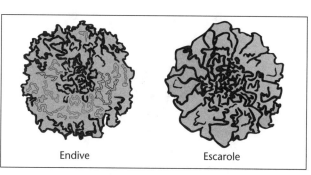

Endive   Escarole

When to Plant

Endive and escarole do not thrive under hot conditions and must be grown as early spring or fall crops. They grow in much the same manner as lettuce and respond well to fertile soil and growing temperatures that average between 60° and 70°F, with a uniform supply of moisture. Seeds may be planted directly into the garden in late March or early April, or as soon as the soil mellows enough to be worked safely in your area.

Spacing of Plants and Depth of Planting

For spring plantings, place seeds ¼ inch deep in rows 18 to 24 inches apart. When seedlings are 1 inch tall, thin or transplant 9 to 12 inches apart. In beds, plants may be spaced 9 to 12 inches apart in all directions. Adequate moisture and space are necessary to assure rapid development and minimal bitterness of the heads.

Summer planting for a fall crop is often quite rewarding. Plant seeds ³/₈ to ½ inch deep in July, and thin the seedlings to 9 to 12 inches apart. Some shade from surrounding crops, which will mature and be removed before the endive or escarole matures, may help germinating seedlings get established in the heat of summer. Water frequently during the hot summer months. Endive is very hardy and withstands frost to give harvest throughout the fall months and into winter in mild areas.

Care

Unless blanched, the spreading plants are likely to be very bitter. When sunlight is kept from the center leaves, their green color is reduced, bitterness is decreased, and texture and flavor are improved. Heads are usually blanched after the leaves spread sufficiently to touch the next plant. Some varieties self-blanch, especially if grown in the fall. For varieties that need artificial blanching, tie the tops of the outermost leaves together as the heads develop. Make sure that the plants are dry before tying the leaves. If the plants are not dry, the inner leaves may rot. Blanching requires 2 to 3 weeks, and the blanched heads should be used soon after their color has faded, as they may begin to deteriorate if left tied up too long, especially in hot or wet weather. Several plants may be blanched at one time, with additional plants tied up every week or so for a continual harvest.

Harvesting

After the blanched heads have developed, cut the plants at ground level. If the weather turns very hot in the summer or hard freezing is expected in the fall, cut the heads. Then wash, drip dry, and store in a polyethylene bag in the refrigerator for later use. Discard the tough, bitter, outer leaves.

Jerusalem artichoke, *Helianthus tuberosus* (also known as sun choke or sunroot), is native to North America. It was one of the few vegetables grown by the native Americans at the time of the European arrival. A perennial, it may persist in the garden as a weed. Any small piece of a tuber missed at harvest may sprout to form a new clump. Jerusalem artichoke, related to the sunflower, is an entirely different plant from the globe artichoke, *Cynura scolymus*, (a thistle) grown in California. The fleshy, oblong tubers may be baked, boiled, or fried like white potatoes or may be sliced raw into salads. They have also been used as animal food, especially for hogs, which are sometimes allowed to root the tubers out of the soil for themselves.

In recent years, jerusalem artichoke selection and breeding have produced plant and tuber types that are more attractive in the garden, with larger, smoother tubers much easier to prepare than the older, knobby ones.

Jerusalem artichoke has also attracted some attention because the tubers contain inulin, which breaks down into the sugar fructose when they are eaten. Fructose is reputed to be of value in the diets of people who have diabetes.

Varieties

The best jerusalem artichoke tubers for garden use are improved seed-stock selections. The most common new variety is Stampede. It flowers earlier in the season, with larger and more attractive flower heads, matures tubers a month sooner, and grows tops much shorter than the old standard type, making plants less likely to fall over as they mature. It produces many large, clean tubers, too. Other selections available for the sun choke enthusiast include Fuseau, a long and smooth yam type; Long Red, the same shape with red skin; Golden Nugget, similar to Fuseau, but about two-thirds the size; Smooth Garnet, with red skin and a more rounded shape; and French Mammoth White, a large but more knobby type.

You may obtain tubers from nurseries, seed supply houses, seed exchanges, the gourmet sections of food stores (under the name "sun chokes" or "sunroots"), or from another gardener. Named varieties are still hard to find—with the exception of Stampede, which has been around for a while. The improved varieties are so superior to the common sort that the search for named varieties is usually worth the effort. Sunroots almost always produce so abundantly that variety sharing is possible after the first year. If you buy seed stock, a very small amount multiplies into enough to eat and plant for another year. For subsequent plantings, you can dig your own tubers and set out a new row when you bring in the spring harvest.

When to Plant

Jerusalem artichoke grows in most parts of temperate North America. It thrives best in a well-drained garden soil with high fertility, responding particularly well to high potassium. Plant the entire tubers in early spring. Beds not dug and reset each year quickly become thick and choked with growth. For peak production, new plantings must be made yearly.

Spacing of Plants and Depth of Planting

Plant individual tubers 2 to 3 inches deep, spacing them 24 to 30 inches apart. Because the plants grow 6 feet tall or taller, you should allow 3 to 4 feet between rows (more if possible, as these plants seem to impede the growth of close neighbors).

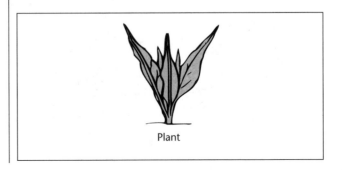

Plant

Care

Early cultivation and hoeing are necessary. As the plants become established, however, little or no further care is required. After frost blackens the foliage, the large, woody tops resembling sunflowers may be cut off above the ground and shredded for composting.

Harvesting

Dig the tubers anytime from September until the ground freezes and in the spring before new growth starts. Usually, the tubers are dug as needed. A supply can be harvested and stored as potatoes are, before the soil freezes. Any tubers that are not harvested regrow and may become troublesome weeds in the garden.

Questions and Answers

Q. What are the best storage conditions for jerusalem artichokes? *A. The best possible storage is in the soil where they grew. Harvest small quantities as needed and a larger amount just before the ground freezes in the winter. Then, if possible, store at a temperature of 32°F with high (95 percent) humidity. Jerusalem artichokes do not form a thick skin like the potato and tend to lose moisture rapidly. The tubers also may be placed in polyethylene bags in the refrigerator. If there are enough sunroots for spring harvest, leave them in place. In most growing areas, winter does not harm the tubers, and it actually keeps them crisp and juicy. Begin to harvest as soon as the frost goes out of the soil in spring. If the bed is mulched heavily in late fall, harvest may continue through the winter by pulling the mulch aside on mild days and digging tubers.*

Kale, *Brassica oleracea* var. *acephala* (also known as borecole), is a hardy, cool-season green of the cabbage family that is rich in vitamins A and C. Although kale tolerates summer heat, it grows best in the spring and fall. The highly curled, bluish green leaves (plain leaves on some varieties) do not form a solid head.

"Flowering" varieties of kale are quite colorful. They are planted as accent or pot plants but can be planted in masses for a striking effect. Because the leaves develop their highest color in cool fall weather, ornamental kale has become a staple of the fall flower border. In addition

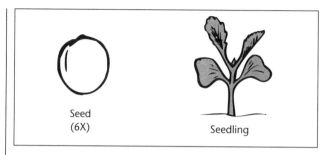

Seed
(6X)

Seedling

to serving as ornamentals, kale plants are used for greens, as a garnish, or in salads; and kale may be cooked in place of cabbage. Flowering kale has become a popular decoration on salad bars as well.

Varieties

Dwarf Blue Curled Scotch (70 days to harvest); Dwarf Curled (Vates) (60 days); and Dwarf Siberian (65 days). Newer hybrid varieties include Blue Surf and Winterbor (65 days). Ornamental kale is sold in open-pollinated, mixed-color packets and in hybrid, separate-color varieties such as Frizzy Hybrid, Nagoya, Peacock Hybrid (all in white or red), and Osaka (in red, white, or pink). Japanese seed companies, in particular, have been very active in developing the ornamental kales recently.

When to Plant

Plant kale in the garden anytime from early spring through early summer. In more southern latitudes, planting in late summer provides harvest from fall into winter until or unless the ground freezes hard. In mild winters, or with protection, kale may overwinter and produce a few new leaves before it blooms in the second year.

Spacing of Plants and Depth of Planting

Sow seeds ¼ to ½ inch deep in rows. Thin the seedlings to 8 to 12 inches apart. The seedlings may be started in late winter and transplanted into the garden for early spring production. For a fall crop, or for ornamental types, plants should be sown or started in flats in late spring, then transplanted to the garden in late June to early July for lush growth by the time cool fall temperatures sweeten and color the leaves.

Care

Kale is relatively easy to grow, requiring only normal cultivation and watering. Most of the standard cabbage pests can also damage kale and must be controlled for best production.

Harvesting

The lower leaves may be individually picked when they are small and tender (8 to 10 inches or shorter). The entire kale plant may also be cut. Quality is improved by frost, and the plant withstands night freezes. Late-summer plantings usually give best results. Kale can be harvested until early winter, when severe freezes injure or kill the plants.

Common Problems

Aphids (see page 40) and **cabbage worms** (page 62).

Questions and Answers

Q. Do new leaves develop if the tip of the plant is removed? *A. No. Removing the tip prevents further growth. If harvest is delayed and lower leaves become tough, harvest from the upper part of the plant where leaves are nearly expanded to full size but are still tender. Take care not to remove the central growing point.*

Kohlrabi, *Brassica oleracea* var. *gongylodes* (also known as stem turnip), is a hardy, cool-season vegetable belonging to the cabbage family. It has a turniplike appearance, with leaves standing out like spokes from the edible portion, which is a rounded, enlarged stem section growing just above the soil line. Kohlrabi is sometimes misclassified as a root vegetable.

Varieties

White (really light green) varieties include the old favorite, Early White Vienna (55 days to harvest); Express Forcer (42 days); Grand Duke (hybrid–50 days); Kolpak (hybrid–38 days); and Triumph (55 days). Purple kohlrabi varieties include Blaro (43 days); the old standard, Early Purple Vienna (62 days); and Rapid (45 days).

When to Plant

Sow seeds in early spring. Make small plantings every 2 to 3 weeks for continuous spring and early summer harvest. For an especially early harvest, plants may be

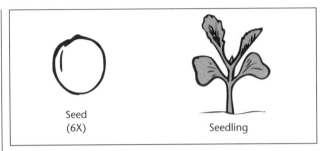

Seed
(6X)

Seedling

started indoors or in the greenhouse in flats to be transplanted into the garden as soon as the ground becomes workable. Like cabbage, kohlrabi plants can stand some frost. One or two late plantings can also be made in midsummer at the same time as late cabbage. In very hot weather, these seedlings may benefit from some shade when they are small.

Spacing of Plants and Depth of Planting

Sow seeds in rows and cover them ¼ to ½ inch deep. Thin the seedlings to 2 to 5 inches apart. Transplant the surplus seedlings to fill in blanks in other parts of the row or into additional row space if more harvest is desired. Discard excess plants or use them for tender, stir-fry greens.

Care

Plant in fertile soil, maintain adequate soil moisture, and keep down weeds. Proper care allows kohlrabi to achieve the rapid growth that results in the best quality.

Harvesting

Kohlrabi has the mildest and best flavor (resembling mild white turnips) when small. Unfortunately, many gardeners allow kohlrabi to grow too large before harvesting it. Large, older kohlrabi is tough and woody, and it may have an off-flavor. Begin harvesting (pull or cut at ground level) when the first stems are about 1 inch in diameter. Continue harvest until the stems are 2 to 3 inches in diameter. When the stems get much bigger than 3 inches, they begin to develop woody fibers, especially in the lower part of the expanded stem. Even overgrown kohlrabi still may have some tender and tasty tissue at the top, where the youngest leaves continue to emerge as the plant grows. The young leaves may be cooked like other greens.

Common Problems

Cabbage worms (see page 62) and **diseases** (page 61).

Leek

Leek, *Allium ampeloprasum* var. *porrum,* is a hardy, mild-flavored vegetable of the onion family that has been cultivated for centuries. The leek plant resembles a large onion plant with flat leaves, but it is composed of a cylindrical sheaf of basal leaves rather than an expanded, rounded bulb. Traditionally, in this country, leeks primarily have been used in place of onions for flavoring soups and stews. Actually, leeks may be eaten raw or cooked, in salads or stir-fries, or any-where their delicate, sweet, mild, and rich flavor can be fully appreciated. Leeks do not have the hot pungency many people find offensive in onions.

Varieties

American Flag, Broad London, Conqueror, Electra, and Giant Musselburgh are dependable, full-season varieties that have been available in the United States for some time. A whole range of leek varieties has recently become available from Europe, where this vegetable has long been popular. Some of these selections include Varna (50 days to harvest), a bunching type designed to be sown thickly and harvested early as with scallions; Titan (70 days, an early sort good for summer crops); King Richard (75 days, an extra-long, early variety); Pancho (80 days; combines earliness, size, and cold tolerance); Splendid (95 days; long, slim shafts; good for dehydration); Unique (100 days, good length and thickness, tolerates cold, stores well); Longina (102 days; blue-green upright leaves that do not trap soil where the base meets the shaft; stores well); Alaska (105 days; thick shafts; best cold tolerance; winter hardy); and Blue Solaise (large and hardy, also overwinters well). Many more varieties are becoming available each year, so read catalog descriptions carefully, and match leek varieties to your needs.

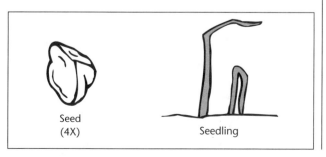

Seed
(4X)

Seedling

When to Plant

Seed 10 to 15 seeds per foot of row directly in the garden in early spring. Thin the seedlings to 4 inches apart. Leeks also may be started indoors or in the green-house during February in the same manner as onion transplants (see page 91). Leek seedlings should be set lower in the garden than they grow in the seed flat so that the long shafts grow longer underground and form more bleached white tissue. Take care not to bury leaf attachments to the stem, as this may encourage rots.

Care

Leeks can grow in any garden that produces good onions. When the plants begin strong growth in the sum-mer, cultivate and draw soil toward the plants to blanch the edible portion. Blanching makes the leeks longer and whiter at harvest. Leeks grow slowly, requiring at least 120 days to reach 1 to 1½ inches in diameter. Leeks of large, thick varieties started in the greenhouse may reach diame-ters approaching 3 inches in good seasons, while longer, thinner varieties may produce shafts of 15 inches or more in length. Do not bank soil around the plants for blanch-ing until they are at least the size of a pencil. Early bank-ing while the leaves are small causes the plants to rot and die by altering soil aeration around the young root system.

Harvesting

Leeks may be harvested for use throughout the sum-mer and fall, depending on the variety. To harvest, loosen the soil with a spading fork or shovel, taking care to dig under the base of the shaft, severing the roots, then pull out the plant. Never try to pull leeks without first digging to loosen the roots. Cut off the roots and all but 2 inches of the green leaves. Leaf trimmings may be used in vege-table soup stocks or, if tender, in the manner of scallion tops. Leeks may be dug before hard freezes and stored under refrigeration (see pages 167 and 168). Plants of cold-tolerant varieties also may be mulched heavily with fresh straw for harvest whenever the ground is not frozen. Spring harvest is usually completed in late March or early April before the leeks begin the second year's growth and send up a seedstalk.

In the second season, as the leek plant flowers, polli-nates, and matures seed, the underground portion forms a small number of cloves, which resemble elephant garlic, *Allium ampeloprasum* var. (see page 153), a very close rela-tive of leek. These bulb structures are very seldom seen in normal garden practice, where leek is treated is treated as an annual crop.

Question and Answer

Q. Why do my leeks rot where the fine roots are attached? *A. This condition may be the result of maggot infestation in the soil. Treat the soil with a suggested soil insecticide in early spring. Choosing a well-drained soil high in organic matter also helps to minimize rots in leeks.*

Lettuce

Lettuce, *Lactuca sativa,* is a fairly hardy, cool-weather vegetable that thrives when the average daily temperature is between 60° and 70°F. It should be planted in early spring or late summer. At high temperatures, growth is stunted, the leaves may be bitter, and the seedstalk forms and elongates rapidly. Some types and varieties of lettuce withstand heat better than others.

There are five distinct types of lettuce: leaf (also called loose-leaf lettuce), Cos or romaine, crisphead, butterhead, and stem (also called asparagus lettuce).

Leaf lettuce, the most widely adapted type, produces crisp leaves loosely arranged on the stalk. Nearly every garden has at least a short row of leaf lettuce, making it the most widely planted salad vegetable. **Cos or romaine** forms an upright, elongated head and is an excellent addition to salads and sandwiches. The **butterhead** varieties are generally small, loose-heading types that have tender, soft leaves with a delicate sweet flavor. **Stem lettuce** forms an enlarged seedstalk that is used mainly in stewed, creamed, and Chinese dishes.

Crisphead varieties, the iceberg types common at supermarkets all over the country, are adapted to northern conditions and require the most care. In areas without long, cool seasons, they generally are grown from transplants, started early, and moved to the garden as soon as the soil can be worked. They are extremely sensitive to heat and must mature before the first hot spell of summer to achieve high-quality heads. If an unseasonably early heat wave hits before they have matured, they almost certainly fail. In many locations, crisphead lettuce plants started in late summer to mature in the cooler weather of fall have a much better chance of success.

Varieties

Green Leaf: Black-Seeded Simpson (earliest to harvest); Grand Rapids (frilly edges; good for cold frames, greenhouse, garden); Green Ice (resistant to heat, slow to bolt, less bitter); Matchless or Deer Tongue (heirloom variety); Oak Leaf (resistant to tipburn, good for hot weather); Salad Bowl (finely cut, large-leaf rosettes, resistant to tipburn); Slobolt (resistant to heat, tipburn); Tango (darker green, deeply cut, pointed leaves); and Waldmann's Green (dark green, resistant to tipburn).

Red Leaf: Lollo Rosso (mild flavor, extra frilly, bolt resistant); Prizehead (upright; frilly red edge; resistant to tipburn); Red Fire (ruffles with red edge, slow to bolt); Red Sails (slowest-bolting red leaf lettuce); Red Salad Bowl (wine red version of salad bowl); and Ruby (darkest red of all, resistant to tipburn).

Cos or Romaine: Cimmaron (unique dark red leaf, Cos type); Green Towers (early; dark green, large leaves); Paris Island (long-standing); Rosalita (attractive red leaves, upright habit); and Valmaine (taller than Paris Island, tolerant to downy mildew).

Butterhead: Bibb or Limestone (crisp texture, delicate flavor, no bitterness); Buttercrunch (resistant to heat); Dark Green Boston (large, more-solid heads); Nancy (excellent quality, texture); Red Boston (rose-red-tinged outer leaves, medium green center); Sangria (thick leaves, tinted with rosy color); Summer Bibb (resistant to heat, holds 2 to 3 weeks in the garden); Summerlong (resistant to heat); Tania (resistant to four strains of downy mildew); and Tom Thumb (delicate miniature butterheads).

Leaf

Butterhead

Cos

Head

Heading or Crisphead: Great Lakes (standard, holds well in warm weather); Iceburg (medium size, tender hearts, leaf edges tinged light brown); Ithaca (tolerates heat, resists bitterness, slow to bolt); Montello (very heat tolerant, tipburn resistant, root-rot resistant); and Summertime (adapts well to high temperature, slow to bolt).

Stem or Asparagus: Celtuce, *L. sativa* var. *asparagina*.

When to Plant

Leaf, Cos, and butterhead lettuce can be planted anytime in the spring when the soil is dry enough to rake the surface. Two or more successive plantings at 10- to 14-day intervals provide a continuous supply of lettuce. Lettuce does not withstand hot summer days well, and spring planting should be completed at least a month before the really hot days of early summer begin. Plantings started in late summer mature during cool fall weather. Watering is essential for seed germination and establishment of seedlings. Some shade may also benefit summer sowings. Heat-tolerant varieties (mainly loose-leaf types) may be grown in the shade of taller crops through most of the summer if extra care is taken about irrigation and soil selection.

Head lettuce must be transplanted in most locations and requires more care than other types of lettuce. Start transplants for a spring crop indoors or in a cold frame (see page 47), and set them in the garden as early in the spring as the weather settles. Harden transplants outdoors so that they become acclimated to the conditions under which they will be grown, but do not allow growth to stop entirely. Cos, butterhead, and leaf varieties also can be transplanted for earlier harvest. In the heat of summer, lettuce seedlings started in a protected location in the shade can be transplanted later into moderate sites for some limited success with summer lettuce.

Spacing of Plants and Depth of Planting

Plant seeds ¼ to ½ inch deep (10 seeds per foot) in single, double, or triple rows 12 to 18 inches apart. Thin seedlings to 4 inches apart for leaf lettuce and 6 to 8 inches apart for Cos or butterhead. The seedlings

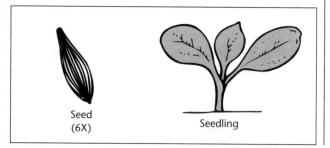

Seed (6X)   Seedling

removed may be transplanted or eaten. Transplant crisphead seedlings 10 to 12 inches apart in the row.

Care

Because lettuce has shallow roots, it should be hoed or cultivated carefully. Frequent light watering causes the leaves to develop rapidly, resulting in high-quality lettuce. Overwatering, especially in heavy soils, can lead to disease, soft growth, and scalding or burning of the leaf margins. Organic mulches can help moderate soil temperature and the microenvironment to produce quality lettuce in less-than-ideal weather conditions.

Harvesting

Leaf lettuce may be cut whenever it is large enough to use. Cutting every other plant at ground level gives the remaining plants more space for growth. Leaf lettuce reaches maximum size (6 to 12 ounces) in 50 to 60 days. Butterhead varieties form small, loose heads that weigh 4 to 8 ounces at harvest (60 to 70 days). The innermost leaves, which tend to blanch themselves, are a delicacy. Cos varieties have an upright growth habit, and form a long, medium-dense head.

To store lettuce, wash, drip dry, and place in a plastic bag in the refrigerator. Lettuce keeps best at 32°F and high (95 percent) humidity (see pages 167 and 168).

Common Problems

Aphids (see page 40).

Tipburn is a physiological condition that causes lettuce to "die back" at the edges of the leaves. It results from a change in the moisture relationship between the soil and the plant. Clip off any brown leaf tissue, and use the remainder of the leaf. Frequent light waterings help prevent tipburn. Some varieties are resistant to this condition.

Foliage rots can be a problem, especially in hot or wet seasons. Providing good soil and air drainage for the lettuce bed can help minimize damage in most years. In severe outbreaks, proper fungicidal materials are required, or the entire crop may be destroyed quickly.

Questions and Answers

Q. Why didn't my lettuce seeds germinate? *A. Failure of seeds to germinate is caused by insufficient moisture or old seed. Lettuce seed does not keep well, and it is advisable to obtain new seed each spring. Store seed for fall gardens in a sealed container in the refrigerator. Some lettuce varieties (especially the white-seeded types) have seed that requires light for germination. These types should not be covered with soil but* *merely pressed into good contact with finely prepared soil. Care then must be taken to keep the seedbed moist, but not soggy, until the seedlings emerge.*

Q. Seedstalks have appeared in the center of my lettuce plants. What should I do? *A. The formation of seedstalks is caused by a combination of long days, warm temperatures, and age. When seedstalks begin to form, harvest your lettuce immediately, and store it in the refrigerator.*

Q. My lettuce tastes bitter. What can I do? *A. Lettuce may become bitter during hot weather and when seedstalks begin to form. Wash and store the leaves in the refrigerator for a day or two. Much of the bitterness will disappear.*

Musk-melon

Muskmelon, *Cucumis melo* var. *reticulatus* (also known as cantaloupe), is a tender, heat-loving vegetable that requires culture similar to that of cucumber, but with a longer season. Most popular varieties have salmon- to orange-colored flesh (a few have green flesh), netted rinds, and deep sutures; and they are properly called "muskmelons." The name describes the aroma (musky perfume) of the ripe fruit. "Cantaloupe" is the name associated popularly with muskmelons of the round-to-oval, firm-fleshed, nonsutured, heavily netted type grown in the U.S. Southwest and shipped to grocery stores around the country. The true cantaloupe, however, has a hard, warty rind and green flesh and is not widely grown or known in the United States.

Honeydew, Crenshaw, and Casaba (all *Cucumis melo* var. *inodorus*) are sometimes referred to as "winter melons." (The true winter melon is a Chinese vegetable.) Their cultural requirements are similar to those of muskmelons. They are generally later in ripening (require a longer season), usually have a smooth rind surface, do not separate from the vine when ripe, and lack as distinctive an odor. Even the earliest varieties may not ripen fully in the northern tier of states.

Varieties

All varieties are hybrids unless designated OP (for open-pollinated).

Orange-Fleshed: Ambrosia (86 days to harvest, very sweet flesh); Burpee Hybrid (85 days, standard eastern sutured melon); Bush Star (88 days; 2 pounds; bush-type plant for limited space); Earlisweet (68 days; very early; 2 to 3 pounds, good sweet flavor, firm flesh); Gold Star (87 days, resistant to fusarium wilt); Harper Hybrid (86 days, resistant to alternaria blight, fusarium wilt, mosaic); Harvest Queen (OP–90 days, resistant to fusarium wilt); Iroquois (OP–85 days, resistant to fusarium, very tasty); Pulsar (80 days; heavily netted; tolerant to powdery mildew, fusarium); Rising Star (84 days, resistant to fusarium race 2); Saticoy (86 days; resistant to fusarium wilt, powdery mildew); Supermarket (88 days; resistant to fusarium wilt, powdery mildew); and Superstar (86 days; resistant to fusarium race 2; large; fine flavor).

Green-Fleshed: Jenny Lind (OP–75 days, heirloom; medium to small, flat melons, with protruding section at blossom end; sweet flesh); Passport (73 days, luscious green flesh); Rocky Sweet (80 days; thick, green, sweet flesh); and Sweet Dream (79 days; delicious, sweet, flavorful).

Hybrid Honeydew-Type: Early Dew (85 days, creamy yellow rind, good flavor); Honey Brew (90 days; high yield; strong, disease-resistant vines); Limelight (96 days; 7 to 8 pounds; thick, juicy, sweet flesh); Morning Dew (96 days; largest honeydew-type; 10 to 12 pounds; thick, sweet flesh); Morning Ice (84 days; resistant to powdery mildew, fusarium race 2); and Venus (88 days; light netting over smooth, golden rind; thick, juicy, aromatic flesh).

Other Specialty Melons: Casaba Golden Beauty (OP–110 days; 7 to 8 pounds; white, spicy-sweet flesh); Early Crenshaw (90 days); Honeyshaw (85 days, salmon pink flesh, delicious); and Marygold (92 days; casaba type; yellow, wrinkled skin with white flesh).

When to Plant

Muskmelons may be directly seeded or started as transplants. If the weather and soil are not warm and the soil moisture level moderate, the seeds do not germinate and the plants do not grow. Plant after the danger of frost has passed and the soil has warmed and dried. (See the maps, page 26.) Gardeners in northern climates or other short-season areas who want early production may need to use transplants. To increase earliness, start seed for transplants 3 to 4 weeks before planting time. Because muskmelons do not transplant well if the roots are disturbed, you should start seeds in individual containers. Proper temperatures for germinating and growing

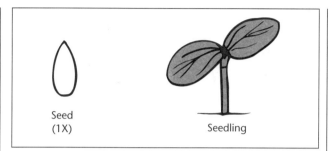

Seed
(1X)

Seedling

the transplants are very important. Do not allow transplants to become too large before planting in the garden, or stunting and crop delays may result. Sterilized media should be used for starting seed to prevent damping-off and other diseases of seeds and seedlings.

Spacing of Plants and Depth of Planting

Plant seeds 1 inch deep, and thin the seedlings 18 to 24 inches apart or the equivalent (two plants every 36 inches or three plants every 48 inches in the hill system). Space rows at least 5 feet apart.

Care

Fertile soils usually grow a fine crop of muskmelons with normal maintenance-fertilizer application plus one side-dress application of high-nitrogen fertilizer when the plants begin to vine. Muskmelons benefit especially from the incorporation of well-rotted manure before planting and also appreciate high potassium. All melons respond favorably to mulching with black plastic, especially early in the season (see page 36). The mulch can be installed when the soil is in good planting condition anytime from a few days to 2 or 3 weeks before planting. Make holes every 2 or 3 feet to plant seed or transplants through the plastic. Use starter fertilizer (see page 20) to help transplants get established. Floating row covers also can be used to advantage over early season melon transplants. These covers exclude the worst of the cold and also early season insect invaders. Covers need not be removed until plants start to flower unless extremely hot weather threatens.

Muskmelons suffer from extremes in soil moisture (too much rain or an extended drought). Irrigation is recommended in case of drought, especially when the vines are growing and the fruits are developing. Trickle irrigation systems used with black plastic mulch work extremely well. Muskmelons ripen to the highest quality when the vines remain healthy throughout the harvest period, when temperatures are warm but not excessively high, and when the weather is comparatively dry at the time of maturity.

Harvesting

Good eating quality depends upon the texture of the melons and the development of sugars from proper ripening on the vines. When muskmelons are ripe, the rind changes from a green to tan or yellow between the netting. They should be picked when the stem separates easily from the vine near the point of attachment ("half-slip" or "full-slip" stages of development). At these stages, there will be a crack near the point of attachment. Do not pick too early because the quality will not be as high as that of vine-ripened melons; sugars continue to be stored in the developing melons up to the moment the stem separates. Once picked, muskmelons soften but do not sweeten further.

Harvest early in the day after the plants are dry, and be careful not to damage the vines. Pick every other day at the beginning of the season, and go over the patch every day at peak season. Especially in dry seasons, wildlife and insects such as picnic beetles quickly attack the sweet, juicy, ripening, and softening fruit.

Honeydew and crenshaw melons are cut off the vine after they turn completely yellow. Their stems do not "slip" at maturity. These melons continue to improve (become soft and mellow) if kept at room temperature for a few days. When they are completely ripe, the blossom end is slightly soft to pressure.

Common Problems

Control **cucumber beetles** (see page 40). They damage muskmelons and spread bacterial wilt by feeding on the plants. When possible, plant varieties that are resistant to fusarium wilt and leaf diseases such as powdery mildew and alternaria blight.

Questions and Answers

Q. Why do the first blossoms drop off my muskmelon plants? *A. The first flowers to appear on the vines are male, and they drop naturally. The female flowers, which open later, have a swelling at the base that forms the fruit. After bees pollinate these female flowers, the fruit develops.*

Q. What causes poor (sparse) fruit set and low yields? *A. The failure of female flowers to set and develop melons can result from lack of proper pollination by bees; cool, wet weather (which also slows bee activity); and planting too close together, resulting in a dense, heavy growth of leaves (which also can suppress effective bee activity).*

Q. How can I grow muskmelons in a small garden? *A. Muskmelon plants can be trained to a fence or trellis. Soon after the fruits begin to enlarge, they should be supported with mesh bags tied to the supporting structures, or their weight may damage the vines.*

Q. Do muskmelons cross-pollinate with other vine crops?
A. No. Muskmelons do not cross-pollinate with cucumbers, watermelons, squash, or pumpkins. Different varieties of muskmelons cross-pollinate readily, but this cross-pollination is not evident unless seeds are saved and planted the following year. Cross-pollination does not make melons bitter.

Q. What causes poor flavor and lack of sweetness or fruits with smooth rinds? *A. Poor soil fertility (especially low potassium), cool temperatures, wet or cloudy weather, choosing a poorly adapted variety, loss of leaves by disease, or picking the melons before they are ripe can all contribute to poor quality.*

Mustard

Mustard, *Brassica juncea* (also known as mustard greens, spinach, leaf mustard, and white mustard), is a quick-to-mature, easy-to-grow, cool-season vegetable for greens or salads. Although mustard is often associated primarily with the Deep South, it is also suitable for gardens in the central and northern United States in the cool parts of the growing season. Mustard greens are high in vitamins A and C.

Varieties

Florida Broadleaf (45 days to harvest, large leaves, slow to bolt); Fordhook Fancy (40 days; frilled, green leaves); Green Wave (45 days; dark green, heavily curled leaves; good in warm temperatures, very slow to bolt); Red Giant (45 days; deep purple-red, white-ribbed, savoyed leaf; best in fall); Savannah (35 days; very vigorous; darker green, thick leaves; slow to bolt); Southern Giant Curled (50 days; bright green, curly, crumpled leaves; slow to bolt; mild flavor); and Tendergreen or Mustard Spinach (45 days, mild, tender, smooth, rounded leaves).

When to Plant

Plant early in the spring (3 weeks before the frost-free date) and again 3 weeks later. (See the maps, page 26.) Plant from midsummer on for fall harvest. Fall plantings are usually of higher quality because they mature under cooler, moister conditions in most locations.

Spacing of Plants and Depth of Planting

Sow seeds ⅓ to ½ inch deep, and thin seedlings to 3 to 5 inches apart. Thinnings can be eaten.

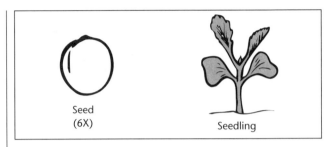

Seed
(6X)

Seedling

Care

Mustard should grow rapidly and without stopping. Give ample fertility, weeding, and water during dry periods.

Harvesting

Harvest the leaves when they are young and tender. Do not use wilted or yellowed leaves. You can cut the entire plant or pick individual leaves as they grow. The leaf texture becomes tough and the flavor strong in summer.

Common Problems

Aphids (see page 40) and **cabbage worms** (page 62).

Questions and Answers

Q. What causes flowers to develop in my spring mustard? *A. Mustard is a cool-season vegetable that naturally flowers during the long, warm days of summer. Pull and compost (or chop and work the spring planting back into the soil) when hot weather arrives and, preferably, before flower stalks develop.*

Q. What causes mustard leaves to have yellow blotches and be misshapen? *A. This condition is caused by downy mildew. It can be controlled by applying a suggested fungicide.*

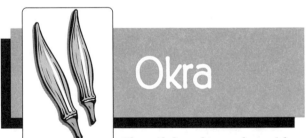

Okra

Okra, *Abelmoschus esculentus* (also known as gumbo), is a tall-growing, warm-season, annual vegetable from the same family as hollyhock, rose of sharon, and hibiscus. The immature pods are used for soups, canning, and stews, or as a fried or boiled vegetable. The hibiscuslike flowers and upright plants (3 to 6 feet or more in height) have ornamental value for backyard gardens.

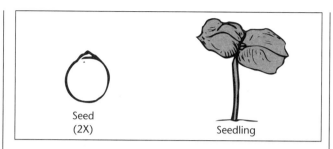

Seed
(2X)

Seedling

Varieties

Annie Oakley (hybrid–52 days to harvest, compact plant, extra-tender pods); Dwarf Green Long Pod (52 days, ribbed pods); Emerald (55 days; dwarf; smooth pods); Clemson Spineless (56 days, AAS winner); and for something novel, try Burgandy (60 days, 1988 AAS winner, deep red pods). Ever-Lucky is a new okra variety that may deserve a trial.

When to Plant

Because okra seeds do not germinate well in cool soils, plant seeds after the soil has warmed in the spring, at about the same time as lima beans, probably a week to 10 days after the date of the last frost for your area. (See the maps, page 26.)

Spacing of Plants and Depth of Planting

Sow seeds 1 inch deep in hills 12 to 24 inches apart. When the seedlings are 3 inches tall, thin all but the one strongest plant per hill. The seeds may be soaked, wrapped in moist paper toweling or in water overnight, to accelerate germination.

Care

Okra usually grows well in any good garden soil. Shallow cultivation near the plants keeps down weeds.

Harvesting

The pods should be picked (usually cut) while they are tender and immature (2 to 3 inches long for most varieties). They must be picked often—at least every other day. Okra plants have short hairs that may irritate bare skin. Wear gloves and long sleeves to harvest okra. Use pruning shears for clean cuts that do not harm the rest of the plant. When the stem is difficult to cut, the pod is probably too old to use. The large pods rapidly become tough and woody. The plants grow and bear until frost, which quickly blackens and kills them. Four or five plants produce enough okra for most families unless you wish to can or freeze some for winter use.

Questions and Answers

Q. Should I remove the old okra pods? *A. Yes. Maturing, older, tough pods sap strength that could go to keeping the plant producing new pods daily. Unless you desire ripe pods for dried arrangements or seed saving, overmature pods should be removed and composted.*

Q. Why doesn't my seed germinate even after soaking? *A. Okra seed does not keep well. Buy fresh seed each season, or save seed of nonhybrid varieties yourself by allowing a few pods on your best plants to mature. When the pods turn brown and begin to split at the seams, harvest them and shell the seeds from the pods. Dry seeds thoroughly for several days, then store in a cool, dry place in tightly closed containers until next season.*

Q. My okra plants grew over 6 feet tall, and the pods were difficult to pick. What should I do? *A. Choose one of the new dwarf or basal-branching varieties, such as Annie Oakley, that grow only 2½ to 5 feet tall.*

Q. What causes yellowing, wilting, and death of plants in midsummer? *A. These conditions are caused by either verticillium or fusarium wilt. Okra varieties, unlike certain tomato varieties, are not resistant to verticillium and fusarium wilt. Rotate crops to prevent buildup of crop-specific strains of these diseases in your garden.*

Onion

Onion, *Allium cepa*, is a cool-season vegetable that can be grown successfully throughout most of temperate North America. Onions may be grown from sets, transplants, or seeds. In each method, onions are planted as soon as the garden can be tilled in the spring, usually late March or early April in prime regions for producing onions. Good fertility, adequate soil moisture, and cool temperatures aid development.

Onions start bulb formation when the day length is of the proper duration, and different varieties of onions require different day lengths to initiate bulbing. In general, most common varieties fall into one of two classes, long-day (for northern latitudes) and short-day (for southern latitudes). For this reason, onion varieties that are grown in the South are not adaptable to the North, and vice versa. Late plantings of the suggested varieties also result in small bulbs or lack of bulbing altogether in any location.

High temperatures and low humidity are advantageous during bulbing and curing. Onions have shallow roots and compete poorly with weeds and grasses. Timely shallow hoeing and cultivation are important, especially when the onions are small.

Onions may be eaten raw, broiled, boiled, baked, creamed, steamed, fried, french fried, and pickled. They are used in soups and stews and in combination with vegetables and meats.

Onions from Sets

Growing green onions from sets is probably the simplest method for the home gardener. The plants are quickly established and become vigorous and strong. Onion sets may be used to produce both green onions and dry onion bulbs, though production of really premium dry onions requires methods described in the following section.

Varieties

Several varieties are used for onion sets. All of these varieties are widely adaptable. The home gardener has little choice of varieties at the store, however, because sets are seldom sold under varietal name, merely by color: yellow, white, or red. Yellow sets are sometimes sold as the varieties Ebenezer or Stuttgarter.

Purchase firm, dormant sets early—before they begin growth in heated salesrooms. Store sets in a cool, dry, dark environment if planting must be delayed after purchase. Divide the sets into two sizes before planting. Large sets (larger than a dime in diameter) are best used for green onions. If allowed to grow, these sets may "bolt" and form flower stalks. The small sets (smaller than a dime in diameter) produce the best bulbs for large, dry onions; and they usually do not "bolt." Extremely cold weather during early season growth also may condition onions from sets to flower.

Round onion sets produce flat onions; elongated or torpedo-shaped sets mature into round onions. Most gardeners prefer white sets for green onions, although red or yellow sets are also acceptable.

Spacing of Plants and Depth of Planting

To produce green onions, plant the larger sets 1½ inches deep and close enough to touch one another (green onions are harvested before crowding becomes a problem). To produce dry onions, plant the smaller sets 1 inch deep, with 2 to 4 inches between sets. Allow 12 to 18 inches between rows. If sets are 2 inches apart, harvest every other plant as green onions so that bulb development of the remaining sets is not impeded by neighboring plants.

Care

Keep free from weeds by shallow cultivation and hoeing. To develop long, white stems for green onions, slightly hill the row by pulling the loose soil toward the onions with a hoe when the tops are 4 inches tall. Do not hill onions that are to be used as dry onions. Hilling may cause the necks of the stored bulbs to rot.

Harvesting

Pull green onions anytime after the tops are 6 inches tall. Green onions become stronger in flavor with age and increasing size. They may be used for cooking when they are too strong to eat raw. Though leaves are traditionally discarded, all parts above the roots are edible.

Remove any plants that have formed flower stalks and use immediately. They do not produce good bulbs for dry storage. Harvest in late July or early August, when most of the tops have fallen over. Allow the plants to mature and the tops to fall over naturally. Breaking over the tops early interrupts growth, causing smaller bulbs that do not keep as well in storage.

Pull the mature onions in the morning, and allow the bulbs to air dry in the garden until late afternoon. On especially hot, bright sunny days, the bulbs may sunburn. On days when this is likely, remove onions to a shaded location and allow them to dry thoroughly. Then, before evening dew falls, place them under dry shelter on elevated slats or screens or hang them in small

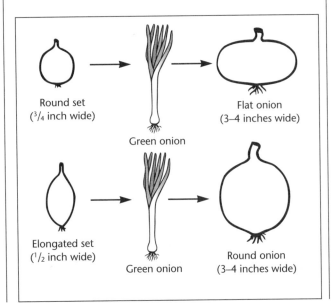

Round set
(³/₄ inch wide)

Green onion

Flat onion
(3–4 inches wide)

Elongated set
(½ inch wide)

Green onion

Round onion
(3–4 inches wide)

bunches. Tops may be braided or tied with string before hanging. Full air circulation for 2 to 3 weeks is necessary for complete drying and curing. Keep the dry wrapper scales as intact as possible on the bulbs, as they enhance the keeping ability. It is best not to wash onions before drying, as this may reduce their keeping ability.

After the bulbs dry, cut the tops 1½ to 2 inches long (at or above the narrow spot where the stem bent over), and place the bulbs in dry storage with good air circulation. Do not try to store bulbs that are bruised, cut, or diseased, or those with green tops or thick necks. Store under cool, dry conditions (see pages 167 and 168). Dry onions may keep until late winter, but check them regularly and use or discard those that begin to soften or rot.

Onions from Transplants

Transplanting young onion seedlings is the method of growing that most regularly produces large, dry, attractive onions for slicing (as shown in the catalog pictures). Transplants are purchased in bundles (usually 60 to 80 plants) from garden stores and through seed and nursery catalogs (though mail-order onion plants often cost as much as buying the 60 to 80 full-size mature bulbs they may produce).

Varieties

Gardeners should try to match varieties to their location. Long-day onions are bred for best performance in the North, and short-day varieties perform best in southern locations. Short-day varieties may perform acceptably in the North if the plants can be set out very early in the season. Long-day types may not get the bulbing signal in the Deep South and so should be avoided there.

The normal garden center may offer Yellow and White Sweet Spanish (long-day varieties), Yellow and White Bermuda (short-day varieties), and a red variety that may or may not be named (Southport Red Globe, perhaps; a long-day variety). Catalog shoppers may choose from a slightly wider variety selection, which may include Texas Grano (short-day), Vidalia Sweet (really a Granex hybrid, short-day), Red Hamburger (short-day), Walla Walla Sweet (long-day), and Texas 1015Y Supersweet (short-day). Prices normally are two to three times as high through catalog sales and may be as much as ten times as high. Only individual consumers can judge if this cost is justified for trying a new variety.

Spacing of Plants and Depth of Planting

Plant in fertile soil in early spring. Space the plants 4 to 5 inches apart in the row to produce large-sized bulbs (closer spacing significantly decreases bulb size), or space 2 to 2½ inches apart and harvest every other plant as a green onion. Allow 12 to 18 inches between rows, or space onions 6 to 8 inches apart in all directions in beds. Set the transplants 1 to 1½ inches deep, and apply 1 cup per plant of a starter-fertilizer solution (see page 20).

Care

Weeds and grass compete with the onion plants for nutrients and moisture during the growing season. Remove all weeds and grass by diligent and repeated shallow cultivation and hoeing. Side-dressing with fertilizer (see page 20) may be necessary.

Harvesting

The earlier varieties are usually ready to harvest in July, with later varieties maturing into August. When most of the tops have fallen over, the onions may be pulled and dried (see "Harvesting," under "Onions from Sets," page 90). The length of storage time varies with the variety, with the sweeter varieties usually being the poorer keepers.

Onions from Seed

Growing onions from seed has been, traditionally, the least popular method with gardeners, though onion farmers have long used seed to produce large crops of excellent onion bulbs. A longer period of time is required for development from seed, especially for dry onions. Both green and dry onions can be grown directly from seed, and the varieties available are different from the varieties sold as transplants. The variety selection goes from 5 or 6 varieties with transplants to perhaps 50 or 60 with seeds. Onions may be seeded in the North as soon as the ground is workable in the spring. In southern areas, short-day varieties can be sown in the fall and then left to overwinter and mature in the spring. This method produces the famous "sweet" onions of various southern states and the island of Maui in Hawaii.

Another method that has recently become more popular is starting onions in flats as bedding plants, indoors or in the greenhouse. Because onions are very hardy plants, onion seeds are sown indoors very early, usually by January or February. This timing does not interfere with greenhouse space needed to start more tender plants, as the onions are planted outdoors by

March or April, depending on location and seasonal weather. This method combines the advantages of seed growing and transplant growing by giving maximal variety selection while allowing precision spacing, with the added advantage of using fresh transplants that grow uninterrupted from flat to garden, unlike other transplants that are grown far away, dug, dried out, and very heavily shocked by the move. Starting your own onion transplants from seed should allow the maturation of a good crop if varieties are matched to the geographic location of the garden.

Varieties

Dry Onions (yellow, long-day): Early Yellow Globe, Norstar, Spartan Banner, Sweet Sandwich, Sweet Spanish Hybrid, Walla Walla Sweet, and Yellow Sweet Spanish.

Dry Onions (white, long-day): Albion Hybrid, Ringmaster, Southport White Globe, White Lisbon, and White Sweet Spanish.

Dry Onions (red, long-day): Benny's Red, Lucifer Hybrid, Red Baron, Red Weathersfield, and Southport Red Globe.

Dry Onions (yellow, short-day): Granex hybrids, Grano hybrids, Yellow Bermuda, and "Vidalia" (really a Granex Hybrid; what makes a Granex hybrid a "Vidalia" is growing in the vicinity of Vidalia, Georgia).

Dry Onions (white, short-day): Crystal Wax, Hybrid White Granex, and White Bermuda.

Dry Onions (red, short-day): Hybrid Red Granex, Red Burgandy, and Red Hamburger.

Green (bunching) Onions (scallions): Beltsville Bunching, Evergreen Bunching, He-Shi-Ko, Red Welsh, Southport White Bunching, Tokyo Long White, White Lisbon, and White Sweet Spanish.

Spacing of Plants and Depth of Planting

For direct-seeded onions, plant seeds 1 inch deep (10 to 15 seeds per foot). Allow 12 to 18 inches between rows. Plant as soon as the garden can be tilled in the spring. This allows the plants to be as big as possible when they get the day-length signal to form bulbs.

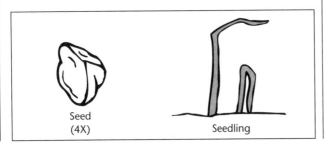

Seed
(4X)

Seedling

Indoors, seed may be sown fairly thickly in small flats, or two or three seeds per cell in a cell pack. In the cells, thin to one plant per cell once germination is complete. Transplant to the garden anytime after plants have grown three or more leaves, as soon as the soil can be worked in the spring. Onions transplant very well, with plants thinned from direct seedings easily taking root when replanted in their own row.

Care

Especially with onions that are direct-seeded, grasses and weeds must be controlled with shallow hoeing and cultivation, especially early in the season. When the seedlings are 3 to 4 inches tall, thin to $1/2$ to 1 inch between plants for green onions. Thin to 2 to 3 inches between plants for most varieties of dry onions and 3 to 4 inches between plants for Sweet Spanish and other large onions.

To develop long, white stems for green onions, draw as much as 1 inch of loose soil around the plants when they are 5 to 6 inches tall. Do not pull soil up to the plants for dry bulbs because it increases the possibility of bulb decay later in storage.

Harvesting

Harvest green onions whenever the base of the plant is $3/8$ inch or larger. Dry bulbs are ready for harvest in September. After most of the tops have fallen over naturally, the onions should be pulled and dried (see "Harvesting," under "Onions from Sets," page 90). When stored under cool, dry conditions (see pages 167 and 168), dry onions from seed keep until spring.

Common Problems

Above 40 degrees north latitude, **root maggots** may attack the roots of onion plants (see page 40). Use a suggested soil insecticide prior to planting if root maggots have been a problem in the past.

Questions and Answers

Q. I harvested my onions in late summer, and they began to rot by fall. Why? A. Onions may rot at either the base or neck. Rotting at the base may be caused by soilborne fungi or carelessness in harvesting and handling, but it is usually caused by damage from root maggots (see page 40). If onion bulbs rot at the neck, either they have been cured insufficiently before storage or the leaves have been severely infected by fungi during the growing season. Onions that were "hilled" or covered with soil before harvest often start to rot soon after harvest. Many of the "sweet" varieties are very poor keepers and should be enjoyed fresh soon after harvest, as no method of storage keeps them from rotting for very long.

Q. What happens when onions are broken over? *A. They stop bulb development at that point and may be immature. As a result, they do not cure or dry properly. In some cases, the rings also separate, yielding bulbs of poor quality.*

Q. My parents came from Europe, where they braided the tops of onions. Why are onions braided? *A. Onions are braided for curing and storage. After the tops are air dried, they are braided and the onions are hung in a dry, sheltered location with good air circulation. Incorporating twine with the braiding adds strength. Individual onions may be cut from the braided "rope" as needed, leaving the rest of the braid intact.*

Q. My grandparents grew winter onions. Can I grow these? *A. Yes. Hardy through most of the country, winter onions (egyptian or walking onions) are planted from sets formed at the tops of the plants in place of flowers. Plant the sets 1 inch deep during August. Space sets 4 to 5 inches apart. The clump also may be divided in early spring (March or April) and transplanted in the same manner as other onion plants. In either case, be sure to place the winter onion bed at the side or end of your garden because these onions are perennials. Sets are available from a limited number of seed houses and can usually be obtained from other gardeners in the area.*

Q. How do I grow multiplier onions? *A. Multiplier onions (sometimes referred to as "potato onions") are planted and handled in exactly the same manner as shallots (see page 142). True multiplier onions, like winter onions, are difficult to obtain, though some specialty seed houses have begun to stock these old-style crops again. They are not normally grown from seed.*

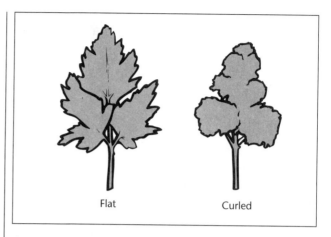

Flat　　　　Curled

Parsley is a green leafy herb that is grown as an annual but is really a biennial. It is the most widely grown herb for garnishing and flavoring. Rarely, parsley seed may be used in cooking. To obtain seed would require allowing the plants to overwinter and flower the second summer, but very little usable foliage is produced in the second season.

Parsley is one of the most popular herb plants grown in vegetable gardens. Because it has a unique ability to blend flavors, parsley may be used as a flavor base with thyme, sweet marjoram, basil, rosemary, summer savory, and a small amount of sage. The combination acts as a unit, rather than the expression of a single herb flavor. Parsley is also used as a garnish; for flavor in salads, soups, and stews; cooked with other vegetables; and dipped into a light batter and served as a french-fried vegetable.

There are two distinct types of parsley. The moss-curled or triple-curled parsley, *Petroselinum crispum* var. *crispum*, forms rosettes of leaves and is frequently used as a garnish. It has been overused as a garnish on restaurant plates and is seldom eaten, though both types are extremely high in vitamins. Good cooks, especially Italians, know that the flat-leaf type, *Petroselinum crispum* var. *neapolitanum*, is where the real flavor is, and they use both its root and leaves. If a good culinary herb is desired, plant flat-leaf parsley; but, if an attractive edging or garnish is desired, plant the curled form. It may be desirable to have a supply of each available. The parsley plant is prized for its ornamental value, makes a fine edging plant, and may be grown in pots and other containers.

Root parsley, *Petroselinum crispum* var. *tuberosum*, which is grown in the same manner as carrots (see page 63), is usually washed, cubed, and added to soups and stews. It can be stored like parnips (see page 95), but cold is not necessary to develop its full flavor. Root parsley has a sweet, mild parsleylike flavor that blends well with other vegetables.

Varieties

Curled Leaf: Banquet, Forest Green, Green River, Krausa, Moss Curled, Pagoda, Paramount, Sherwood, and Triple Curled. **Plain or Flat Leaf:** Catalogno, Flatleaf, Giant Italian, Italian Dark Green, and Plain or Single Italian. **Root Parsley:** Early Sugar, Fakir, Hamburg, and Short Sugar.

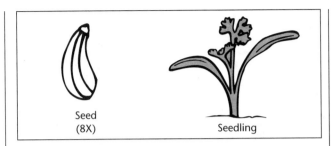

Seed
(8X)

Seedling

When to Plant

Parsley seeds can be planted in the spring in cold frames or window boxes, or directly in the garden. Parsley is hardy, and seeds may be planted as soon as the soil is warm in the spring. For the most consistent results, start the plants indoors or in a protected cold frame (see page 47), and transplant into the garden. Parsley transplants very well if the taproot can be moved intact.

Spacing of Plants and Depth of Planting

Because parsley seed is short-lived, and fresh seed is important in establishing a crop, new seed should be purchased each year. Plant 10 to 15 seeds per inch of row, no more than 1/4 inch deep. Seeds germinate relatively slowly, so be patient and do not overwater. Because parsley seeds are slow to germinate, they may be soaked overnight before planting. Radish seeds may be sown every 6 to 8 inches in the row as a marker so that weeds can be controlled while the parsley germinates. Thin the seedlings to 4 to 6 inches apart. (The seedlings of root parsley are usually thinned to 3 to 5 inches apart.) Allow 12 to 18 inches between rows, or space plants 8 to 12 inches apart in all directions in a bed.

Harvesting

Parsley is usually picked leaf by leaf for daily use after the plants are well established. Whole plants can be sheared off at the ground if the plant is allowed to recover fully before further harvest. Most varieties will allow several such pickings per growing season. The green leaves may be harvested anytime during the growing season. Once plants are established, foliage can be cut regularly and will grow back. The plants remain green in the garden until early winter, and many gardeners harvest the entire plant to dry in late fall. Once dried, parsley leaves are usually placed in a closed container and stored in the dark so that they do not lose their healthy green color. Loss of color usually means loss of flavor.

When the summer supply is adequate, the leaves may be harvested and dried (see page 163). To store fresh parsley leaves, wash them, drip dry, and place in a plastic bag or widemouthed jar in the refrigerator. Parsley may be covered lightly with straw and used continuously over the winter in southern locations.

You also can carefully dig a few plants, pot them in 4- to 6-inch pots, and continue to grow them in the house for a fresh winter supply. The plants need a cool location and ample light. Discard these plants the following spring. If they are set outside, the leaves become tough and strong in flavor, and the plants develop seedstalks. Parsley is a biennial, so plants that survive the winter bolt to seed the following spring. If you are growing a choice or hard-to-find variety, some of these seedstalks may be allowed to mature seed for future plants. If more than one variety is allowed to seed in the garden, crossing may occur, so limit seed production to one variety per year.

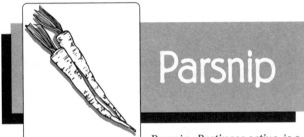

Parsnip

Parsnip, *Pastinaca sativa,* is a hardy biennial, grown in the garden as a full-season annual for its long, tapered storage root that resembles a large, white carrot. It is considered a winter vegetable because its flavor is not fully developed until the roots have been exposed to near-freezing temperatures for 2 to 4 weeks in the fall and early winter. The starch in the parsnip root then changes into sugar, resulting in a strong, sweet, unique, nutlike flavor admired by many but despised by a few.

Varieties

All American; Cobham Improved Marrow (high sugar; half-long shape; better for heavy soils); Harris Model; and Hollow Crown. New varieties that may deserve a trial include Andover and Lancer.

When to Plant

Plant seed in early April or May in a deep, fertile soil that is well prepared. Because parsnip seed is very short-lived, you must obtain a fresh supply each spring.

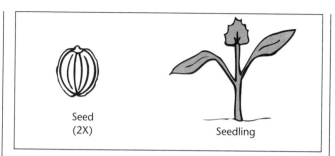

Seed
(2X)

Seedling

Depth of Planting and Spacing of Plants

Plant seeds ½ to ¾ inch deep. Because germination of even the freshest parsnip seed is often mediocre, seed thickly, at least two or three seeds per inch to ensure a good stand. Space rows 18 to 24 inches apart, or plants 8 to 10 inches apart in a bed. Parsnip seed is slow to germinate, and some gardeners drop a radish seed every foot in the furrow to mark the row and help break the soil crust. Once parsnip seedlings are up and growing, pull the radishes and thin parsnip seedlings to 2 to 4 inches apart.

Care

Keep young parsnip plants free of weeds by shallow hoeing or cultivation. Watch for swallowtail-butterfly caterpillars, which feed on most members of the carrot family. Handpicking the caterpillars from the leaves normally gives adequate control. Water thoroughly once a week in periods of extended dry weather to keep growth from slowing in summer.

Harvesting

Parsnips should remain in the ground until the tops freeze in late fall. In lighter-textured soils, long-rooted types may reach down 12 to 18 inches after a good season's growth, so dig deeply and carefully, trying to stay back far enough from the root to safely undercut these deep roots. At this time, the roots may be harvested and stored, or they may be left in the garden to be used as needed. Gardeners who do not have storage facilities often mulch parsnips with straw so that they can be dug throughout the winter. In spring, before new growth begins, the roots still can be dug and should have excellent flavor and quality. Once growth really gets under way, the root becomes flabby and fibrous and should be removed and composted unless seed production of a variety is desired.

Like beets and carrots, parsnips may be stored in outdoor vegetable pits or underground cellars or under refrigeration at 32°F with high (95 percent) humidity (see pages 167 and 168). Dig the roots (usually 1½ to 2 inches in diameter and 8 to 12 inches long) with a shovel, tilling spade, or spading fork. Yields frequently exceed 1 pound per foot of row (single roots may weigh more than 1 pound each).

Common Problems

Low soil fertility is a common problem. However, in well-maintained garden soils adequately supplied with organic matter and fertilizer, this ordinarily should not be a problem. If plants begin to look light green or stunted during the season due to low fertility, the problem usually can be overcome by side-dressing a complete fertilizer in late June (see page 20). Where parsnips will be grown, avoid fertilizing with fresh clumps of organic matter, which can cause misshapen or forked roots. Parsnips are relatively free of both insects and diseases.

Pea

Pea, *Pisum sativum* var. *sativum,* is a frost-hardy, cool-season vegetable that can be grown throughout most of the United States, wherever a cool season of sufficient duration exists. For gardening purposes, peas may be classified as garden peas (english peas), snap peas, and snow peas (sugar peas). The garden pea varieties have smooth or wrinkled seeds. The smooth-seeded varieties tend to have more starch than the wrinkled-seeded varieties. The wrinkled-seeded varieties are generally sweeter and usually preferred for home use. The smooth-seeded types are used more often to produce ripe seeds, which are used like dry beans and to make split-pea soup. Snap peas have been developed from garden peas to have low-fiber pods that can be snapped and eaten along with the immature peas within. Snow peas are meant to be harvested as flat, tender pods before the peas within develop at all. The southern pea (cowpea) is an entirely different warm-season vegetable that is planted and grown in the same manner as beans (see page 53).

Varieties

GARDEN

The following varieties (listed in order of maturity) have wrinkled seeds and are resistant to fusarium wilt unless otherwise indicated.

Early: Daybreak (54 days to harvest, 20 to 24 inches tall, good for freezing); Alaska (57 days, 25 inches, smooth seeds); and Spring (57 days, 22 inches, dark green freezer pea).

Main-Season: Sparkle (60 days, 18 inches, good for freezing); Maestro (61 days, 24 inches, double pods, resistant to powdery mildew); Progress #9 (62 days, 15 inches, dark green pods); Knight (62 days, 18 to 22 inches; long, well-filled pods); Olympia (62 days; 18 inches; resistant to fusarium, powdery mildew, bean yellows mosaic); Little Marvel (63 days, 18 inches, holds on the vine well); Frosty (64 days, 28 inches, resistant to fusarium); Novella II (65 days, 28 inches, "leafless" type); Bounty (67 days; 24 inches; pods set double; exceptional flavor; resistant to fusarium race 1, powdery mildew); Green Arrow (68 days; 28 inches; pods in pairs; resistant to fusarium and powdery mildew); Bolero (69 days, 29 inches, excellent for freezing); and Wando (70 days, 24 to 30 inches, withstands some heat, best variety for late-spring planting.)

SNAP, *Pisum sativum*

Sugar Bon (59 days, 18 to 24 inches, resistant to powdery mildew); Early Snap (60 days; 18 to 22 inches; thick-walled, fleshy pods); Sugar Ann (60 days, 16 to 20 inches, sweet); Honey Pot (70 days); Super Sugar Mel (70 days; 24 to 28 inches; largest pod; resistant to powdery mildew); Sugar Daddy (72 days, 24 to 30 inches, stringless); and Sugar Snap (74 days, 5 to 6 feet, original snap pea, needs trellis or fence).

SUGAR, *Pisum sativum var. macrocarpon*

Snowbird (58 days, 18 inches, double or triple pods in clusters); Little Sweetie (60 days, 16 inches, tolerant to heat and disease); Blizzard (63 days, 30 inches, two pods per node); Dwarf Gray Sugar (65 days, 24 to 30 inches); Oregon Sugar Pod II (68 days; 24 to 30 inches; resistant to pea enation, fusarium, powdery mildew); Mammoth Melting Sugar (68 days, 4 to 5 feet, wilt resistant); Super Sugar Pod (70 days, over 4 feet, wilt resistant); and Snowflake (72 days, 22 inches, high yield).

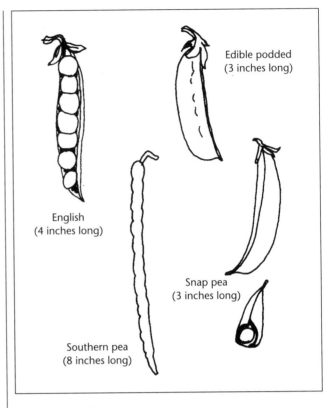

English
(4 inches long)

Edible podded
(3 inches long)

Snap pea
(3 inches long)

Southern pea
(8 inches long)

When to Plant

Peas thrive in cool, moist weather and produce best in cool, moderate climates. Early plantings normally produce larger yields than later plantings. Peas may be planted whenever the soil temperature is at least 45°F and the soil is dry enough to till without its sticking to garden tools.

Plantings of heat-tolerant varieties can be made in midsummer to late summer, to mature during cool fall days. Allow more days to the first killing frost than the listed number of days to maturity because cool fall days do not speed development of the crop as do the long, bright days of late spring.

Spacing of Plants and Depth of Planting

Plant peas 1 to 1½ inches deep and 1 inch apart in single or double rows. Allow 18 to 24 inches between single or pairs of rows. Allow 8 to 10 inches between double rows in pairs.

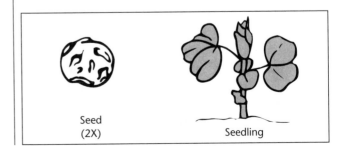

Seed
(2X)

Seedling

Care

The germinating seeds and small seedlings are easily injured by direct contact with fertilizer or improper cultivation. Cultivate and hoe shallowly during the early stages of growth. Most dwarf and intermediate varieties are self-supporting. The taller varieties (Green Arrow and Bolero) are more productive and more easily picked when trained to poles or to a fence for support; but they are no longer popular. Peas can be mulched (see page 35) to cool the soil, reduce moisture loss, and keep down soil rots. Some of the snap and sugar peas are vining types with heights of 6 feet or more that require fencing or other supports.

Harvesting

Garden peas. When the pea pods are swollen (appear round), they are ready to be picked. Pick a few pods every day or two near harvest time to determine when the peas are at the proper stage for eating. Peas are of the best quality when they are fully expanded but immature, before they become hard and starchy. Peas should be picked immediately before cooking because their quality, especially sweetness (like that of sweet corn), deteriorates rapidly. The pods on the lower portion of the plant mature earliest. The last harvest (usually the third) is made about one week after the first. Pulling the entire plant for the last harvest makes picking easier. All the listed varieties, excellent as fresh peas, may be canned or frozen.

Sugar snap peas. Snap peas should be harvested every 1 or 2 days, similarly to snow peas, to get peak quality. Sugar snaps are at their best when the pods first start to fatten but before the seeds grow very large. At this point, the pods snap like green beans, and the whole pod can be eaten. Some varieties have strings along the seams of the pod that must be removed before cooking. Sugar snaps left on the vine too long begin to develop tough fiber in the pod walls. These must then be shelled and used as other garden peas, with the fibrous pods discarded. Vining types of both sugar snap and snow peas continue to grow taller and produce peas as long as the plant stays in good health and the weather stays cool.

Snow peas. These varieties are generally harvested before the individual peas have grown to the size of BBs, when the pods have reached their full length but are still quite flat. This stage is usually reached 5 to 7 days after flowering. Snow peas must be picked regularly (at least every other day) to assure sweet, fiber-free pods. Pods can be stir-fried, steamed, or mixed with oriental vegetables

or meat dishes. As soon as overgrown pods missed in earlier pickings are discovered, remove them from the plants to keep the plants blooming and producing longer. Enlarging peas inside these pods may be shelled and used as garden peas. Fat snow pea pods (minus the peas enlarging inside) should be discarded. Fibers that develop along the edges of larger pods, along with the stem and blossom ends, are removed during preparation. Pea pods lose their crispness if overcooked. The pods have a high sugar content and brown or burn quickly. Do not stir-fry over heat that is too intense.

Pea pods can be stored in a plastic bag in the refrigerator for 2 weeks. Unlike fresh green peas, pea pods deteriorate only slightly in quality when stored.

Common Problems

The first signs of **fusarium wilt** and **root-rot diseases** are the yellowing and wilting of the lower leaves and stunting of the plants. Infection of older plants usually results in the plants' producing only a few poorly filled pods. These diseases are not as prevalent on well-drained soils. Double-dug raised beds amended with abundant organic matter can greatly improve soil aeration and drainage. Fusarium wilt can be avoided by growing wilt-resistant varieties.

Questions and Answers

Q. Should I inoculate my peas with nitrogen-fixing bacteria before planting? *A. When peas are planted on new land, you may increase the yield by inoculating peas with a commercial formulation of nitrogen-fixing bacteria. In an established garden, however, inoculation is less necessary. If you are in doubt, inoculation is a relatively inexpensive process that is easy to do and ensures better plant-nutrient status.*

Pepper, *Capsicum annuum* (also known as mango), is a tender, warm-season vegetable. Technically speaking, all peppers are also known as "chiles," though hot peppers (*Capsicum annuum*, *C. chinense*, and *C. frutescens*) more usually are associated with this name. Pepper plants require some-

Variety	Color progression, comments	Days to maturity
Hybrid bell peppers:		
Bell Boy	green to red	70
Camelot	green to red	67
Cardinal	green to red	70
Four Corners	green to red	67
King Arthur	green to red	70
Lady Bell	green to red	72
North Star	green to red	66
Canary	green to yellow	72
Klondike Bell	green to yellow	72
Marengo	green to yellow	72
Orobelle	green to yellow	76
Dove	"white" (immature yellow) to red	71
Gold Finch	"white" to bright yellow	72
Ivory	"white" to bright yellow	70
Corona	green to orange	66
Orange Grande	green to orange	76
Oriole	green to orange	74
Peppourri Orange	green to orange	75
Valencia	green to orange	72
Blue Jay	immature purple (lavender) to red	73
Islander	immature purple (lavender) to red	72
Lilac	immature purple (lavender) to red	74
Peppourri Lilac	immature purple (lavender) to red	75
Blackbird	immature purple (black) to red	73
Purple Belle	immature purple (black) to red	70
Secret	immature purple (black) to red	70
Chocolate Bell	green to chocolate brown	75
Hybrid elongated bell peppers:		
Clovis	green to red	68
Elisa	green to red	72
Marquis	green to red	72
Ori	green to yellow	70
Pimento peppers:		
Super Red	green to red, sutured	70
Sweetheart	green to red, top-shaped	75
Yellow Cheese	green to yellow, sutured	73
Sweet frying or salad type:		
Biscayne	pale green to red	65
Gypsy	pale yellow to orange to red	65
Key Largo	pale green to red	66
Sweet Banana	pale yellow to orange to red	70

Variety	Comments	Days to maturity
Hot peppers:		
Anaheim		78
Cayenne, large, thick		70
Cayenne, long, slim		73
Cherry	small, round	75
Gold Spike		75
Habanero (Scotch Bonnet)	extremely hot!	85–90
Hungarian Wax		70
Jalapeno		80
Mexi Belle Hybrid	mild	70
Red Chili		84
Serrano Chile		75–80
Super Chile Hybrid		75
Tam Jalapeno	mild	65–70
Zippy Hybrid	mild	(to green harvest) 57

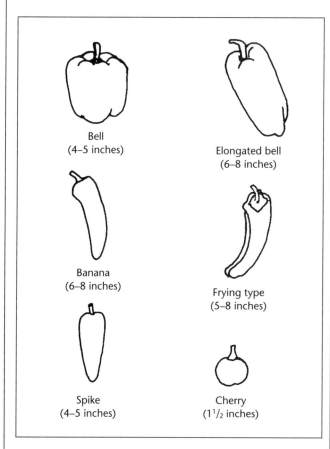

Bell
(4–5 inches)

Elongated bell
(6–8 inches)

Banana
(6–8 inches)

Frying type
(5–8 inches)

Spike
(4–5 inches)

Cherry
(1^1/$_2$ inches)

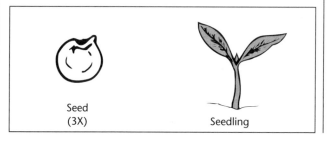

Seed
(3X)

Seedling

what higher temperatures, grow more slowly, and are smaller than most tomato plants. Brightly colored, sweet bell pepper varieties have recently burst onto the scene. A vast range of other garden peppers (pimiento, tabasco, cayenne, chili, and paprika) may be grown for food, spices, or as ornamentals.

The sweet varieties of peppers, especially the bells, traditionally have been by far the most popular in the United States. They are eaten green or ripe and are used for salads, stuffing, soup, stews, relishes, and pickling. New developments in color and form have done nothing to dull the popularity of sweet peppers. Hot pepper varieties have also enjoyed a rebirth of popularity recently, mainly due to various ethnic cuisines that use their unique flavors and heat creatively.

Many pepper types listed in the preceding paragraphs should be familiar to you from names on the spice rack at the grocery store. Many people do not realize that most of these diverse types can be grown in much of this country if plants are started indoors and transplanted into the garden after frost danger passes. Do not confuse these peppers (*Capsicum* species) with black pepper (*Piper nigra*), the familiar table condiment. The two species are not related, though Columbus's confusion on his arrival in the Western Hemisphere cemented the problem in the language.

When to Plant

Peppers are best started from seeds indoors in late winter and then transplanted into the garden after the soil and air have warmed in the spring. The plants cannot tolerate frost and do not grow well in cold, wet soil. When night temperatures are below 50° to 55°F, the plants grow slowly, the leaves may turn yellow, and the flowers drop off. Raised beds, black plastic mulch, and floating row covers may be used to advantage with peppers to warm and drain the soil and to enhance the microenvironment of the young pepper plants in spring, when cool weather may persist. Earlier, more uniform harvests usually result.

Spacing of Plants

Set transplants 18 to 24 inches apart in the row, or 14 to 18 inches apart in all directions in beds. A dozen plants, including one or two salad and hot types, may provide enough peppers for most families; but with so many colors, flavors, and types available, more may be necessary for truly devoted pepper lovers or for devotees of ethnic cuisines.

Care

Peppers thrive in a well-drained, fertile soil that is well supplied with moisture. Use a starter fertilizer when transplanting (see page 20). Apply supplemental fertilizer (side-dressing) after the first flush of peppers is set. Because a uniform moisture supply is essential with peppers, especially during the harvest season, irrigate during dry periods. Hot, dry winds and dry soil may prevent fruit set or cause abortion of small immature fruits.

Harvesting

Fruits may be harvested at any size desired. Green bell varieties, however, are usually picked when they are fully grown and mature—3 to 4 inches long, firm, and green. When the fruits are mature, they break easily from the plant. Less damage is done to the plants, however, if the fruits are cut rather than pulled off. The new, colored bell pepper fruits may be left on the plant to develop full flavor and ripen fully to red, yellow, orange, or brown; or they may be harvested green and immature. Some (including "white," light yellow, lilac, and purple) are colors that develop in the immature fruit and that should be harvested before actually ripening, when they turn red.

Hot peppers are usually harvested at the red-ripe stage; but "green chiles," the immature fruits, are also required for some recipes. Some dishes may actually call for a specific variety of chile to be authentic. Hot pepper flavor varies more from variety to variety than was previously appreciated.

To dry chiles, individual fruits can be picked and strung in a "ristras" or entire plants can be pulled in the fall before frost and hung in an outbuilding or basement to dry. Always exercise caution when handling hot varieties, because skin, noses, and eyes may become painfully irritated. Plastic or rubber gloves may be helpful when picking or handling hot peppers.

Common Problems

People who use tobacco should wash their hands with soap and water before handling pepper plants to prevent spread of **tobacco mosaic disease.** Grow resistant varieties if possible.

Watch for accumulation of **aphids** (see page 40) on the underside of the leaves, especially near growing branch tips. When a large aphid population is present, sticky "honeydew" appears on the lower leaves and fruit. If this situation occurs, apply a suggested insecticide.

Bacterial diseases may be transported on purchased transplants, so look over potential purchases carefully for any leaf spotting or stem cankers.

Questions and Answers

Q. Why do my pepper plants grow large but not develop fruits? They are dark green and do not appear to be diseased. *A. Several weather conditions can reduce fruit set of peppers. Early in the season, extreme cold may prevent fruit set. The most common problems later in the season are hot, dry winds and warm nights (above 70°F). Periods of extreme heat, with or without wind, may prevent fruit set, especially in some varieties. Although overfertilization, especially with nitrogen, is often suspected in these cases because the growth is luxuriant, peppers can actually produce fruit quite well under almost ridiculously high fertility programs. Pepper plants that have no developing fruit attached normally maintain a greener, healthier appearance because all the nutrients can go into producing leaves and stems instead of fruit.*

Q. What causes small, dry, sunken black areas near the ends of the peppers? *A. This condition is blossom-end rot, a condition more commonly associated with tomato. It is caused by drought, uneven water availability, or pruning roots through improper cultivation. Blossom-end rot is more severe on some varieties of peppers than on others. Remove infected fruits and throw them away. Irrigation and mulching can help to prevent blossom-end rot. Though the condition is caused by a calcium deficiency in the affected fruit tissue, addition of calcium to the soil seldom alters the condition. The problem is one of calcium mobility in the plant, not lack of calcium in the soil.*

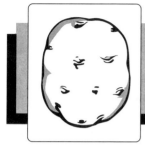

Potato

Potato, *Solanum tuberosum,* is a cool-season vegetable that ranks with wheat and rice as one of the most important staple crops in the human diet around the world. The white potato is referred to as the "irish potato" because it is associated with the potato famine in Ireland in the 19th century. Potatoes are not roots but specialized underground storage stems called "tubers." Maximal tuber formation occurs at soil temperatures between 60° and 70°F. The tubers fail to form when the soil temperature reaches 80°F. Potatoes withstand light frosts in the spring and can be grown throughout most of the country in the cooler part of the growing season, but they prefer the northern tier of states for maximal yield and quality.

Varieties

There are more than 100 varieties of potatoes. White-skinned (actually very light brown) and red-skinned varieties with white flesh are the most common in home gardens. Some russets and yellow-fleshed types are also grown. Russet Burbank is the most important commercial variety produced in the United States, but the weather over most of the country is too warm and the moisture fluctuation too great for the production of smooth tubers and good yields. Common garden varieties offer better taste, texture, and cooking quality for home use anyway.

The following varieties are well adapted to a variety of conditions. If possible, use northern-grown seed potatoes that are certified disease free.

Early: Caribe (magenta skin; good size, attractive, smooth); Irish Cobbler (light brown skin; often irregularly shaped); Norgold Russet (russet skin, attractive "baker" shape, poor keeper); Norland (red skin, smooth, resistant to scab); and Superior (light brown skin; often irregularly shaped).

Midseason: Red Lasoda (red skin, smooth); Red Pontiac (red skin, deep eyes); and Viking (red skin, very productive).

Late: Katahdin (light brown skin; smooth; resistant to some viruses, verticillium, bacterial wilts) and Kennebec (light brown skin, smooth; resistant to some viruses, late blight).

Green Mountain is an old semi-rough white variety noted for its great taste. Due to a fairly high number of misshapen tubers, it has all but disappeared from commercial production. For dependable production in all seasons and the greatest-tasting baked potato ever, Green Mountain is worth the effort to find certified seed.

Yukon Gold is the most famous of the new wave of yellow-fleshed varieties now available. Long popular in Europe, these have good flavor and more moist flesh, which many people claim requires less of the fattening condiments required by dry-as-dust Russet Burbanks. Yukon Gold is a very early bearer of large, round, attractive tubers with a hint of pink around the eyes. Many grocery stores around the country now feature some name-brand version of "golden" potatoes, usually this variety. If the flavor of these market potatoes suits you, look for seed of Yukon Gold.

When to Plant

Potatoes are among the earliest vegetables planted in the garden. Early, midseason, and late varieties all may be planted in March or early April. Planting too early in damp, cold soils makes it more likely that seed pieces rot before they can grow. Potatoes planted in March also may be frozen back to the ground by late frosts. Plants usually recover fully, but the blackened shoots are always demoralizing to the gardener. Medium-early plantings, when soils have dried and warmed, may do as well as extremely early, winter-defying plantings. Midseason and late varieties may be planted as late as the first of July. Late potatoes are best for winter storage.

Spacing of Plants and Depth of Planting

Potatoes are started from "seed pieces" rather than from true seed. These seed pieces may be small whole potatoes or potatoes that are cut into 1½- to 2-ounce pieces. Plant the pieces soon after cutting. Be sure that there is at least one good "eye" in each seed piece. Some

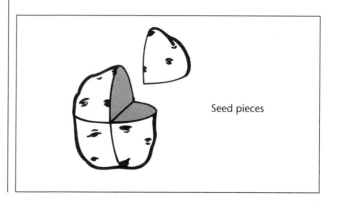

Seed pieces

garden centers and seed suppliers sell "potato eyes" that weigh less than an ounce. These may be too small for optimal production. Small, whole, certified seed potatoes are often the best choice for home gardeners.

Plant seed pieces 10 to 12 inches apart, and cover in a furrow between 2 and 3 inches deep. Space rows 24 to 36 inches apart. The 24-inch spacing is often beneficial because the plants shade the soil and prevent high soil temperatures that inhibit tuber development.

Care

The soil should be fertile and well drained. Clay soils should be improved with organic matter and plowed deeply in the fall. If space allows, a cover crop such as clover, buckwheat, or winter rye grown in the potato bed the year before potatoes are planted improves soil structure, organic-matter content, and subsequent potato production.

Mulching is usually beneficial in growing potatoes. After the potato plants have emerged, organic mulch can be applied to conserve moisture, help keep down weeds, and cool the soil (see page 35). Some gardeners cover rows of early potatoes with clear plastic film at planting (see page 36) to warm the soil and promote early growth when the soil temperature is low. When the plants emerge, remove the film to allow the plants to grow unrestricted.

After the potatoes break the surface of the ground, gradually build up a low ridge of loose soil by cultivation and hoeing toward the plants. This ridge, which may become 4 to 6 inches high by summer, reduces the number of "sunburned" (greened) tubers. The object of potato cultivation is to eliminate competition from weeds, to loosen and aerate the soil, and to ridge the row. Misshapen potatoes develop in hard, compact soil. Use extreme caution when hoeing near potato plants because developing tubers are easily cut and ruined.

Irrigate to assure uniform moisture while the tubers are developing (see page 37). A uniform moisture supply also helps to cool the ground and eliminate knobs caused by secondary growth.

Harvesting

Harvest potatoes after the vines have died. Handle as gently as possible during harvest. Because the tubers develop 4 to 6 inches beneath the soil surface, a shovel or spading fork is a useful tool for digging potatoes.

Potatoes for use in early summer ("new" potatoes) may be dug before the vines die (usually in July). When the potatoes reach 1 to 2 inches in size, you may wish to dig a few hills to use for soup or to cook with creamed peas or to butter and roast.

Late potatoes are usually dug in August or early September. They keep in the garage or basement for several weeks in their natural dormancy. Store over the winter in a dark room at a temperature between 38° and 40°F with high humidity (see pages 167 and 168). Check periodically for spoilage. Temperatures below 38°F cause internal damage to the tubers.

"Straw Potatoes"

Potatoes grown by a special cultural method in that they are not hilled or cultivated after planting are called "straw potatoes." The seed pieces and rows should be spaced the same as for conventional cultivation, but the seed pieces are planted at the soil surface. Place loose straw 4 to 6 inches deep over the seed pieces and between the rows. Potato sprouts should emerge through the straw cover. Cultivation should not be necessary. Pull any weeds that manage to emerge through the straw cover, and add more straw through the season if decomposition starts to thin the layer. Harvest by carefully removing the straw and picking up the tubers that lie on the soil surface. In addition to weed control, strawing has several other advantages. The straw keeps the soil temperature more uniform and about 10°F cooler, reduces water loss, and results in better-shaped tubers. It is usually more rewarding to straw late varieties than early ones because there is a longer period for tuber development. Many gardeners who grow potatoes for competition in exhibits and fairs use the strawing method because the potatoes are of excellent size, color, shape, and smoothness.

Colorado potato beetle
(1/2 inch)

Common Problems

Early blight causes yellowing and dying of the leaves. The first signs of the disease are the presence of brown spots and yellowing of the lower leaves. The entire plant becomes infected if the disease is not controlled. Early blight is best controlled by weekly applications of suggested fungicides, beginning when the seedlings are 6 to 8 inches tall.

The **potato scab disease** (indicated by scabby, rough skins) does not develop when the soil pH is 5.6 or lower. Plant resistant varieties when available.

Colorado potato beetles, flea beetles, and **leafhoppers** (see page 40) can significantly reduce potato yields. These insects can be controlled with suggested insecticides.

Questions and Answers

Q. Should I save some of my potatoes for seed? *A. No, unless you are saving seed of an heirloom variety not commercially available. Saving your own seed potatoes can lead to a buildup of viruses and diseases. Whenever possible, plant seed potatoes certified to be free from certain viruses and diseases.*

Q. My potato plants flowered and formed green fruits that resemble small tomatoes. What are they? *A. These small seed balls are the fruits that contain the true seeds. They are not edible. Except for breeding purposes, growing potato plants from the true seeds in these fruits is a troublesome and unrewarding exercise.*

Q. What causes green skin on my potatoes? *A. The green areas on tubers develop where the potato was exposed to the sun. This condition occurs when the potatoes were not planted deeply enough or not covered with straw. The green portions taste bitter because they contain a moderately poisonous alkaloid. These green areas should be cut off and discarded. Exposure of potato tubers to fluorescent light or sunlight causes greening during storage.*

Q. How should potatoes that are cut into seed pieces be cured? *A. They can be cured by holding them for a week at 60° to 65°F with high humidity (85 percent or higher). This treatment is of questionable value for the home gardener.*

Q. Can I make chips from homegrown potatoes? *A. Yes. Almost any potato variety can be used to make chips when the potatoes are freshly dug and starchy. Commercial chips are made from selected varieties that are naturally high in solids, carefully handled, and properly stored to preserve starch and avoid buildup of sugars. Chips made from potatoes stored at low temperatures for long periods are brown or have a dark ring because they contain excessive amounts of sugar.*

Q. Can I use grocery store potatoes for planting? *A Probably not. They may have been treated with a sprout retardant, in which case, they will not grow. Even if they are sprouting, they have not been inspected and certified free of disease. While results occasionally may be acceptable, the risk of introducing a nematode, disease, or other pest is much higher than from quality-certified seed potatoes.*

Pumpkin

Pumpkin (*Cucurbita pepo, C. maxima, C. moschata,* and *C. mixta*) is a warm-season vegetable that can be grown throughout much of the United States. Besides being used as jack-o'-lanterns at Halloween, pumpkins are used to make pumpkin butter, pies, custard, bread, cookies, and soup. The flowers may be picked just before or as they open, dipped in batter, and fried as a delicacy. The small, immature pumpkin fruit (before the seed develops) may be prepared like a summer squash. These young, tender fruits may be either steamed or boiled and then served as a buttered vegetable; or sliced, dipped in batter, and fried. The immature pumpkin is sometimes cut into strips and eaten raw with dips for snacks. The seeds of "naked-seeded" varieties do not have tough seed coats and can be roasted in the oven or sauteed for snacks.

Varieties

Small *Cucurbita pepo* pumpkins are grown primarily for fall decorations or for cooking and pies and are usually referred to as "pie" types because they are associated with cooking. They vary in size from less than 2 pounds in the case of Baby Bear to more than 5 pounds with some of the larger varieties. In general, small-fruited varieties produce more fruit per vine than larger ones because each individual fruit takes less plant energy to produce.

Intermediate and large *C. pepo* varieties are used primarily for jack-o'-lanterns, for stock feed, and very rarely for cooking. Recent variety developments have greatly strengthened the walls of these pumpkins so that much rounder, more attractive fruit are produced with fewer flat sides. Generally, these varieties take up more space in the garden and produce fewer fruits per plant. Flesh quality is pretty uniformly poor, and they are consequently almost never used for cooking.

Processing pumpkins of the species *C. moschata* are almost exclusively canned commercially, yielding the familiar dark orange, fine-textured, dry-fleshed product most consumers expect to find when they begin to make their holiday "pumpkin" pies. Because these varieties look more like buff-colored watermelons than pumpkins,

Dickinson Field
(12 inches long)

Triple Treat (naked-seeded)
(7 inches long)

Connecticut Field
(18 inches long)

Sugar Pie
(8 inches long)

their *C. pepo* cousin's picture graces the can; but the true, high-quality flesh desired for pumpkin pies comes from these relatives of butternut squash.

Jumbo or mammoth pumpkin varieties of the species *C. maxima* have recently begun to attract much attention. While these varieties have long been used for exhibits at county fairs, annual weigh-offs now take place at numerous locations around the country and throughout the world. The most recent winner topped 900 pounds, with 1,000 pounds the goal of these professional growers by the year A.D. 2000. Here, genetics is everything. The better and larger the pumpkin your seed comes from, the better your chance of producing a whopper of your own. Seeds are so valuable that some giants on display in malls or other businesses actually have been destroyed by night raiders and their seeds stolen. Buy your seed from a reliable source, and try your hand at producing the Great Pumpkin.

White painting types are *C. pepo* or *C. maxima* but have light, creamy white skin instead of the orange more typical of these species. This colorless background is regarded as ideal by some pumpkin painters. Flesh is pale yellow, similar to the orange varieties. Fruits of these types are often marketed as "ghost" pumpkins.

Cushaws are relatively large and long necked, with an enlarged, bell-shaped base at the blossom end. Most cushaws are of the species *C. mixta*, though some, like Golden Cushaw, are *C. moschata*. The long necks have solid flesh, with a characteristically coarse texture that is preferred by some people for cooking. The large size and unusual color patterns make them popular, as well, for fall decorations. Cushaws, especially the *C. mixta* types, typically produce long, less-branched vines than other species.

Naked-seeded types produce seeds without the tough seed coats of common varieties. These "naked" seeds are ready to roast and eat as they come from the fruit with-

out hulling. Newer varieties in this classification include small pie types and at least one variety that produces very acceptable jack-o'-lantern-sized fruit. Because the seeds are not protected by a seed coat, however, they are much more vulnerable to soil insects or to rotting in damp soil. Soil should be thoroughly warm and reasonably well dried to get these types to germinate acceptably and quickly. Fresh seed also helps. These types may be worth the trouble to germinate in cell-tray flats of sterilized seed-starting medium or in peat pellets, where temperature and moisture can be controlled. Transplant to the garden when they have two to three true leaves.

Chinese pumpkins, developed in Asia, are the type most recently introduced into the United States. Although they are eaten pureed, baked, or stir-fried (and in soups and pies in Asia), they are more frequently used as fall decorations here. They are typically flattened, with prominent sutures and bright orange color. Where space is limited, they may be trained on a fence or other support. Although they resemble gourds in both plant habit and size of the miniature pumpkins, these are good tasting, unlike gourds, though almost as durable. Production is heavy in terms of number of fruit per plant.

The following varieties of pumpkins are well adapted to a variety of conditions. All are vining types that require considerable growing space and are best suited for large gardens, unless otherwise indicated. The bush and semi-vining types are best suited to be grown in smaller gardens.

STANDARD ORANGE (*C. pepo*)

Small: All 2 to 5 pounds, 100 to 110 days to harvest: Baby Bear (small, flattened shape; fine stem); Baby Pam; Oz (hybrid, semi-bush; very smooth skin, heavy stem, immature yellow color); Small Sugar or New England Pie (the standard pie type); Spooktacular (hybrid; bright orange; ribbed; strong stem); Sugar Treat (hybrid; semi-bush; bright color); and Winter Luxury (old variety, good for cooking; unique netted skin).

Intermediate: All 8 to 15 pounds, 100 to 110 days to harvest: Autumn Gold (hybrid, yellow when immature); Bushkin (hybrid, bush type); Frosty (hybrid; smooth-textured skin); Funny Face (hybrid); Harvest Moon (hybrid); Jack-O-Lantern; Spirit (hybrid, semi-bush); and Young's Beauty.

Large: All 15 to 25 pounds, 100 to 110 days to harvest: Aspen (hybrid, deep orange, uniformly large); Big Autumn (hybrid, yellow when immature); Big Tom (selection of Connecticut Field); Connecticut Field (the old standard, continually reselected); Ghost Rider (dark orange; very dark green handle); Happy Jack (uniform, dark orange; good handle); Howden Field (the industry standard for the last 20 years); Jackpot (hybrid; round; compact vine habit); Jumpin' Jack (large, dark orange, heavy, tall fruit); and Pankow's Field (large, variable pumpkins with exceptionally large, long handles). Rouge Vif d'Estampes is a *C. maxima* type that is deep red-orange, flattened, heavily sutured. It was the prototype for Cinderella's carriage pumpkin and is sometimes sold as "Cinderella" pumpkin.

SPECIALTY

Processing: All *C. moschata,* tan skin color, widely used for commercially canned pumpkin: Buckskin (hybrid); Chelsey (hybrid); Dickinson Field; and Kentucky Field.

Jumbo: All *C. maxima,* 50 to 100 pounds, or much more; 120 days to harvest: Atlantic Giant (most true giants come from selections of this variety); Big Max; Big Moon; Mammoth Gold; and Prizewinner (hybrid; most uniform size, shape, orange color; not the largest, but the most dependable).

White Painting: Casper, Lumina, and Snowball (all *C. maxima*); and Little Boo (*C. pepo*).

Cushaw group: Green-Striped Cushaw, Sweet Potato, Tennessee, and White Cushaw (all *C. mixta*); and Golden Cushaw (*C. moschata*).

Naked-Seeded: All *C. pepo:* Trick or Treat (hybrid, semi-bush, 10 to 12 pounds, good for carving); Tricky Jack (hybrid; small; bush type); and Triple Treat (thick flesh; 6 to 8 pounds; cooks, carves well).

Miniature: All *C. pepo:* Baby Boo (white); Jack-Be-Little (standard orange miniature); Jack-Be-Quick (taller, darker orange); Munchkin (uniform, attractive orange fruit); and Sweetie Pie (small, scalloped, medium orange fruit).

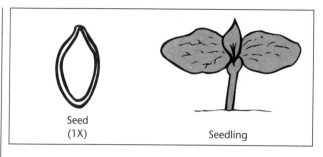

Seed (1X) Seedling

When to Plant

Pumpkin is a very tender vegetable. The seeds do not germinate in cold soil, and the seedlings are injured by frost. Do not plant until all danger of frost is past and the soil has thoroughly warmed. Plant pumpkins for Halloween from late May in northern locations to early July in extremely southern sites. If pumpkins are planted too early, they may soften and rot before Halloween.

Spacing of Plants and Depth of Planting

Vining pumpkins require a minimum of 50 to 100 square feet per hill. Plant seeds 1 inch deep (four or five seeds per hill). Allow 5 to 6 feet between hills, spaced in rows 10 to 15 feet apart. When the young plants are well established, thin each hill to the best two or three plants.

Plant semi-bush varieties 1 inch deep (four or five seeds per hill), and thin to the best two plants per hill. Allow 4 feet between hills and 8 feet between rows.

Plant miniature varieties 1 inch deep, with two or three seeds every 2 feet in the row. Rows should be 6 to 8 feet apart, with seedlings thinned to the best plant every 2 feet when they have their first true leaves.

Plant bush varieties 1 inch deep (1 or 2 seeds per foot of row), and thin to a single plant every 3 feet. Allow 4 to 6 feet between rows.

Care

Pumpkin plants should be kept free from weeds by hoeing and shallow cultivation. Irrigate (see pages 37 and 38) if an extended dry period occurs in early summer. Pumpkins tolerate short periods of hot, dry weather pretty well.

Bees, which are necessary for pollinating squash and pumpkins, may be killed by insecticides. When insecticides are used, they should be applied only in late afternoon or early evening when the blossoms have closed for the day and bees are no longer visiting the blossoms. As new blossoms open each day and bees land only inside the open blossoms, these pollinating insects should be safe from contact with any potentially deadly sprays.

Harvesting

Pumpkins can be harvested whenever they are a deep, solid color (orange for most varieties) and the rind is hard. If vines remain healthy, harvest in late September or early October, before heavy frosts. If vines die prematurely from disease or other causes, harvest the mature fruit and store them in a moderately warm, dry place until Halloween. Cut pumpkins from the vines carefully, using pruning shears or a sharp knife, and leave 3 to 4 inches of stem attached. Snapping the stems from the vines results in many broken or missing "handles." Pumpkins without stems usually do not keep well. Wear gloves when harvesting fruit because many varieties have sharp prickles on their stems.

Avoid cutting and bruising the pumpkins when handling them. Fruits that are not fully mature or that have been injured or subjected to heavy frost do not keep. Store in a dry building where the temperature is between 50° and 55°F (see pages 167 and 168).

Common Problems

Powdery mildew causes a white, powdery mold growth on the upper surfaces of the leaves. This growth can kill the leaves prematurely and interfere with proper ripening. Apply a suggested fungicide if powdery mildew appears before the fruits are fully grown and ripened.

Cucumber beetles and **squash bugs** (see page 40) attack seedlings, vines, and both immature and mature fruits. They can be controlled with a suggested insecticide. Be alert for an infestation of cucumber beetles and squash bugs, as populations build in late summer, because these insects can damage the mature fruits, marring their appearance and making them less likely to keep properly.

Questions and Answers

Q. The first flowers that appeared on my pumpkin plants did not form fruits. Why not? *A. This condition is natural for cucurbits (such as cucumber, gourd, muskmelon, pumpkin, squash, and watermelon). The first flowers are almost always male. The pollen on these first male flowers attracts bees and alerts them to the location of the blooming vines. By the time the first female blossoms open, the bees' route is well established and the male flowers' pollen is transferred to the female flowers by the bees. Male flowers bloom for one day, then drop off the plants. The male flowers may predominate under certain conditions, especially early in the season, or under certain kinds of stress. The small fruits, visible at the bases of the female flowers, identify them. There is no swelling on the bases of the male flower stems.*

Q. How can I grow pumpkins that weigh more than 100 pounds? *A. Use one of the jumbo varieties. Plant in early June, and allow 150 square feet per hill. Thin to the best one or two plants. High fertility, proper insect control, and shallow cultivation are essential. Remove the first two or three female flowers after the plants start to bloom so that the plants grow larger with more leaf surface before setting fruit. Allow a single fruit to develop, and pick off all female flowers that develop after this fruit has set on the plant. Do not allow the vine to root down at the joints near this developing fruit because these varieties develop so quickly and so large that they may actually break from the vine as they expand on a vine anchored to the ground.*

Q. My grandmother made pies with a green-striped, long-necked pumpkin. Is this variety still available? *A. Yes. The variety is Green-Striped Cushaw. Because it has a unique texture, some cooks prefer it for custards and pies.*

Q. Will pumpkins, squash, and gourds cross-pollinate and produce freak fruit if I interplant several kinds in my garden? *A. Pumpkins, squash, and gourds are members of the vine crops called "cucurbits." The name is derived from their botanical genus classification of Cucurbita (often abbreviated C.). There are four main species of Cucurbita usually included in the pumpkin, squash, and gourd grouping. The varieties within a botanical species (which may be referred to as pumpkins, squash, or gourds) can cross-pollinate. Varieties from different species do not. For example, zucchini crosses with Howden's Field pumpkin, acorn or spaghetti squash, small decorative gourds, or Jack-Be-Little miniature pumpkins because they are all members of the same botanical species (C. pepo). However, cross-pollination does not affect the taste, shape, or color of the current season's fruit. Crosses show up only if seeds from these fruits are saved and grown the following year. Butternut squash, Small Sugar pumpkin, White Cushaw pumpkin, and Big Max pumpkin could all be grown in the same area without crossing because each variety comes from a different species. Because bees carry pollen for distances of a mile or more, in suburban areas where many gardens are in close proximity, fruits must be bagged and pollinated by hand if pure seed of nonhybrid varieties is desired.*

Q. What is the difference a pumpkin and a squash? *A. It is all in what you call it. Varieties of each of the four species discussed in this section are popularly called "pumpkins," and varieties of each are called "squash," more by tradition than by system. In fact, orange color sometimes helps determine what is a pumpkin. Two varieties of the same species, C. maxima, hold the records for the world's largest squash and pumpkin. The variety called squash is gray to green, and largest one called a pumpkin is pinkish to orange. Shape may vary slightly, but these two freely interpollinate and are botanically pretty much indentical. Unless you are dealing with specific rules or regulations at a show, you can pretty much interchange the words squash and pumpkin, though you can expect a fight with purists, no matter what you do.*

The table on pages 113 and 114 shows many common varieties of pumpkins, squashes, and gourds belonging to the botanical species of C. pepo, C. maxima, C. moschata, and C. mixta. This table is meant to classify many of the diverse varieties of these four species. Not all varieties listed in the table are recommended in this book.

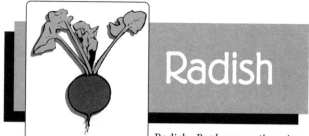

Radish

Radish, *Raphanus sativus*, is a cool-season, fast-maturing, easy-to-grow vegetable. Garden radishes can be grown wherever there is sun and moist, fertile soil, even on the smallest city lot. Early varieties usually grow best in the cool days of early spring, but some later-maturing varieties can be planted for summer use. The variety French Breakfast holds up and grows better than most early types in summer heat if water is supplied regularly. Additional sowings of spring types can commence in late summer, to mature in the cooler, more moist days of fall. Winter radishes are sown in midsummer to late summer, much as fall turnips. They are slower to develop than spring radishes; and they grow considerably larger, remain crisp longer, are usually more pungent, and hold in the ground or store longer than spring varieties.

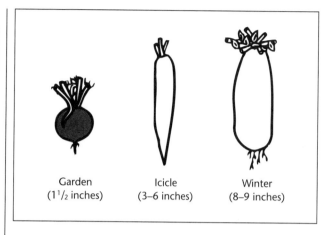

Garden
(1½ inches)

Icicle
(3–6 inches)

Winter
(8–9 inches)

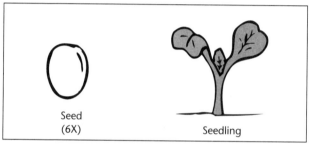

Seed
(6X)

Seedling

Varieties

Spring: Burpee White (25 days to harvest; round; smooth white skin); Champion (28 days, large, round, red); Cherry Belle (22 days, round, red); Cherry Queen Hybrid (24 days, deep red, round, slow to become pithy); Early Scarlet Globe (23 days; globe-shaped, small taproot, bright red); Easter Egg (25 days; large, oval; color mix includes reddish purple, lavender, pink, rose, scarlet, white); Fuego (25 days; round, red; medium tops; resistant to fusarium, tolerant to black root/black scurf); Plum Purple (25 days, rounded, large, deep magenta); and Snow Belle (30 days, attractive, round, white, smooth).

For Spring or Summer Use: French Breakfast (23 days, oblong red with white tip) and Icicle (25 days, long, slim, tapered white).

Winter (for storage): China Rose (52 days, white); Chinese White (60 days; large, long, square-shouldered, blunt-tipped, creamy white roots); Round Black Spanish (55 days; rough, black skin, white flesh); and Tama Hybrid (70 days; daikon type; roots as long as 18 inches, with 3-inch diameter; smooth, white; blunt tip).

When to Plant

Spring radishes should be planted from as early as the soil can be worked until midspring. Make successive plantings of short rows every 10 to 14 days. Plant in spaces between slow-maturing vegetables (such as broccoli and brussels sprouts) or in areas that will be used later for warm-season crops (peppers, tomatoes, and squash). Spring radishes also can be planted in late winter in a protected cold frame, window box, or container in the house or on the patio. Later-maturing varieties of radishes (Icicle or French Breakfast) usually withstand heat better than the early maturing varieties and are recommended for late-spring planting for summer harvest. Winter radishes require a much longer time to mature than spring radishes and are planted at the same time as late turnips (usually midsummer to late summer).

Spacing of Plants and Depth of Planting

Sow seed ¼ to ½ inch deep. Thin spring varieties to ½ to 1 inch between plants. Winter radishes must be thinned to 2 to 4 inches, or even farther apart to allow for proper development of their larger roots. On beds, radishes may be broadcast lightly and thinned to stand 2 to 3 inches apart in all directions.

Care

Radishes grow well in almost any soil that is prepared well, is fertilized before planting, and has adequate moisture maintained. Slow development makes radishes hot in taste and woody in texture.

Radishes mature rapidly under favorable conditions and should be checked often for approaching maturity.

Harvest should commence as soon as roots reach edible size and should be completed quickly, before heat, pithiness, or seedstalks can begin to develop.

Harvesting

Pull radishes when they are of usable size (usually starting when roots are less than 1 inch in diameter) and relatively young. Radishes remain in edible condition for only a short time before they become pithy (spongy) and hot. Proper thinning focuses the harvest and avoids disappointing stragglers that have taken too long to develop.

Winter varieties mature more slowly and should be harvested at considerably larger size. Once they reach maturity, they maintain high quality for a fairly long time in the garden, especially in cool fall weather. Size continues to increase under favorable fall conditions. Daikon, or chinese radish, can achieve particularly large size and still maintain excellent quality. Winter radishes can be pulled before the ground freezes and stored in moist cold storage for up to several months.

Common Problems

Root maggots (see page 40) may tunnel into radishes. These insects are more common above 40 degrees north latitude. Apply a suggested soil insecticide before planting if this insect previously has been a problem.

Questions and Answers

Q. What causes my radishes to crack and split? *A. The radishes are too old. Pull them when they are younger and smaller. A flush of moisture after a period of relative dryness also may cause mature roots to burst and split. Try to avoid uneven moisture availability.*

Q. Why do my radishes grow all tops with no root development? *A. There may be several reasons: seed planted too thickly and plants not thinned (though some roots along the outside of the row usually develop fairly well even under extreme crowding), weather too hot for the spring varieties that do best in cool temperature (planted too late or unseasonable weather), and too much shade (must be really severe to completely discourage root enlargement).*

Q. What causes my radishes to be too "hot"? *A. The "hotness" of radishes results from the length of time they have grown rather than from their size. The radishes either grew too slowly or are too old.*

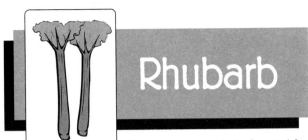

Rhubarb

Rhubarb, *Rheum rhabarbarum* (also known as pie plant), is a very hardy perennial garden vegetable that grows well in most of the country. Although considered a vegetable, rhubarb is used as a fruit in pies, tarts, and sauces. Because rhubarb produces yields for 5 years or longer in the same location, it should be planted at the end or one side of the garden where it will not be disturbed by normal activities to prepare the soil each year. A half-dozen plants should provide enough rhubarb for all but truly rhubarb-loving families.

Varieties

Red Petioles (leafstalks): Canada Red (long, thick stalks, extra sweet); Cherry Red (rich red inside and out); Crimson Red (tall, plump petioles); MacDonald (tender skin; brilliant red); Ruby; and Valentine (petioles 22 by 1½ inches, good flavor).

Green Petioles (leafstalks): Victoria (shaded with red).

When to Plant

Plant or divide rhubarb roots in early spring while the plants are still dormant. Planting seeds is not recommended except in extremely southern parts of the country because it may take too long for the plants to become established. Also, the seedlings do not come true to color and size. Seed-grown rhubarb also tends to produce more seedstalks, which sap strength from the developing leaves, than do the cultivars selected for moderate to light seed production.

Spacing of Plants and Depth of Planting

Plant the roots with the crown bud 2 inches below the surface of the soil. Space the roots 36 to 48 inches apart in rows 3 to 4 feet apart. Good garden drainage is essential in growing rhubarb. Planting on raised beds

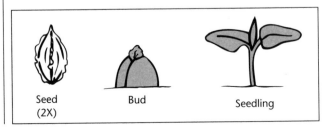

Seed
(2X)   Bud   Seedling

ensures against rotting of the crowns. Working plenty of well-rotted manure into the rhubarb bed before planting greatly increases production.

Old roots may be dug and divided to make new plantings. Cut the roots into four to eight pieces. Each piece must have at least one strong bud. To improve vigor and leaf size, many gardeners divide the old plants and establish a new planting after at least 5 years of full harvest. Plantings older than this tend to begin crowding themselves out. Dig the roots of the most vigorous, healthy plants to establish a new bed the spring before the old planting is to be discarded.

Care

Cultivate shallowly as often as necessary to remove weeds. Apply a complete garden fertilizer before growth begins in the spring and side-dress with manure tea or other high-nitrogen fertilizer in late June (see page 20). Except in poorly drained sites, organic mulches help moderate soil temperature and moisture. Irrigate during extended dry periods. An application of manure or compost is beneficial in late fall or early winter. Do not cover the crowns.

Harvesting

Do not harvest rhubarb during the first year of planting. Newly set plants need all their foliage to build a strong root system. Stalks may be harvested for 1 or 2 weeks during the second year, and for 8 to 10 weeks (a full harvest season) during the third and subsequent years. Harvest in the fall only when the plants are to be discarded the next season. To harvest, pull the leafstalks from the plant, and trim off the leaf blades. The leaf blades contain large amounts of oxalic acid and should not be eaten. To keep the plants healthy, vigorous, and producing well, remove only about one-third of the leaves from a plant at any one time.

If seedstalks and flowers develop during the spring and summer, cut them from the base of the plant as soon as they appear and discard them. Vegetatively propagated, named varieties usually have been selected to produce many fewer seedstalks than cheaper, seed-produced plants. The petioles (leafstalks) are of the highest quality (maximum color, flavor, and tenderness) in early spring. They should be crisp and fairly thick. Yield and quality are highest if petioles that have just reached full size are harvested before any coarse fiber can develop.

You can grow tender stalks out of season by "forcing" rhubarb at home during the late winter and early spring. Forcing is most successful with the Victoria variety because it normally produces stalks with large diameters. Dig the roots of plants that are to be forced (3-year-old plants are best) and allow them to freeze on top the ground. Keep excess soil on the roots to prevent damage from subzero freezing. After the roots are thoroughly chilled (about 45 to 50 days), take them indoors to a warm, dark place (such as a cellar or hotbed) and cover with peat, soil, or sawdust. Place the crowns close together and keep them moist. The ideal temperature is 55° to 60°F. Harvest when the stalks are 12 to 18 inches tall, the leaves small, and the petioles tender and uniformly bright pink. The harvest period for forced roots is about 1 month. It is usually best to discard roots after forcing.

Rhubarb curculio
(1/5 inch)

Common Problems

Rhubarb curculio, a snout beetle, bores into the stalks, crowns, and roots of rhubarb plants. It also attacks wild dock, a weed that is prevalent in many areas of the country. Destroy all wild dock growing around the garden. Treat the base of plants with a suggested insecticide. Burn badly infected rhubarb plant parts in July after the beetles have laid their eggs.

Questions and Answers

Q. A severe freeze has damaged my rhubarb. Can I safely eat the leafstalks? *A. No. The leafstalks will be of poor texture and flavor, and oxalic acid may have migrated from the leaf blades.*

Q. Why do my rhubarb plants send up seedstalks and produce small leaves and leafstalks? The petioles are not as large as they have been in previous years. *A. These conditions may result from excessive crowding, old plants, or low soil fertility. Allow more space between rhubarb plants, divide parent plants, and fertilize regularly. Some seed-propagated plants produce small foliage and many seedstalks even under the best conditions. Buy only named, vegetatively propagated varieties; or get divisions from another gardener who has a high-quality planting.*

Salsify

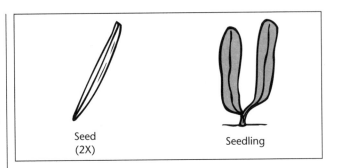

Seed
(2X)

Seedling

Salsify, *Tragopogon porrifolius,* and Black Salsify, *Scorzonera hispanica,* are both known as vegetable oyster or oyster plant, from the flavor of the cooked roots. Both are hardy biennials that produce foliage and an edible root the first year. Salsify is a creamy white root that produces purple flowers the second season. Scorzonera is a black-skinned root that produces yellow flowers. The tops form a spreading rosette of narrow, pointed leaves, giving salsify and scorzonera a somewhat exotic appearance compared to most other garden vegetables. Because they are able to withstand hard freezing in the winter, either crop may be harvested anytime frozen ground allows until early spring, when new growth depletes the overwintered roots. The tapered roots (½ to ¾ inch in diameter and 8 to 10 inches long) are made into a chowder or cooked and served cold as a salad vegetable. The roots of salsify are usually peeled after cooking, while the roots of scorzonera are not because a large proportion of their flavor is in the skin of the roots. Spring shoots of either plant may be eaten like asparagus. Scorzonera is reputed to be a good companion plant to carrots, repelling the carrot fly.

Varieties

Salsify: Mammoth Sandwich Island (120 days to harvest; creamy white, 8-inch roots) and Lange Jan (115 days, European variety, very resistant to bolting).

Scorzonera: Gigantia (120 days; long, cylindrical, thick roots).

Either salsify or scorzonera is sometimes sold without variety names, simply by the name of the vegetable.

When to Plant

Salsify and scorzonera are both grown in much the same way as parsnip. Plant seeds in a deep, well-prepared, fertile soil in early spring (about 100 days before freezing weather in the fall).

Spacing of Plants and Depth of Planting

Plant seeds ½ to ¾ inch deep (10 to 12 seeds per foot of row) in rows 18 to 24 inches apart. When the seedlings are 2 inches tall, thin to 2 to 4 inches apart.

Care

Salsify grows slowly when young, and frequent shallow cultivation is necessary to remove weeds. It is free from most garden diseases and insects and withstands dry conditions once it is well established.

Harvesting

The flavor of salsify and scorzonera, like that of parsnip, is improved after several hard frosts in the fall sweeten the roots. Harvest anytime through April. Top growth in the spring may be cut when young and tender and used like asparagus. To store the roots, cut off the leaves 1 inch above the roots and hold the roots under conditions similar to those for storing parsnips (see page 95). Gardeners without storage facilities may mulch the vegetable oyster rows with straw and dig the roots as needed throughout the winter. If allowed to grow a second year, salsify sends up a seedstalk and bloom.

Spinach

Spinach, *Spinacia oleracea,* is a hardy, cool-season vegetable. It is grown in early spring or late fall because long, hot summer days cause it to "bolt" (form premature seedstalks), making it unusable. Rich in vitamins, spinach is one of the more important vegetable greens grown in the United States for both salads and cooking, and it can be grown in certain seasons in all parts of the country.

Savoy (crinkled) leaf spinach catches fine soil particles, like tiny grains that are splashed by rainfall. This makes the spinach slightly "gritty" when chewed. If you

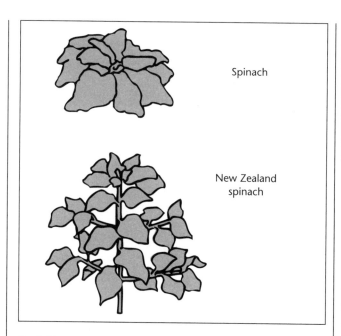

Spinach

New Zealand
spinach

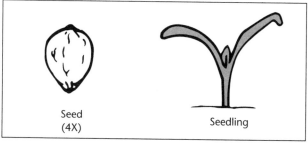

Seed
(4X)

Seedling

find this unacceptable, plant one of the the plain-leaf sorts, which do not catch and hold as many soil particles, and wash cleaner. Much of commercial spinach production is on organic muck soils, which have little or no mineral content, and, thus, do not make the spinach gritty.

Varieties

Choose the best varieties for spring or fall planting.

Crinkled-Leaf: Bloomsdale Long Standing (48 days to harvest; thick, very crinkly, glossy dark green leaves) and Winter Bloomsdale (45 days, tolerant to cucumber mosaic virus, slow to bolt, cold tolerant, good for over-wintering).

Hybrid Savoy: Indian Summer (39 days; semi-savoy; resistant to downy mildew races 1 and 2, tolerant to spinach blight); Melody (42 days; lightly crinkled; resistant to downy mildew, mosaic; good spring or fall); Tyee (39 days; dark green; heavily savoyed; tolerant to downy mildew; spring, fall, or winter); and Vienna (40 days; very savoyed; medium- to long-standing; tolerant to downy mildew races 1 and 2 as well as spinach blight).

Plain-Leaf: Giant Nobel (43 days; large, smooth leaves; long-standing).

Plain-Leaf Hybrid: Olympia (46 days; slow to bolt; spring, summer harvest).

When to Plant

The first planting can be made as soon as the soil is prepared in the spring. If the soil was prepared in the fall, seeds can be broadcast over frozen ground or snow cover in late winter and germinate as the soil thaws. Plant

successive crops for several weeks after the initial sowing to keep the harvest going until hot weather. Seed spinach again in late summer for fall and early winter harvest. Chill seeds for summer or fall plantings in the refrigerator for 1 or 2 weeks before planting. In southern locations, immature spinach seedlings survive over winter on well-drained soils and resume growth in spring for early harvest. With mulch, borderline gardeners should be able to coax seedlings through the winter for an early spring harvest. Spinach can be grown in hotbeds, sunrooms, or protected cold frames for winter salads.

Spacing of Plants and Depth of Planting

Sow 12 to 15 seeds per foot of row. Cover ½ inch deep. When the plants are 1 inch tall, thin to 2 to 4 inches apart. Closer spacing (no thinning) is satisfactory when the entire plants are to be harvested. The rows may be as close as 12 inches apart, depending upon the method used for keeping weeds down. In beds, plants may be thinned to stand 4 to 6 inches apart in all directions. Little cultivation is necessary.

Care

Spinach grows best with ample moisture and a fertile, well-drained soil. Under these conditions, no supplemental fertilizer is needed. If growth is slow or the plants are light green, side-dress with nitrogen fertilizer (page 20).

Harvesting

The plants may be harvested whenever the leaves are large enough to use (a rosette of at least five or six leaves). Late thinnings may be harvested as whole plants and eaten. Cut the plants at or just below the soil surface. Spinach is of best quality if cut while young. Two or three separate seedings of short rows can provide harvest over an extended period. Some gardeners prefer to pick the outer leaves when they are 3 inches long and allow the younger leaves to develop for later harvest. Harvest the entire remaining crop when seedstalk formation begins because leaves quickly lose condition as flowering begins.

Common Problems

Cucumber mosaic virus causes a condition in spinach called blight.

Downy mildew and other fungal leaf diseases are a problem, especially in seasons that are wet, humid, or both. Some resistance is available through variety selection. Raised beds create excellent air and water drainage in the spinach bed, which also helps prevent infections.

Questions and Answers

Q. What causes spinach to develop flower stalks (seed-stalks) before a crop can be harvested? *A. Spinach bolts quickly to seed during the long days in late spring or summer. Warm temperatures accelerate this development. Varieties that are "long standing" or slow to bolt are best adapted for spring planting.*

Q. What causes yellowing, stunting, and early death of plants? *A. These conditions are caused by blight disease (cucumber mosaic virus). Grow resistant varieties.*

New Zealand Spinach

New Zealand spinach, *Tetragonia tetragonioides*, is a vegetable that thrives under summer heat and is used for salads or greens. It is not true spinach, but an entirely different species grown as a warm-season substitute for spinach because it is similar in taste and texture and because it is tolerant to heat and drought. The large, spreading plants produce succulent leaves and branch tips that are used in the same way as spinach.

Varieties

This vegetable green is indeed native to New Zealand, and it is listed in garden catalogs simply as "New Zealand Spinach." There is some variation in plant type, but named varieties are seldom, if ever, seen in this country.

When to Plant

Because New Zealand spinach plants are cold tender, seeds should not be planted before the frost-free date. (See the maps, page 26.) Seeds can also be started indoors for transplanting.

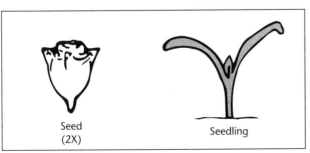

Seed
(2X)

Seedling

Spacing of Plants and Depth of Planting

Plant seeds 1 inch deep where they are to grow in the garden, or start them early in flats. Soak seeds overnight in lukewarm water before planting, and keep the soil moist after planting because they are sometimes slow to germinate. Thin or space plants 12 inches apart in the garden. Starting plants in flats allows precision spacing. Be sure to allow space between rows because the plants may spread 4 to 6 feet by the end of the season, depending on how diligently you harvest them.

Care

New Zealand spinach requires no special care other than normal cultivation.

Harvesting

The young, tender leaves and tips of shoots (3 to 4 inches) are cut as needed throughout the summer. Plants may be cut back (sheared) occasionally to force new growth. Harvest until the first hard freeze in the fall. As fall plantings of true spinach begin to mature about the same time, the supply of "spinach" can be relatively uninterrupted.

Squash, Summer

Summer squash, *Cucurbita pepo* and *C. maxima* (also known as vegetable or italian marrow), is a tender, warm-season vegetable that can be grown throughout the United States anytime during the warm, frost-free season. The true English vegetable marrow is a vining type that is of good quality when immature. It is not commonly grown in the United States, where summer squash varieties are virtually all bush types. Summer squash differs from fall and winter squash in that it is selected to be harvested before the rind hardens and the fruit matures. It grows on bush-type plants that do not spread like the plants of fall and winter squash and pumpkin. A few healthy and well-maintained plants produce abundant yields.

Botanical species	Pumpkin	Summer squash	Winter squash	Gourds and ornamental squash
Cucurbita pepo		**green elongated**	**acorn type**	
	Aspen	Ambassador	All-Season	Apple
	Autumn Gold	Black Beauty	Autumn Queen	Bicolor
	Baby Bear	Black Jack	Cream of the Crop	Crown of Thorns
	Baby Pam	Black Zucchini	Ebony	Nest Egg
	Big Autumn	Boss	Raven	Orange
	Big Tom	Classic	Royal Acorn	Pear
	Connecticut Field	Cocozelle	Swan White	Shenot
	Early Sweet Sugar	Cousa (Lebanese	Table Ace	Spoon
	Extra Early Sugar	zucchini)	Table Gold	
	Frosty	Elite	Table King	
	Funny Jack	Fiorentino (hybrid	Table Queen	
	Ghost Rider	cocozelle)	Tay-Belle	
	Half Moon	Greyzini		
	Halloween	Midnite	**spaghetti type**	
	Happy Jack	Milano	Orangetti	
	Howden Field	Napolini	Pasta	
	Jack-O-Lantern	Pale face	Tivoli (compact plant)	
	Jackpot	President		
	Jumpin' Jack	Senator	**delicata type**	
	New England Pie	Spineless Beauty	Delicata	
	Pankow's Field	Viceroy	Heart of Gold	
	ProGold 500	Zucchini	Honey Boat	
	Seneca Harvest		Sugar Loaf	
	Moon	**green round**	Sweet Dumpling	
	Spirit	Garnet Globe		
	Spookie	Ronde de Nice		
	Spooktacular	Scallopini		
	Tallman			
	Winter Luxury	**yellow round**		
	Wizard	Sun Drops		
	Young's Beauty	Suntop		
		yellow elongated		
	naked-seeded	Blondie		
	Lady Godiva	Butterbar		
	Mini Jack	Classic		
	Sugar Treat	Condor		
	Trick or Treat	Crescent		
	Triple Treat	Early Prolific		
		Straightneck		
		Eldorado		
	miniature	Gold Finger		
	Baby Boo (white)	Gold Slice		
	Jack-Be-Little	Goldbar		
	Jack-Be-Quick	Golden Girl		
	Munchkin	Goldie		
	Sweetie Pie	Medallion		
		Seneca		
		Sundance		
		Super Spike		
		Superpik		
		Supersett		
		flat-shaped		
		Patty Pan		
		Peter Pan		
		Sunburst		

Botanical species	Pumpkin	Summer squash	Winter squash	Gourds and ornamental squash

Cucurbita maxima	Atlantic Giant
	Big Max
	Big Moon
	Casper (white painting)
	Hungarian Mammoth
	King of the
	   Mammoths
	Lumina (white)
	Mammoth Prize
	Prizewinner
	Rouge Vif d'Estampes
	   (also called
	   Cinderella;
	   flattened, dark
	   orange)
	Snowball (white)
			All Season Bush
			Baby Blue Hubbard
			Banana
			Buttercup
			Delicious
			Emerald
			Gold Nugget
			Golden Hubbard
			Green Warted Hubbard
			Honey Delight
			Kindred
			Marblehead
			Mooregold
			NK 530
			NK 580
			NK 4000
			Red Kuri
			Sweet Mama
			Sweet Meat
				Aladdin
				Turk's Turban

Cucurbita moschata	Buckskin Cheese Dickinson Field Golden Cushaw Kentucky Field Palomino		**butternut type** Butternut Early Butternut Hercules Hybrid Butternut Patriot Ponca Puritan Supreme Ultra Waltham Zenith	
Cucurbita mixta	Green-Striped Cushaw Japanese Pie Sweet Potato Tennessee White Cushaw			

Varieties

Summer squash appears in many different fruit shapes and colors: scallop (or Patty Pan), which is round and flattened like a plate with scalloped edges, usually white but sometimes yellow or green; constricted neck (thinner at stem end than blossom end, classified as either "crookneck" or "straightneck" depending on if the stem end is straight or bent), which is usually yellow; and the cylindrical to club-shaped italian marrows, such as zucchini, cocozelle, and caserta, which are usually shades of green but may be yellow or nearly white.

The varietal selection of summer squash has markedly changed in recent years, and the number of varieties offered has greatly expanded as the result of new interest, hybridization, and introduction of disease resistance. The number of varieties is staggering. See table starting on page 113 for a wider (yet still far from complete) listing of varieties.

Recommended varieties of summer squash include:

Zucchini (open-pollinated): Black Zucchini (best-known summer squash; greenish black skin, white flesh);

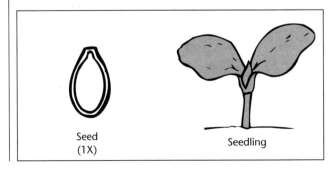

Seed
(1X)

Seedling

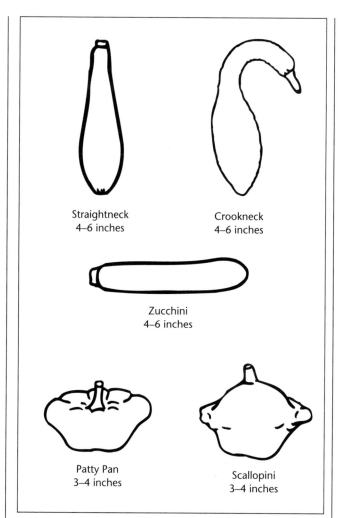

Straightneck
4–6 inches

Crookneck
4–6 inches

Zucchini
4–6 inches

Patty Pan
3–4 inches

Scallopini
3–4 inches

Black Beauty (slender, with slight ridges, dark black-green); Cocozelle (dark green overlaid with light green stripes; long, very slender fruit); and Vegetable Marrow White Bush (creamy greenish color, oblong shape).

Zucchini (hybrid): Aristocrat (AAS winner; waxy; medium green); Chefini (AAS winner; glossy, medium dark green); Classic (medium green; compact, open bush); Elite (medium green; lustrous sheen; extra early; open plant); Embassy (medium green, few spines, high yield); President (dark green, light green flecks; upright plant); and Spineless Beauty (medium dark green; spineless petioles).

Golden Zucchini (hybrid): Gold Rush (AAS winner, deep gold color, superior fruit quality, a zucchini not a straightneck).

Yellow Crookneck: Early Yellow Summer Crookneck (classic open-pollinated crookneck; curved neck; warted; heavy yields) and Sundance (hybrid; early; bright yellow, smooth skin).

Yellow Straightneck: Early Prolific Straightneck (standard open-pollinated straightneck, light cream

color, attractive straight fruit) and Goldbar (hybrid; golden yellow; upright, open plant).

Scallop: White Bush Scallop (old favorite Patty Pan type, very pale green when immature, very tender); Peter Pan (hybrid, AAS winner, light green); Scallopini (hybrid, AAS winner); and Sunburst (hybrid, bright yellow, green spot at the blossom end).

Other: Butter Blossom (an open-pollinated variety selected for its large, firm male blossoms; fruit may be harvested like summer squash, but remove female blossoms for largest supply of male blossoms); Gourmet Globe (hybrid; globe-shaped; dark green, with light stripes; delicious); and Sun Drops (hybrid, creamy yellow, unique oval shape, may be harvested as baby with blossom attached).

When to Plant

Plant anytime after the danger of frost has passed, from early spring until midsummer. (See the maps, page 26.) Some gardeners have two main plantings—one for early summer harvest and another for late summer and fall harvest.

Spacing of Plants and Depth of Planting

Sow two or three seeds 24 to 36 inches apart for single-plant production, or four or five seeds in hills 48 inches apart. Cover 1 inch deep. When the plants are 2 to 3 inches tall, thin to one vigorous plant or no more than two or three plants per hill.

Care

Any well-drained garden soil produces excellent yields of summer squash. Certain mulches (see page 36) increase earliness and yields because the roots are shallow.

Harvesting

Because they develop very rapidly after pollination, summer squash are often picked when they are too large and overmature. They should be harvested when small and tender for best quality. Most elongated varieties are picked when they are 2 inches or less in diameter and 6 to 8 inches long. Patty Pan types are harvested when they are 3 to 4 inches in diameter. Slightly larger fruit may be salvaged by hollowing out and using them for stuffing. These larger fruits may also be grated for baking in breads and other items. Do not allow summer squash to become large, hard, and seedy because they sap strength from the plant that could better be used to produce more young fruit. Pick oversized squash with developed seeds and hard skin, and throw them away. Go over the plants every 1 or 2 days. Squash grow rapidly, especially in hot weather, and are usually ready to pick within 4 to 8 days after flowering.

Although summer squash has both male and female flowers, only the female flowers produce fruits. Because the fruits are harvested when still immature, they bruise and scratch easily. Handle with care, and use immediately after picking. Be careful when picking summer squash, as the leafstalks and stems are prickly and can scratch and irritate unprotected hands and arms. Use a sharp knife or pruning shears to harvest, and wear gloves if possible. Some gardeners also pick the open male and female blossoms before the fruits develop. Especially the female blossoms, with tiny fruit attached, are a delicacy when dipped in a batter and fried.

Common Problems

Cucumber beetle (see page 40) and **squash vine borer** (page 40).

Questions and Answers

Q. Will summer squash cross with winter squash? *A. Summer squash varieties can cross with one another, with acorn squash, and with jack-o'-lantern pumpkins. (See table on pages 113 and 114). Cross-pollination is not evident in the current crop, but the seed should not be sown for the following year. Summer squash does not cross with melons or cucumbers.*

Squash, Winter

Winter squash *(Cucurbita pepo, C. maxima, C. moschata,* and *C. mixta),* is a warm-season vegetable that can be grown in most of the country. It differs from summer squash in that it is harvested and eaten in the mature fruit stage, when the seeds within have matured fully and the skin has hardened into a tough rind. When ripened to this stage, fruits of most varieties can be stored for use throughout the winter.

Winter squash may be steamed, baked, or made into pies; and it is frequently used in place of irish potatoes, sweet potatoes, or rice. Squash blossoms may be dipped in batter and fried in the same manner as pumpkin blossoms.

Varieties

The following varieties of squash are adapted to a wide variety of conditions. They are vining types unless otherwise indicated. Vining squash plants require considerable growing space and are best suited for large gardens. The bush and semi-vining types can be grown in smaller gardens. Occasionally, some of these varieties may be listed as pumpkins by certain seed companies. The distinction between squash and pumpkins is mainly in what you choose to call them. Here, open-pollinated varieties are identified as OP.

Acorn *(C. pepo):* 80 to 100 days to harvest: Cream of the Crop (hybrid–AAS winner; uniform white acorn type; creamy smooth, tasty flesh); Ebony (early; glossy dark green; flaky flesh texture); Swan White (OP–creamy white skin; pale yellow flesh; smooth, delicate, sweet flesh); Table Ace (hybrid–semi-bush; uniform, near black fruit; excellent, low-fiber flesh); Table Gold (OP–compact bush habit, attractive bright golden yellow, may also be harvested as summer squash when light yellow); Table King (OP–compact bush; dark green, color holds well); Table Queen (OP–standard dark green acorn type); and Tay-Belle (OP–semi-bush, dark green).

Delicata *(C. pepo):* Delicata (also known as sweet-potato squash; long cylindrical shape; cream color with dark green stripes); Honey Boat (shaped like Delicata, tan background with dark green stripes, very sweet flesh); Sugar Loaf (tan background, dark green stripes, elongated oval, very sweet); and Sweet Dumpling (flattened round, fluted; light cream to white background, with dark green stripes).

Spaghetti *(C. pepo):* Orangetti (hybrid–semi-bush plant, orange version of spaghetti, high in carotene); Pasta (yellowish cream fruit, improved flavor); Stripetti (hybrid of Spaghetti and Delicata, great taste, stores better); Tivoli (hybrid–bush habit; AAS winner; light yellow, uniform fruit, 3 to 4 pounds); and Vegetable Spaghetti (OP–good keeper; light yellow, oblong fruit).

Butternut *(C. moschata):* Butterbush (bush habit; early, 1- to 2-pound fruit); Early Butternut (hybrid–AAS winner, early, medium size, high yield); Ponca (extra early, small seed cavity, stores well); Puritan (OP–uniform, blocky, smooth, slightly smaller than Waltham); Supreme (hybrid–thick neck; early, uniform, sweet); Ultra (largest fruit 6 to 10 pounds; good leaf canopy); Waltham (OP–uniform, thick-necked, 10- to 12-inch fruits); and Zenith (hybrid; smooth, attractive fruit; high yield).

True Winter Squash *(C. maxima):* All Season (bush; orange skin, flesh; 8 or more small fruit per plant);

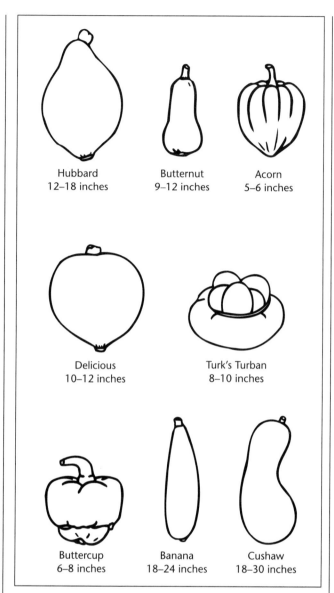

Hubbard
12–18 inches

Butternut
9–12 inches

Acorn
5–6 inches

Delicious
10–12 inches

Turk's Turban
8–10 inches

Buttercup
6–8 inches

Banana
18–24 inches

Cushaw
18–30 inches

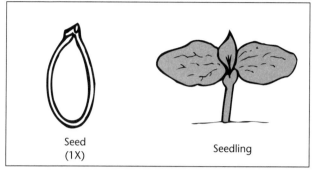

Seed
(1X)

Seedling

orange; teardrop-shaped; smooth-textured flesh; 3 to 5 pounds). For giant varieties, see "Pumpkin" (page 103).

When to Plant

Squash is a very tender vegetable. The seeds do not germinate in cold soil, and the seedlings are injured by frost. Do not plant until all danger of frost is past and soil is thoroughly warmed.

Spacing of Plants and Depth of Planting

The vining types of squash require at least 50 to 100 square feet per hill. Plant seeds 1 inch deep (four or five seeds per hill). Allow 5 to 6 feet between hills. When the young plants are well established, thin each hill to the best two or three plants. Allow 7 to 12 feet between rows.

Plant semi-vining varieties 1 inch deep (four or five seeds per hill), and thin to the best two plants per hill. Allow 8 feet between rows.

Plant bush varieties 1 inch deep (1 or 2 seeds per foot of row), and thin to a single plant every 3 feet. Allow 5 feet between rows.

Care

Squash plants should be kept free from weeds by hoeing and shallow cultivation. Irrigate (see page 37) if an extended dry period occurs in early summer. Squash requires minimal care after the vines cover the ground.

Bees, which are necessary for pollinating squash and pumpkins, are killed by insecticides. If insecticides are used, they should be applied in late afternoon or early evening after the bees stop visiting blossoms for the day.

Harvesting

Winter squash can be harvested whenever the fruits have turned a deep, solid color and the rind is hard. Harvest the main part of the crop in September or October, before heavy frosts hit your area. Cut squash from the vines carefully, leaving 2 inches of stem attached if possible. Avoid cuts and bruises when handling. Fruits

Banana (pink, blue, or gray; long, slim, pointed at the ends; 10 to 30 pounds); Buttercup (dark green fruit with distinct gray cap at blossom end; the standard for fine-grained, sweet flesh; 3 to 4 pounds); Delicious (5 to 12 pounds; large, top-shaped, green or gold fruit, smoother than Hubbard); Emerald Bush Buttercup (bush habit); Honey Delight (hybrid–3 to 4 pounds; buttonless buttercup type; excellent flesh quality); Gold Nugget (5-inch, flattened round; 1 to 2 pounds; orange skin, flesh; bush habit); Baby, Blue, Chicago, Golden, Green, and Warted Hubbard (large teardrop shape, pointed at ends; warted skin; 8 to 25 pounds); Mooregold (bright orange skin, flesh; excellent keeper with tough rind; buttercup type; 2 to 3 pounds); Sweet Mama (hybrid–AAS winner; semi-vining, buttercup type; uniform; tasty; 2 to 3 pounds); Sweet Meat (OP–old time favorite; flattened; slate gray skin; 10 to 15 pounds); and Red Kuri (OP–bright red-

that are not fully mature, have been injured, have had their stems knocked off, or have been subjected to heavy frost do not keep and should be used as soon as possible or be composted (watch for seedlings in the compost). Store in a dry building where the temperature is between 50° and 55°F (see pages 167 and 168). For prolonged storage, do not pile squash more than two fruits deep. It is preferable, where space allows, to place the fruits in a single layer so that they do not touch each other. This arrangement minimizes the potential spread of rots.

Common Problems

Cucumber beetles (see page 40) attack seedlings, vines, and both immature and mature fruits. They can be controlled with a suggested insecticide applied weekly either as a spray or dust. Be alert for an infestation of cucumber beetles in early September because these beetles can damage the mature fruits.

Squash bugs (see page 40) attack vines as the fruit begin to set and increase in number through the late summer, when they can be quite damaging to maturing fruit. They hatch and travel in groups, which seem to travel in herds until they reach maturity. Using the proper insecticide when the numbers of this pest are still small minimizes damage.

Questions and Answers

Q. Can squash varieties cross-pollinate with one another or with pumpkins in the garden? *A. Yes. Any variety of squash or pumpkin in the same species can cross-pollinate (see table on pages 113 and 114). Cross-pollination does not affect the current crop, but the seed does not come true the following year.*

Q. Does squash make as good a pie as pumpkin? *A. Yes. Most people cannot tell whether pumpkin or squash is used in a pie. This finding is not surprising given the whimsical application of the names pumpkin and squash. Many cooks prefer winter squash to pumpkin because they make a nonfibrous pie, much more akin to the* C. moschata *processing pumpkins commonly bought canned. (*C. moschata *is closely related to butternut squash.)*

Q. I have vine borers in my squash. Can I control them with insecticides? *A. No. Vine borers cannot be controlled effectively with insecticides. You can reduce potential damage the following season by disposing of infested plants. Vining types of squash can be encouraged to root at the nodes, giving the plant some ability to withstand attacks of vine borers. Some success in control of an active infestation may be achieved by carefully splitting open areas being fed upon and removing the larvae.*

Q. Is Turk's Turban an edible squash? *A. Yes, but it has relatively poor flesh quality and is more often grown for its ornamental value than for cooking. (See "Gourd," page 138, and the table on pages 113 and 114.)*

Sweet Potato

Sweet potato, *Ipomoea batatas,* is a tender, warm-weather vegetable that requires a long frost-free growing season to mature large, useful roots. It is one of the most important food crops in tropical and subtropical countries, where both the roots and tender shoots are eaten as a vital source of nutrients. Commercial production in the United States is mainly in the southern states, particularly North Carolina and Louisiana.

Sweet potatoes, which are related to morning glory, grow on trailing vines that quickly cover the soil, rooting at the nodes along the way. "Bush" varieties with shorter vines are available for situations where space may be limiting.

Though orange-fleshed varieties are most common today in commerce, white- or very light yellow-fleshed types were once considered the finest types for sophisticated people. Some white-fleshed types are still available, though they may be hard to find outside the Deep South.

For their ornamental value, sweet potatoes are often grown as ground cover or in hanging baskets, in planters, and even in bottles of water in the kitchen. Cut-leaf types exist that are particularly attractive. The sweet potato is rich in vitamin A. It is not related to the yam, though in the marketplace the two names are often used interchangeably. The true yam, *Dioscorea* sp., is an entirely separate species that grows only in the tropics.

Varieties

Beauregard (100 days to harvest, light purple skin, dark orange flesh, extremely high yielder from Louisiana State University); Bush Porto Rico (110 days, compact vines, copper skin, orange flesh, heavy yield); Centennial (100 days; orange skin, flesh; good keeper; resistant to internal cork, wilt); Georgia Jet (100 days, red skin, orange flesh, somewhat cold tolerant); Jewel (100 days, orange flesh, good yield, excellent keeper); Sumor (ivory to very light yellow flesh, may be substituted for irish potatoes in very warm regions); and Vardaman (110 days, golden skin, orange flesh, compact bush type, young foliage purple). Commercial production is currently dominated by Jewell in North Carolina and Beauregard in Louisiana.

When to Plant

Sweet potatoes are started from plants called "slips." Transplant the slips as soon as the soil warms up after the last frost to allow the maximal warm-weather growing period. Always buy plants grown from certified disease-free roots. To grow your own plants, place several sweet potato roots about 1 inch apart in a hotbed, and cover with 2 inches of sand or light soil. Add another 1 inch of sand when the shoots begin to appear. Keep the soil in the bed moist throughout the sprouting period, but never allow it to become waterlogged. Keep soil temperature between 70° and 80°F. Plants are ready to pull in about 6 weeks (when they are rooted and 6 to 8 inches tall). You can allow roots to continue possibly producing additional flushes of plants if more are desired. The sprouts (slips) are planted directly in the garden from the sprout bed.

Spacing of Plants

Set the plants 12 to 18 inches apart, preferably on a wide, raised ridge about 8 inches high. A ridge not only dries better in the spring but also warms earlier than an unridged area. Black plastic mulch can be a good way to speed early season growth by capturing and storing more of the sun's heat in the soil under the plastic cover. Because the vines of spreading varieties need a great deal of space, allow at least 3 to 4 feet between rows.

Care

After early cultivation (which is not necessary with black plastic), sweet potatoes need minimal care to keep down weeds. Once the vines spread to cover the ground, little weeding is required. Irrigate if an extended drought occurs. Do not water during the last 3 to 4 weeks before harvest to protect the developing roots.

Harvesting

Early roots may be "robbed," starting in late summer, by digging into the side of the ridge and carefully removing some developing roots while leaving the plant in place. Dig the main crop of sweet potatoes around the time of the first frost in the fall. Use a spading fork or stout shovel, and be careful not to bruise, cut, or other-

wise damage the roots. Dig below the level of the ridge, and gradually move closer toward the plants, removing soil until the fat roots are exposed. Carefully dig under these roots to gauge the depth to dig as you go down the row.

Proper curing can be a problem in the cool fall season. Ideally, the roots should be allowed to dry on the ground for 2 to 3 hours, then placed in a warm room for curing (85°F and 85 percent humidity if possible) for 10 to 14 days, and then stored in a cool (55°F) location (see pages 167 and 168). Sweet potatoes should be handled as little as possible to avoid scuffing and bruising. In case of frost, cut the vines from the roots immediately to prevent decay spreading from the vines to the roots; and dig sweet potatoes as soon as possible. Cold soil temperatures quickly lessen the roots' ability to keep in storage. Do not allow roots drying in the garden to be frosted because they are quickly ruined. For best quality, use the potatoes as soon as possible after they have been stored.

Common Problems

To prevent **diseases**, plant varieties with multiple resistance, use "certified" plants, and rotate sweet potatoes' location in the garden.

At certain sites, **mice** may become a problem by burrowing into the mound and eating the tasty, nutritious roots before harvest can commence. Check for evidence of mouse infestation regularly, and apply appropriate control measures as needed.

Questions and Answers

Q. My sweet potato roots are covered with black splotches in the skin. What can I do to prevent this condition? *A. This condition is probably caused by a disease known as "scurf" that is superficial in the skin of the root. The sweet potatoes are still good to eat, although they may not keep as well in storage. Check for varieties resistant to this problem.*

Q. Why did my sweet potato roots grow long and stringy instead of short and plump? *A. Too much rain, irrigation, or poorly drained soil prevents proper root formation. Sweet potatoes prefer hot, dry weather once the vines cover the ground.*

Q. What makes sweet potatoes crack and split? *A. Heavy rains or too much irrigation during the final 3 to 4 weeks before harvest may cause the roots to split, especially if conditions have been dry for a period before late water application begins.*

Q. Are sweet potatoes ruined if the vines were frosted before digging? *A. No, but they should be harvested immediately. The length of time that they can be stored may be reduced, and some experts say that taste and quality of the roots may be adversely affected.*

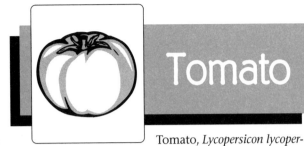

Tomato

Tomato, *Lycopersicon lycopersicum,* is today the most popular garden vegetable in America. For many years, however, tomatoes (then called "love apples") were considered poisonous and were grown solely for their ornamental value. Tomatoes are usually easy to grow, and a few plants provide an adequate harvest for most families. The quality of fruit picked in the garden when fully ripe far surpasses anything available on the market, even in season. The tomato plant is a tender, warm-season perennial that is grown as an annual in summer gardens all over the continental United States. Spring and fall freezes limit the outdoor growing season.

Varieties

Hundreds of varieties of tomatoes are now available for the home gardener. They range widely in size, shape, color, plant type, disease resistance, and season of maturity. Catalogs, garden centers, and greenhouses offer a large selection of tomato varieties; and choosing the best one or two varieties can be extremely difficult. Evaluate your needs, then choose the varieties best suited to your intended use and method of culture.

Tomato plants fall into one of two types, which affect ultimate plant height and cultural requirements. Tomatoes are "determinate" if they eventually form a flower cluster at the terminal growing point, causing the plant to stop growing in height. Plants that never set terminal flower clusters, but only lateral ones, continue indefinitely to grow taller and are called "indeterminate." Older varieties are almost all indeterminate. These can be counted upon to produce abundant foliage and to ripen flavorful fruit. They may, however be extremely late in maturing. The first determinate varieties developed had real problems with inadequate foliage cover and taste, but they ripened very early. Newer determinates produce better foliage, may grow taller, and ripen fruit of similar quality to modern indeterminate varieties. They still tend to ripen their fruit over a shorter period of time, so successive plantings may be desirable with determinates to keep the harvest coming through the entire season. Determinate vines are easier to control and support

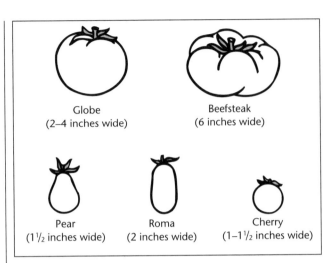

Globe
(2–4 inches wide)

Beefsteak
(6 inches wide)

Pear
(1½ inches wide)

Roma
(2 inches wide)

Cherry
(1–1½ inches wide)

during the growing season. Some of the extreme dwarf types are determinate as well as dwarf, producing some truly tiny mature plants.

Tomato varieties are listed in order of maturity in the table on pages 121 and 122. Most of the varieties listed here are widely adapted to a variety of conditions and produce good yields around the country.

FIRST-EARLY RED (60 or fewer days to harvest)

These varieties have more compact plant growth than the main-season varieties, and sunburning of the fruit is a problem in hot weather. The main-crop varieties are generally far superior for summer-long harvest. First-early varieties are better suited for northern areas, where the growing seasons are shorter and the summers cooler. They have small- to medium-sized red fruit and are usually not suitable for pruning.

MEDIUM-EARLY RED (60 to 69 days)

These varieties are intermediate between the extreme earliness of the first earlies and the sounder plant type and production characteristics of the main-crop types. Fruit size is improved, as is quality. The real tomato harvest season begins with the medium-early varieties.

MAIN-CROP

Most of these main-crop varieties bear medium-sized to large fruit, have adequate foliage cover, and are relatively free from fruit cracking and other deformities. They are suitable for growing on mulch, in wire cages, or on trellises. Many of them can be pruned and trained to stakes. As the name implies, they should make up the bulk of the main-crop harvest because they have superior yield, better staying power in the garden, and fruit of high quality.

Variety	Disease resistance	Days to harvest	Plant type	Weight	Comments
First-early red					
Sub Arctic Plenty		45	det.	3 to 4 oz	fruit concentrated in center clusters
Early Cascade	VF	55	ind.	4 oz	trailing plant, large fruit clusters
Early Girl	V	54	ind.	5 oz	earliest full size
Quick Pick	VFFNTA	60	ind.	4 oz	round, smoth, heavy yield
Medium-early red					
Champion	VFNT	65	ind.	10 oz	solid, smoth, large
Mountain Spring	VF	65	det.	9 oz	globe, very smooth
Main-crop red					
Celebrity	VFFNT	70	det.	10 oz	large, productive
Mountain Delight	VF	70	det.	10 oz	no green shoulders
Fantastic		70	ind.	9 oz	deep globe, high yield
Better Boy	VFN	72	ind.	12 oz	easy-to-find plants
Mountain Pride	VF	74	det.	10 oz	smooth, flat globe
Floramerica	VF	75	det.	12 oz	AAS winner, bright red
Burpee's Big Girl	VF	78	ind.	16 oz	crack-resistant, attractive fruit
Supersonic	VF	79	ind.	12 oz	solid, crack resistant
Extra-large red					
Delicious (OP)		77	ind.	over 1 lb	world record (7 lb 12 oz) with this variety
Supersteak	VFN	80	ind.	1 to 2 lb	extra meaty
Beefmaster	VFN	81	ind.	1 to 2 lb	large Beefsteak type
Yellow or orange					
Mountain Gold (OP)	VF	70	det.	8 oz	deep tangerine orange
Lemon Boy	VFN	72	ind.	7 oz	lemon yellow, mild flavor, productive
Jubilee (OP)		72	ind.	8 oz	deep orange-yellow
Golden Boy		80	ind.	8 oz	deep golden fruit, few seeds
Pink					
Pink Girl	VF	76	ind.	7 oz	smooth, crack resistant
Brandwine (OP)		80	ind.	12 oz	large, rough, heirloom; juicy, great taste
Other colors and types					
White Wonder (OP)		85	ind.	8 oz	creamy white flesh and skin
Evergreen (OP)		85	ind.	8 oz	green skin tinged with yellow; flesh bright green at maturity
Long Keeper (OP)		78	ind.	6 oz	orange skin, orange-red flesh; solid, keeps for weeks
Yellow Stuffer (OP)		80	ind.	4 oz	lobed, lemon yellow, shaped like pepper; semi-hollow, easy to stuff
Red paste types					
Veeroma (OP)	VF	72	det.	2 to 3 oz	early Roma type, deep square shape
Roma (OP)	VF	75	det.	2 oz	standard red plum, tolerant to early blight
San Marzano (OP)		80	det.	3 oz	deep red, crack resistant, meaty, and dry
Viva Italia	VFN	80	det.	3 oz	meaty, sweet; good fresh

Variety	Disease resistance	Days to harvest	Plant type	Weight	Comments
Small-fruited salad types					
Super Sweet 100	VF	70	ind.	1 in.	red, cherry-sized fruit in large clusters
Sweet Million	FNT	65	ind.	1 in.	red, sweet, crack resistant; large clusters
Yellow Pear (OP)		70	ind.	1 in.	clusters of yellow, pear-shaped fruit
Large Red Cherry (OP)		70	ind.	1½ in.	solid, deep red, tasty fruit
Mountain Belle	VF	65	det.	1¼ in.	red, crack resistant, ripens uniformly and holds on the vine
Dwarf container types					
Tiny Tim		45	det.	1 in.	very dwarf, red cherry fruit
Cherry Gold		45	det.	1 in.	golden version of Tiny Tim
Red Robin		55	det.	1 in.	super-dwarf plant, 6 inches tall; mild taste
Yellow Canary		55	det.	1 in.	similar to Red Robin, but yellow fruit
Pixie Hybrid II		52	det.	2 oz	compact dwarf plants
Patio Hybrid		65	det.	3 oz	strong dwarf plants, relatively large fruit, ideal container plant
Small Fry		72	det.	1 in.	red, good in hanging baskets
Husky Red Hybrid	VF	68	ind.	6 oz	dwarf plant, large fruit; extended harvest
Husky Gold Hybrid	VF	70	ind.	6 oz	AAS winner; same plant type as Red and Pink; gold fruit
Husky Pink Hybrid	VF	72	ind.	6 oz	smooth pink fruit on same husky-type plant

Abbreviations used for disease resistance:

A = Alternaria; F = Fusarium; FF = Fusarium Races 1 and 2; N = Root-knot nematodes; T = Tobacco mosaic virus; V = Verticillium

EXTRA-LARGE RED

These varieties are relatively late maturing. The fruits may be extremely large but also can be misshapen, with rough scar tissue ("cat-facing") on the blossom end. When this scar tissue must be cut away, some of the advantage of extra-large size is lost. Large size, though, is almost never about total yield, but more often about the novelty of huge size. Some of the newer hybrid large types like Supersteak and Beefmaster have fruit with much more consistent shape.

YELLOW OR ORANGE

Contrary to popular belief, yellow- and orange-fruited varieties are not significantly lower in acid content than red tomatoes, and they are equally safe to can or process. They "taste" sweeter than red varieties because they have a higher sugar content. Current varieties in this classification have much earlier maturity and better plant-growth characteristics than older yellows and oranges, which tended to be big, sprawling, and late maturing.

PINK

These varieties always have maintained a loyal following in certain regions of the country. Pinks traditionally have been similar to yellows with regard to plant type and maturity. Recent breeding work has developed disease-resistant plants with very attractive fruit. For the highest eating quality, some of the older types may still be at the top for flavor.

OTHER COLORS AND TYPES

Although odd colors and types have been around for a long time, they have experienced a resurgence of popularity, fueled in part by the upscale salad bar. As these outlets have competed to offer the newest and brightest assortment of produce, some almost-forgotten tomatoes have been "rediscovered."

Red Paste

Paste tomatoes are usually used for making catsup, paste, and sauces and for canning whole. Their solid, meaty, low-moisture flesh makes processing these products less complicated. Recently, some of them are becoming trendy and popular for eating fresh. These are usually short plant types that tend to set up a large load of fruit in a short time and then ripen a large proportion of this fruit at once. With tomatoes used fresh, it is usually seen as an advantage to have fruit ripening over an extended season on individual plants, but ripening most of the crop in a short period has been a bonus for paste tomatoes because processing activities are best done in fairly large lots.

Small-Fruited/Salad

These varieties are generally vigorous growing and productive. They vary in size from 1 to 1½ inches in diameter and are usually suitable for pruning. Production per plant is very high, to the point that picking may become tedious. Whole clusters may sometimes be picked at one time to speed the harvest. Splitting seems to be more of a problem with cherries, though newer hybrids have attempted to lessen the problem. These types are usually described as especially sweet and tasty.

Dwarf/Container

These tomatoes are popular for use in containers, hanging baskets, and garden or patio locations where space is limited. Because more people now live where traditional vegetable gardening is not possible, container and patio gardens have become more popular. Their ornamental value is an added benefit, and their fruit quality has recently been improved as well. They have fruit in red and some other colors and are not suitable for pruning (except the new Husky hybrids).

Greenhouse

Gardeners interested in growing greenhouse tomatoes should know that specific varieties have been developed for this environment. Some catalogs now routinely list these types, which should be used for the most satisfactory results. Consult catalogs for varieties available.

Heirloom

A particularly large number of heirloom tomato varieties are available today, mainly because tomatoes normally do not cross-pollinate. Seed saved from fruits of nonhybrid varieties produce plants fairly identical to the parent plant. Many of the odder colors and types that have resurfaced lately have their origins in these older, self-saved varieties. The plant type is usually large, sprawling, and late compared to current commercial varieties. Disease resistance may also be suspect. If, however,

the gardener wants to try a few truly weird or tasty types, these usually mature some fruits almost anywhere except in the shortest-season areas. Specialty seed houses and exchanges are a source of the widest variety of heirloom tomatoes imaginable.

The table on pages 121 and 122 gives currently recommended varieties in most of the listed classifications.

When to Plant

Buying transplants, or starting seeds indoors early, gets tomatoes off to the best start in the garden when warm weather finally arrives, and it saves several weeks in growing time. Some gardeners transplant their tomatoes soon after the soil is prepared for spring gardening, when there is a high risk of damage from freezing. (See page 26 for the average frost-free date for your area). Be prepared to cover early set plants overnight to protect them from frost. For best results with very early plantings, consider black plastic mulch and floating row covers for heat accumulation and frost protection. For best results with minimal risk, plant when the soil is warm, soon after the frost-free date for your area.

For fall harvest and early winter storage of tomatoes, late plantings may be made from late spring until midsummer, depending on the length of the growing season. These plantings have the advantage of increased vigor and freedom from early diseases, and they often produce better-quality tomatoes than later pickings from early spring plantings. Time late plantings for maximal yield before killing freezes in your area (up to 100 days from transplanting for most varieties).

Spacing of Plants

The space required depends upon the growth pattern of the variety and method of culture. Space dwarf plants 12 inches apart in the row, staked plants 15 to 24 inches apart, and trellised or ground bed plants 24 to 36 inches apart. Some particularly vigorous indeterminate varieties may need 4 feet between plants and 5 to 6 feet between rows to allow comfortable harvest room.

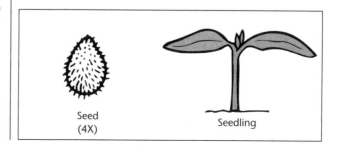

Seed
(4X)

Seedling

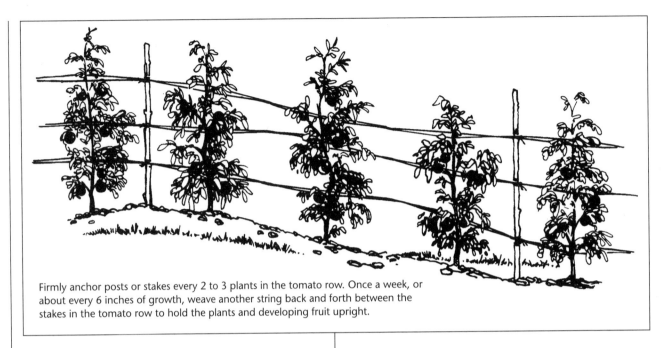

Firmly anchor posts or stakes every 2 to 3 plants in the tomato row. Once a week, or about every 6 inches of growth, weave another string back and forth between the stakes in the tomato row to hold the plants and developing fruit upright.

Care

Apply starter fertilizer when transplanting (see page 20). Hoe or cultivate shallowly to keep down weeds without damaging roots. Mulching is recommended, especially for gardeners who wish to maintain their plants for full-season harvest. Black plastic or organic materials are suitable for mulching (see page 35). Delay application of organic materials until after the soil has warmed completely in early summer so that growth is not retarded by cool soil temperatures early in the season.

Water the plants thoroughly and regularly during prolonged dry periods. Plants confined in containers may need daily or even more frequent watering. Side-dress nitrogen fertilizer (ammonium nitrate) at the rate of 1 pound per 100 feet of row (equivalent to 1 tablespoon per plant) after the first tomatoes have grown to the size of golf balls. (If ammonium nitrate is not available, use 3 pounds of 10-10-10 fertilizer.) Make two more applications 3 and 6 weeks later. If the weather is dry following these applications, water the plants thoroughly. Do not get fertilizer on the leaves.

Many gardeners train their tomato plants to stakes, trellises, or cages with great success. Not all varieties, however, are equally suitable for staking and pruning. The advantages and disadvantages of various cultural systems are shown in the table on page 125.

Tomato cages may be made from concrete-reinforcing wire, woven-wire stock fencing, or various wooden designs. Choose wire or wooden designs that have holes large enough to allow fruit to be picked and removed without bruising. The short, small, narrow type often sold at garden centers is all but useless for anything but the smallest of the dwarf types. Most modern determinate tomatoes easily grow 3 to 4 feet tall, and indeterminates continue to get taller until frozen in the fall, easily reaching at least 6 feet in height. Use cages that match in height the variety to be caged, and firmly anchor them to the ground with stakes or steel posts to keep the fruit-laden plants from uprooting themselves in late-summer windstorms.

Trellis-weave systems have recently been developed for commercial operations and can work just as well in a garden planting. Tall stakes are securely driven into the tomato row about every two or three plants in the row. Make sure the stakes are tall enough to accommodate the growth of your tomato varieties, and make sure they are driven very securely into the ground to prevent wind damage. (The woven rows of tomatoes can catch much wind.) As the tomatoes grow upward, strings are attached to the end posts and woven back and forth between the supports, holding the tops of the plants up and off the ground. This operation is repeated about as often as the tomatoes grow another 6 inches, until the plants reach maturity. The fruit is held off the ground as with staked or caged plants; but the foliage cover is better than with staked plants, and the fruit is more accessible than with cages. (See the illustration, page 125).

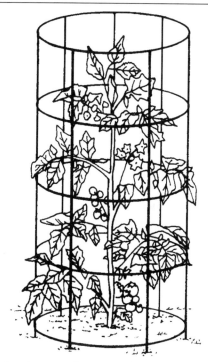

Wire cages placed over small tomato plants (left) hold the vines and fruit off the ground. Short cages (2½ to 3 feet tall) usually support themselves when the wire prongs at the bottom are pushed into the ground. Taller cages require a stake, post, or wire for support. Large (6-inch by 6-inch) mesh permits easy harvest. Tomato plants must be tied to supporting stakes or a trellis because (unlike cucumber plants) they do not support themselves with tendrils. Loop ordinary soft twine, cord, or cloth loosely around the main stem and tie tightly to the stake (right). Tying the stems too tightly injures them.

Cultural system	Variety	Pruning	Mulching	Advantages	Disadvantages
Plants allowed to sprawl on ground	All varieties are suitable.	not recommended	highly recommended	high yields (15–25 pounds per plant); least work; normal size and maturity	most space; sunburn, ground spots, and rots
Plants tied to stake or trellis	Use recommended vining types.	recommended: increases size and earliness; may use single-stem, double-stem, or multiple-stem pruning systems	highly recommended	intermediate yields (10–15 pounds per plant); least space; plants can be closer together; fruits are larger and easy to pick	more fruit cracking and blossom-end rot; lowest yield per plant; labor and time to tie and prune the plants
Plants grown inside wire cage	Most varieties are suitable.	not generally recommended; some gardeners prune early and allow plants to grow naturally later in the season	highly recommended	high yields (15–25 pounds per plant); intermediate space; best ripening in hot weather; normal size; no tying necessary	cost of cage; storage and handling of cage; latest to mature; difficult to pick inside foliage

Harvesting

Tomatoes should be firm and fully colored. They are of highest quality when they ripen on healthy vines and daily summer temperatures average about 75°F. When temperatures are high (air temperature of 90°F or more), the softening process is accelerated and color development is retarded, reducing quality. For this reason, during hot summer weather, pick your tomatoes every day or two, harvest the fruits when color has started to develop, and ripen them further indoors (at 70° to 75°F). On the day before a killing freeze is expected, harvest all green mature fruit that is desired for later use in the fall. Wrap the tomatoes individually in paper and store at 60° to 65°F. They continue to ripen slowly over the next several weeks. Whole plants may be uprooted and hung in sheltered locations, where fruit continues to ripen.

Tomato hornworm
(2–3 inches)

Common Problems

Tomato hornworms are large (2 to 3 inches long when fully grown), green caterpillars with white stripes on the body. A horn protrudes from the top rear end of the worm. Tomato hornworms feed on the leaves and fruit, and several worms on one plant can quickly defoliate it and ruin developing fruit. Because their green coloring so closely resembles tomato foliage and stems, they are difficult to see. Handpick in cooler parts of the day or use suggested biological insecticides. If you see hornworms with small, white cocoons protruding, leave them alone. These structures are the pupae of parasitic insects that help control the hornworm population, and the individual wearing them is already doomed.

Verticillium and fusarium wilts are soilborne diseases that cause yellowing of the leaves, wilting, and premature death of plants. These diseases persist in gardens where susceptible plants are grown. Once they build up, the only practical control is the use of resistant (VF) varieties.

Early blight is characterized by dead brown spots that usually start on the lower leaves and spread up the plant. Upon close inspection, you can see concentric rings within the spots. Although early blight is most severe on the leaves, it sometimes occurs on the stems and can cause severe defoliation. In some seasons, you may need to use fungicide sprays to achieve high yields and high-quality fruit. Certain varieties (Roma and Supersonic) are more tolerant of early blight than others.

Septoria leafspot is characterized by numerous small black spots on the leaves. The centers of these spots later turn white, and tiny black dots appear in the white centers. The disease starts on the bottom leaves and may become severe in wet weather. Use suggested fungicides for control.

Blossom-end rot is a dry, leathery brown rot of the blossom end of the fruit that is common in some seasons on tomatoes. It is caused by the combination of a localized calcium deficiency in the developing fruit and wide fluctuations of soil moisture. The problem is especially bad in hot weather. Soil applications of calcium seldom help, though foliar calcium sprays may minimize the occurrence of the problem. Make sure the formulation is designed for foliar application, or severe damage could result. Pruning causes stress to the plants that may increase the incidence of blossom-end rot. Some tomato varieties are much more susceptible to this condition than others. Mulching and uniform watering help to prevent blossom-end rot. Once the blackened ends appear, affected fruits cannot be saved. They are best removed and destroyed so that healthy fruit setting later can develop more quickly.

Poor color and sunscald occur when high temperatures retard the development of full red color in tomatoes exposed directly to the hot sun. Sunscald occurs as a large, whitish area on the fruit during hot, dry weather. It becomes a problem when foliage has been lost through other diseases such as early blight, or on early varieties that normally have poor foliage cover as the fruit ripens.

Questions and Answers

Q. What causes the lower leaves of my tomato plants to roll up? *A. Leaf roll (curling of the leaflets) is a physiological condition that occurs most commonly when plants are trained and pruned. It should not affect fruiting or quality.*

Q. What causes the flowers to drop off my tomato plants? *A. During unfavorable weather (night temperatures lower than 55°F, or day temperatures above 95°F with drying hot winds), tomatoes do not set and flowers drop. The problem usually disappears as the weather improves.*

Q. What can I do to prevent my tomatoes from cracking? *A. Cracking varies with the variety. Many of the newer varieties are resistant to cracking. Severe pruning increases cracking. Keep soil moisture uniform as the tomatoes develop, and plant resistant varieties to minimize this problem.*

Q. What causes small, irregular, cloudy white spots just under the skin of my tomatoes. *A. These spots on green or ripe fruits are caused by the feeding of stink bugs.*

Q. What causes the young leaves of my plants to become pointed and irregular in shape? I noticed some twisting of the leaves and stems after spraying the plants for the first time. *A. Judging from the description, it seem likely that your tomato plants have been injured by 2,4-D or a similar growth-regulator weed killer. Never use the same sprayer in your vegetable garden that you use for weed control in your lawn. Drift from herbicides originating 1/2 mile or more away also can injure your tomato plants. For this reason, use extreme caution when applying lawn-care chemicals near vegetable or fruit plantings.*

Q. What is a tree tomato? *A. The treelike plant sold as a "tree tomato," Cyphomandra betacea, is a different species from garden tomatoes. It is a woody tree that grows 8 feet or taller and bears after 2 years. The tree tomato is a tropical plant and does not overwinter outside anywhere the temperature drops below freezing. The fruits are small (1 to 2 inches in diameter) and are used primarily in stews or preserves rather than in salads. Some of the common, vigorous, indeterminate garden tomato varieties that are suitable for training and pruning (such as Ponderosa) are also sold as climbing or "tree tomatoes" by some seed stores.*

You may wish to prune staked or caged tomato plants to stimulate early maturity. Be sure that your variety is suitable for pruning (see list of varieties). To prune the plants properly, remove the shoots (suckers) when they are 1 to 2 inches long. The shoots develop in the axil of each leaf (the angle between the leaf petiole and the stem above it). Breaking off the shoots by hand is preferable to cutting them. Bend the shoots in opposite directions until they snap. Prune the plants every 5 to 7 days. Be careful not to prune the developing flower clusters that grow from the main stem or to pinch off the growing tip (terminal) of the plant. Remember—the more severely you prune the foliage (for example, a single stem rather than two or more stems), the more you limit plant growth, including root development. Double-stem or multiple-stem pruning systems sacrifice some of the earliness and fruit size for less risk of cracking, blossom-end rot, and sunburn.

Q. What is a "potomato?" *A. Although both potato and tomato plants can be intergrafted, the "potomato" (sometimes called "topato") commonly advertised is simply a tomato seed inserted into a potato tuber and planted together, producing both a tomato plant and a potato plant in the same hill. The results are not likely to be particularly successful.*

Q. My grandpa grew a heart-shaped, dark pink tomato that was thick and meaty, yet juicy with great flavor. Grandpa's gone, and I can't find a source for the seed. What can I do? *A. Fortunately, there are a number of seed exchanges like Seed Savers Exchange, RR #3, Box 239, Decorah, IA 52101, which have been finding and rescuing old varieties. More old and heirloom varieties are also available from conventional seed sources these days. Perhaps, by doing some homework and contacting one or several of these sources, you can find a variety that is exactly (or very nearly) like those you remember from your grandfather's garden. As a guess, the variety sounds like one called Oxheart, which used to be fairly commonly offered and has recently become rare.*

Turnip-Rutabaga

Rutabaga, *Brassica napus* var. *napobrassica* (also known as swede or swede turnip), and turnip, *Brassica rapa* var. *rapifera,* are frost-hardy, cool-season vegetables that are often used as substitutes for potatoes in the diet. In fact, these roots, along with parsnips, were staples in parts of Europe before the introduction of the white potato from the Western Hemisphere in the late 15th century.

Turnips are easy to grow if sown in the proper season. They mature in 2 months and may be planted either in the spring, late summer, or fall for roots or greens. The spring crop is planted for early summer use. The fall crop, which is usually larger and of higher quality, is often stored for winter use.

Because rutabagas require 4 weeks longer to mature than turnips, they are best grown as a fall crop. The leaves are smoother; and the roots are rounder, larger, and firmer than those of turnips. Rutabaga is most commonly grown in the northern tier of states and Canada but should perform fairly well anywhere there is a fairly long cool period in the autumn or early winter.

Varieties

Turnip (white-fleshed unless noted): Just Right (hybrid–28 days to harvest for greens and 60 days for roots; smooth, high-quality, mild roots, pure white; for fall); Gilfeather (75 days; Vermont heirloom; egg-shaped, uniform, large; creamy white, smooth texture, delicate flavor, smooth foliage, almost like a rutabaga); Golden Ball (60 days, sweet, fine-grained yellow flesh); Market Express (earliest, 38 days for baby turnips, pure white roots); Purple Top White Globe (55 days, the standard purple and white; smooth, globe roots); Royal Crown (hybrid–52 days, purple top, fast growth, uniform roots, resistant to bolting); Scarlet Ball (red skin, white flesh; cooked or pickled in the skin, the flesh turns red as well); Scarlet Queen (hybrid–45 days, bright scarlet root, smooth white flesh, resistant to downy mildew, slow to get pithy); Tokyo Cross (hybrid-35 days; AAS winner; all-white, uniform, round roots; slow to get pithy); White Knight (75 days, smooth, uniform, pure white, flattened-globe roots); and White Lady (hybrid–pure white, sweet, tender, delicious roots, slow to get pithy; smooth tops).

Turnip Greens: Alltop (hybrid–35 days, vigorous, high-yielding, rapid regrowth, resistant to mosaic); Seven Top (open-pollinated–40 days; dark green leaves; for tops only); Shogoin (42 days; tender, mild; roots good when young); and Topper (hybrid–35 days; heavy yields, vigorous regrowth; good bolt resistance; resistant to mosaic; pale green roots also edible).

Rutabaga (yellow-fleshed): Altasweet (92 days; purple shoulders, light yellow below; mild, sweet flavor); American Purple Top (90 days, large globe-shaped roots with purple top and light yellow flesh); Improved Long Island (90 days; large, spherical; purplish red shoulders, light yellow below; small taproot); Laurentian (90 days; dark purple shoulders, pale yellow below; smooth, uniform roots, small necks); Pike (100 days; purple shoulders; similar to Laurentian, better leaf cover, may be left in field later in fall); and Red Chief (90 days).

When to Plant

For summer use, turnips should be planted as early in the spring as possible. (See the maps, page 26.) For fall harvest, plant rutabagas about 100 days before the first frost, and plant turnips about 3 to 4 weeks later.

Fall turnips may also be broadcast after early potatoes, cabbage, beets, and peas, or between rows of sweet corn. Prepare a good seedbed, and rake the seed in lightly. No cultivation is necessary, but you may find that a few large weeds must be removed by hand. Provide ample water for seed germination and vigorous plant growth. Both turnips and rutabagas have been used for excellent fall and early winter stock feed when broadcast onto fields left vacant by earlier crop harvest.

Spacing of Plants and Depth of Planting

Plant seeds ½ inch deep (3 to 20 seeds per foot of row). Allow 12 to 24 inches between rows. Water if necessary to germinate the seed and establish the seedlings (especially for summer sowings). Thin rutabaga seedlings to 6 inches apart when they are 2 inches tall.

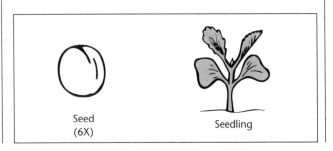

Seed
(6X)

Seedling

Thin turnip seedlings to 2 to 4 inches apart when they are 4 inches tall. The removed plants are large enough to use as greens. If you have planted turnips for greens, harvest the tops as needed when they are 4 to 6 inches tall. If the growing points are not removed, tops continue to regrow. Successive plantings at 10-day intervals provide later harvests of quality roots or greens. Old turnips tend to be tough and woody. Rutabagas are not usually sown in succession due to their longer time requirement before harvest. In mild areas, large rutabagas may hold in the garden well into the winter.

Care

When the plants are small, cultivate 2 to 3 inches deep between rows. As the plants become larger, cultivate more shallowly to prevent injury to the tender feeder roots. Pull weeds that appear in the row before they become too large.

Harvesting

Spring turnips should be pulled or cut when the roots or tops reach usable size. Harvest fall roots starting in early autumn or as needed. Turnips and rutabagas are of best quality (mild and tender) when they are of medium size (turnips should be 2 to 3 inches in diameter and rutabagas 3 to 5 inches in diameter) and have grown quickly and without interruption. Both are hardy to fall frosts and may, in fact, be sweetened by cool weather. A heavy straw mulch extends harvest through the early part of the winter. Turnips and rutabagas keep well in refrigeration, in an outdoor pit, or in an underground cellar (see pages 167 and 168). They may be dipped in warm (but not hot) wax to prevent loss of moisture.

Common Problems

Root maggots (see page 40) can be a problem in areas where radishes, turnips, or rutabagas were grown the previous year. The soil should be treated with a suggested insecticide before the next planting.

Question and Answer

Q. Why are my rutabagas small, tough, and bitter tasting? *A. Rutabagas are best grown in northern areas or as a fall crop. When they develop and mature in hot weather, they do not develop typical sweetness and flavor. In southerly locations, try adjusting the planting season so that root development takes place in the cooler days of fall, whenever that may be in your area.*

Watermelon, *Citrullus lanatus,* is a tender, warm-season vegetable. Watermelons can be grown in all parts of the country, but the warmer temperatures and longer growing season of southern areas especially favor this vegetable. Gardeners in northern areas should choose early varieties and use transplants. Mulching with black plastic film (see page 36) also promotes earliness by warming the soil beneath the plastic. Floating row covers (see page 32) moderate temperature around the young plants, providing some frost protection in unseasonable cold spells.

Seedless watermelons are self-sterile hybrids that develop normal-looking fruits but no fully developed seeds. The seeds for growing them are produced by crossing a normal diploid watermelon with one that has been changed genetically into the tetraploid state. The seeds from this cross produce plants that, when pollinated by normal plants, produce seedless melons.

In seedless watermelons (genetic triploids), rudimentary seed structures form but remain small, soft, white, tasteless, and undeveloped tiny seedcoats that are eaten virtually undetected along with the flesh of the melon. Seed production for these seedless types is an extremely labor-intensive process, which makes the seeds relatively expensive. Because germination of these types is often less vigorous than normal types, it is recommended that they be started in peat pots or other transplantable containers, where the germinating conditions can be closely controlled. Once transplanted, cultivation is similar to that for regular watermelons.

For pollination necessary to set fruit, normal seeded types must be interplanted with seedless melons. The pollinator should be distinct from the seedless cultivar in color, shape, or type so that the seedless and seeded melons in the patch can be separated at harvest. Because seedless types do not put energy into seed production, the flesh is often sweeter than normal types, and the vines are noticeably more vigorous as the season progresses.

Varieties

Early (70 to 75 days to harvest): Golden Crown (red flesh, green skin; skin turns yellow when ripe); Sugar Baby (red flesh, 6 to 10 pounds); Yellow Baby (hybrid–yellow flesh, 6 to 10 pounds); and Yellow Doll (hybrid–yellow flesh, 6 to 10 pounds).

Main-Season (80 to 85 days): Charleston Gray (red, 20 to 25 pounds); Crimson Sweet (red, 20 to 25 pounds); Madera (hybrid–red, 14 to 22 pounds); Parker (hybrid–red, 22 to 25 pounds); Sangria (hybrid–red, 22 to 26 pounds); Sunny's Pride (hybrid–red, 20 to 22 pounds); and Sweet Favorite (hybrid–red, 20 pounds).

Seedless (all are triploid hybrids, 80 to 85 days): Cotton Candy (red, 15 to 20 pounds); Crimson Trio (red, 14 to 16 pounds); Honey Heart (yellow flesh, 8 to 10 pounds); Jack of Hearts (red, 11 to 13 pounds); King of Hearts (red, 14 to 18 pounds); Nova (red, 15 to 17 pounds); Queen of Hearts (red, 12 to 16 pounds); and Tiffany (red, 14 to 22 pounds).

When to Plant

Plant after the soil is warm, and when all danger of frost is past. Watermelons grow best on a sandy loam soil, although yields on clay soils can be increased significantly by mulching raised planting rows with black plastic film.

Spacing of Plants and Depth of Planting

Watermelon vines require considerable space. Plant seeds 1 inch deep in hills spaced 6 feet apart. Allow 7 to 10 feet between rows. After the seedlings are established, thin to the best three plants per hill. Plant single transplants 2 to 3 feet apart or double transplants 4 to 5 feet apart in the rows.

Start the seeds inside 3 weeks before they are to be set out in the garden (see "Starting Plants at Home," pages 45 to 48). Plant 2 or 3 seeds in peat pellets, peat pots, or cell packs, and thin to the best one or two plants. For expensive seedless types, plant one seed to a pot or cell, and discard those that do not germinate. Do not start too early—large watermelon seedlings transplant poorly.

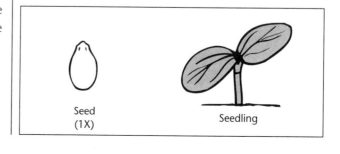

Seed
(1X)

Seedling

Growing transplants inside requires a warm temperature, ideally between 80° and 85°F. Place black plastic film (see page 36) over the row before planting. Use a starter fertilizer (see page 20) when transplanting. If you grow seedless melons, you must plant a standard seeded variety alongside. The seedless melon varieties do not have the fertile pollen necessary to pollinate and set the fruit.

Care

Watermelons should be kept free from weeds by shallow hoeing and cultivation. The plants have moderately deep roots, and watering is seldom necessary unless the weather turns dry for a prolonged period. In cooler areas, experienced gardeners may find floating row covers, drip irrigation, and black plastic mulch advantageous in producing a good crop in a short season.

Harvesting

Many home gardeners experience difficulty in determining when watermelons are ripe. Use a combination of the following indicators: (1) light green, curly tendrils on the stem near the point of attachment of the melon usually turn brown and dry; (2) the surface color of the fruit turns dull; (3) the skin becomes resistant to penetration by the thumbnail and is rough to the touch; and (4) the bottom of the melon (where it lies on the soil) turns from light green to a yellowish color. These indicators for choosing a ripe watermelon are much more reliable than "thumping" the melon with a knuckle. Many watermelons do not emit the proverbial "dull thud" when ripe. For these, the dull thud may indicate an over-ripe, mushy melon.

Common Problems

Cucumber beetles (see page 40) attack watermelon plants. Apply a suggested insecticide for control. If row covers are used in the early season for temperature moderation, early-season insect pests may also be excluded if the covers are applied so that the pests cannot penetrate to the crop below. These covers may be left in place until the plants start to bloom, at which time pollinating insects must be allowed to reach the flowers.

Questions and Answers

Q. My watermelons are not very sweet or flavorful. Is the low sugar content caused by the watermelons' crossing with other vine crops in the garden? *A. No. Although watermelon varieties cross with one another, cross-pollination is not apparent unless seeds are saved and planted the following year. Watermelons do not cross with muskmelons, squash, pumpkins, or cucumbers. The poor quality of your melons may result from wilting vines, high rainfall, cool weather, or a short growing season in extreme northern areas.*

Q. What can I do to prevent my watermelons from developing poorly and rotting on the ends? *A. This condition is probably caused by an extended period of extremely dry weather when the melons were maturing. It may be aggravated by continued deep hoeing or close cultivation. Mulching the plants with black plastic film helps to reduce this problem.*

Q. What causes deep holes in the tops of my watermelons? *A. The holes were probably made by pheasants or other wildlife searching for water during dry weather.*

Minor Vegetables

Minor Vegetables

Amaranth Greens

Amaranth greens, *Amaranthus tricolor* and other *Amaranthus* species, are also know as tampala, chinese spinach, hon-toi-moi, or pigweed. Leaf shapes are varied, with red, green, purplish, and variegated color patterns. Tampala is a broad-leaf variety, which is most often available in the United States.

Seeds should be sowed about ½ inch deep, in rows 18 to 24 inches apart. Soil temperature should be at least 55°F, and the planting planned so that the seeds do not germinate until after the average last-frost date, as the seedlings are frost tender. Thin seedlings to stand 3 to 6 inches apart. Thinned plants may be eaten, composted, or discarded. Greens are usually cooked like spinach; and the taste is similar, with an added zesty tang. Harvested at the proper stage (about 7 weeks after sowing) these greens have more iron and calcium than kale, chard, spinach, or collards.

The shoot tips and young leaves are ready for harvest about 3 weeks after sowing. Plants should branch and regrow after harvest. Eventually, they will attempt to flower, at which time a new planting may be made. Amaranth should grow and produce well through the warm season. Frost marks the end of harvest for the year.

Arugula

Arugula, *Eruca vesicaria* var. *sativa,* is also know as roquette, rocket salad, and white pepper. Roquette was the preferred common name until recently, when this plant has enjoyed a surge in popularity, and arugula has now become the name of choice in the trendy greens trade. Arugula is commonly used in mixed salads or as a cooked green. The taste is probably too strong to be eaten alone, though it can add considerable zest and interest to salad mixes.

Arugula is a cool-season plant in the Cruciferae (cabbage) family, closely related to the mustards. Under favorable growing conditions, it quickly forms a low rosette of succulent, dull green, deeply cut,

compound leaves with a biting, pungent, spicy flavor reminiscent of peppercress or horseradish. Leaves should be harvested in the young-tender stage, as a bitter flavor develops in older leaves, especially as flowers develop. Arugula quickly bolts to seed when exposed to hot temperatures.

Plant seeds in the garden about the same time as radishes or spinach, in either early spring or fall. Sow seeds ½ to 1 inch deep in rows 12 to 18 inches apart. Thin plants to stand about 4 inches apart. Thinned plants may be added to salads or mixed greens as they are removed from the row. Starting about 6 weeks after sowing, individual young, tender leaves may be harvested from the remaining plants, as they enlarge, until the plant bolts to seed. Remove flowering plants to avoid self-seeding problems.

Successive plantings may be made every 7 to 10 days through the early spring season, so long as the plants have enough cool days to mature the crop before summer's heat. Each planting remains in peak eating condition for only a short time. Resume plantings in late summer for fall harvest.

Few pests normally bother this plant, though it is probably wise to be on the lookout for common pests of the cabbage family.

Bean

Adzuki bean, *Vigna angularis,* has been cultivated for hundreds of years in the Far East. Because the beans are high in protein, low in sugar, and easy to digest and have a slightly sweet flavor, they are often used in desserts. Many of the adzuki beans imported into the United States are used for sprouting (see "Sprouting Seeds," page 169). Some gardeners harvest the immature pods, saute or boil them briefly, and eat adzukis as a fresh vegetable.

Plant seed in the spring after frost danger is past. Successive plantings may be made to extend the season. Rich, loamy soil is best, with seeds planted about 1 inch deep in rows 24 to 36 inches apart, with plants thinned to 3 inches apart. The beans mature in late summer or early fall. Pull and dry the plants once they are fully mature, and the seeds then are removed easily by shelling.

Fava bean, *Vicia faba* (horse bean, broad bean, or windsor bean), pods are edible when young and may be cooked as snow peas. They have never been popular in the United States, as they require cool summers. Young fresh beans may be shelled from pods and eaten like green peas; or mature dry pods may be shelled, and the favas prepared like dry beans for use in casseroles.

Fava beans are a cool-season vegetable, hardier than green beans, and should be planted earlier in the season, more like garden peas. They grow to 40 to 50 inches in height, depending on the variety. Plant in 30-inch rows, with seeds 5 to 6 inches apart and 2 inches deep. Favas also make a good cool-season cover crop for green-manure soil building. Care should be taken when eating favas for the first time because a few people carry a genetic allergy to them. Favas are popular in Italy, Portugal, and Spain. Some sources offer them simply as fava beans, but varietal names used may include Long Pod, Windsor, or Broad Windsor Long Pod.

Garbanzo bean, *Cicer arietinum* (also known as chickpea, chestnut bean, and egyptian pea), is a tender annual that is neither a pea nor a bean. It is grown for its chestnut-flavored seeds, which are dried or roasted for soups and salads. Garbanzo beans are a long-season crop (about 100 days to harvest) and are not a common garden vegetable in the United States. They are listed as garbanzo or chickpea in garden catalogs. Commonly, no variety name is listed.

Garbanzo beans grow in any well-drained garden soil. Because they do not require high fertility, side-dress fertilizer applications are not necessary. After the soil warms, plant seeds 1 inch deep in rows 24 to 36 inches apart. Thin seedlings to 3 inches apart. The bushy plants grow about 2 feet tall. White flowers are followed by short, rounded green pods, which turn brown when ripe. Pick fully mature pods as they turn brown, shell as dried beans, and store in airtight jars or cans.

Hyacinth bean, *Dolichos lablab*, is also called lablab, chinese flowering, pharaoh, wild field, and indian bean. Although the ripe seeds and green pods are widely used for food in southern Asia and Africa, in the United States the plant is more often cultivated as an ornamental vine. Its appearance is somewhere between a southern pea and a pole bean. The trifoliate leaflets are broad, oval, and pointed. With support, the vines may grow 15 to 20 feet tall where the frost-free season is long enough.

The most spectacular feature of the hyacinth bean is the 4- to 6-inch clusters of sweet-scented flowers in shades of pink, purple, or white. Fruits resemble lima bean pods and may be either glossy green or reddish purple. The pods contain three to six seeds, which may be red, brown, or white. There is a distinctive, long white seed scar along most of one side of each seed.

Immature seed pods may be harvested and cooked like snap beans or asparagus beans. Both mature shellout beans and dried seeds also can be cooked and eaten.

Culture is much like pole beans, with seeds planted 1 to 2 inches deep after all danger of frost is past and the soil has warmed thoroughly. In areas of short growing seasons, plants may be started early indoors or in a greenhouse and transplanted outside after warm weather arrives. The stems are twining and will climb strings, wires, poles, or most other common supports. Culture without supports is not advised. This is a gorgeous plant to be grown where the vegetable and flower gardens meet, or where all plants are freely interplanted.

Mung bean, *Vigna radiata* (chinese bean), is popular with gardeners interested in oriental vegetables. An ancient crop of India, mung beans may be eaten as a vegetable when the pods are green, or as a dry bean when they mature. There are two types, one with green seed coats and one with yellow. Selections are available that are adaptable to long or short day length. In the United States, where mung beans are mostly used for sprouting, seeds may be ordered from a very limited number of seed houses and catalogs and very rarely are found on garden-center seed racks. If no other source can be found, seeds may be purchased in gourmet food stores and planted in your garden.

Berken and Oklahoma-12 are two commercial varieties, sometimes available, that are suitable to many U.S. locations. They are listed simply as "mung bean" in most seed catalogs.

Plant mung beans 1 inch deep and 1 inch apart. Allow 24 to 30 inches between rows. Keep free of weeds by shallow hoeing and cultivation. The beans start forming when the plants are 15 to 18 inches tall and begin to flower.

Mung beans are ready to harvest as dry beans in about 100 days. Harvest by pulling up the entire plant. Tie the plants in bunches and hang them overhead, or dry them on clean papers on the floor of a shed or garage that is well-ventilated. The beans can be easily shelled or flailed from the pods when they are completely dry. They can be stored for sprouting or for planting the following year. See "Sprouting Seeds," page 169, and gourmet and specialty vegetable references for more information about sprouting and using mung beans or sprouts.

Edible soybean, *Glycine max* (also called soya bean), can be successfully grown as a shellout or dry bean in most parts of the country. A food naturally high in protein, it is prepared as a fresh vegetable. Cooking makes the vegetable protein in soybeans more easily digestible and palatable.

Varieties available include Black Jet, Butterbeans, Envy, Fiskeby V, Maple Arrow, and Prize. These garden varieties of soybeans are usually larger-seeded, shorter plants than the field varieties. They also mature earlier and are easier to shell. Field soybeans, harvested when immature, also may be used as edible soybeans; but their flavor may be more bitter.

Edible soybeans are planted and grown much like snap beans. Plant seeds 1 inch deep (8 to 10 seeds per foot) after the danger of frost has passed and the soil has warmed. (See the maps, page 26.) Allow 24 to 30 inches between rows.

Edible soybeans reach the green-shell stage of maturity in about 70 to 90 days. Dry beans can be harvested in 95 to 110 days. Green-shell beans are ready to harvest when the seeds are fully enlarged, but before the pods become brown and the seeds harden. At this time, the pods are plump, green, rough, and hairy. Because nearly all the beans are the same size and maturity, you can pull the entire plant and pick off the beans in the shade.

As they come from the garden, soybeans are difficult to shell, but boiling them for 1 to 3 minutes or steaming them in a covered pan for 5 minutes makes shelling a comparatively easy task. The beans may be frozen if you are not ready to use them. To harvest dry soybeans for sprouting, tofu, seed, or other uses, wait until the leaves have turned yellow and fallen. At this time, the pods are brown. When completely dry, they may be easily shelled or flailed in the same manner as mung beans. Most edible soybeans have some tendency to shatter (burst from the pods) once the pods dry; you may want to begin harvest before the beans are completely dry to avoid having too many of them spontaneously popping out of their pods in the garden. Harvest carefully, too, to avoid losing beans because the pods may burst when touched. If this is a problem, harvesting early in the day while dew still moistens the pods may help.

Winged bean, *Psophocarpus tetragonolobus* (goa bean or four-angled bean), has been cultivated for centuries in parts of Asia but in recent years has drawn much attention in the United States for its high protein content and the edible nature of the entire plant at various stages. Immature pods, mature seeds, tender shoots, flowers, and leaves all can be eaten.

After frost danger is past, seeds are planted 2 to 3 feet apart, in rows 4 feet apart. Flowering occurs under short days. Plants should be grown on wires to facilitate the harvesting of tips, leaves, and the young beans.

Yard-long bean, *Vigna unguiculata* subspecies *sesquipedalis* (asparagus bean); see "Southern Pea," page 143.

Burdock

Burdock, *Arctium lappa* (also called gobu in Japanese or ngau pong in Chinese), has enlarged storage roots valued both for food and as a tonic to purify the blood and relieve arthritis. Burdock is a hardy biennial plant that is grown as an annual because the large storage root forms the first year, quickly toughens, and becomes inedible in the second, flowering, season.

There are two closely related species, *A. lappa* and *A. minus*. The one most commonly found growing wild around the United States is *A. minus*. *A. lappa,* however, is the choice one for eating; if you had a bad experience digging burdock out of the raspberry patch to eat, then maybe you have not tried the true gobu.

In the garden, sow seeds of burdock in the spring when the soil has warmed to at least 50°F. Fall sowings are possible, but fall-planted seedlings may flower in the spring without making a root big enough to use. Seeds prefer light to germinate, so press them into the soil at a spacing of 4 to 8 inches. Soaking or scarifying (somehow piercing or breaking the seed coat) may speed germination. Seeds also may be started in flats indoors, but they should be transplanted before the taproot becomes distorted within the container. Thin or space transplants to stand 1 to 2 feet apart. Almost any soil where weedy burdock grows can produce cultivated gobu. Added compost or fertilizer helps make more spectacular results. Some plants of burdock actually grow roots the size of baseball bats if left to grow through one whole season.

Space can be a problem. The leaves of a thriving burdock plant may spread 2 to 3 feet in all directions. Allow enough space so a neighboring crop is not smothered. If allowed to go to seed the second year, the plants may grow seedstalks up to 8 feet tall.

Because mature roots often may be 2 feet or more in length, digging the crop can be a challenge, especially in stony or heavy soil. Care should be taken to dig the bed deeply before planting the seeds, so that the young roots will not be deformed by encountering impediments in the soil. Small root pieces that break off in the soil may form new plants and become moderately weedy, so dig carefully alongside the plants, and pull cautiously to minimize breakage. Harvest can begin about 10 weeks after seed sowing in most years. Roots allowed to grow too large develop a tough outer bark that requires peeling of the roots.

To prepare tender, young roots for eating, scrape the outer layer from them, down to the white fiber beneath. Slice or julienne the roots, and soak in cool water or place directly in the cooking utensil. Changing the water two to three times improves the color and flavor. Cook until tender, though cooked gobu remains more crunchy than a cooked carrot and is slightly stringy. It can be used as an ingredient in oriental stir-fry dishes or combined with carrots as a vegetable side dish. The roots also add a pleasantly aromatic flavor to soups and stews.

Celeriac

Celeriac, *Apium graveolens* var. *rapaceum* (also known as celery root, knob celery, turnip-rooted celery, and german celery), is a novel form of celery. It is grown for the swollen root that develops at the ground line. The attractive dark green stems and leaves are generally free from pests. Celeriac, popular with many European cultures, is grated or sliced in salads and cooked in soups and stews.

Celeriac requires a minimum growing period of 120 days and can be grown successfully throughout most of the United States. Alabaster, Giant Prague, and Large Smooth Prague are the varieties most frequently found in the United States; but new introductions now include Alba, Brilliant, Diamant, Dolvi, Jose, and Monarch. The seed should be planted in the early spring in cell packs, either in a cold frame or greenhouse. Plant two or three of the fine seeds ¼ inch deep in each cell of the seed flat. Thin to a single plant per cell after the plants have at least two true leaves. When the plants are 2 to 2½ inches tall, they can be transplanted into the garden. Space the plants 6 inches apart in rows 18 to 24 inches wide. Though the plants later become very robust, the seedlings are rather delicate, so use caution when handling the transplants. Use a starter fertilizer solution (see page 20) to get the plants established. Because celeriac, like celery, appreciates moist soil and interruptions of growth seriously decrease the size of the roots, the plants should be watered uniformly, especially during periods of drought.

Celeriac does not attain its full sweetness and flavor until after the first frost in the fall. In southern locations, celeriac may be left in the garden to be harvested as needed. Above 40 degrees north latitude, the roots should be harvested before freezing weather and stored in some sort of protected cold storage. Some gardeners mulch the plants with straw or leaves to protect the roots, permitting harvesting at any time during the winter months. The yield should exceed 1 pound of usable root per foot of row. Celeriac can be blanched by slightly hilling the plants to cover the roots as they develop. Although the exterior is brown in color, the flesh remains a bright white.

Chicory

Chicory, *Cichorium intybus*, is a hardy vegetable that is used in three basic forms. The roots are dried, roasted, and prepared as a coffee substitute or in coffee blends. The slightly bitter, curled, dandelionlike greens (sometimes called italian dandelion) are grown and used as potherbs. Witloof chicory (also called french or belgian endive) is forced as a blanched, tender, fresh-salad delicacy. It is sold at high prices in some produce markets.

The following varieties are listed according to intended use. **Greens:** Catalongna (asparagus type); Radichetta; San Pasquale; and Sugarhat (cut-leaf). **Chicory Root:** Brunswick, Madgeburg, and Zealand. **Forcing:** Flash; Mitado; Monitor Hybrid; Robin (pink color when forced; unique); Turbo Hybrid; Witloof; and Zoom hybrid.

Plant seeds ½ inch deep (12 to 15 seeds per foot of row). Allow 18 to 24 inches between rows. When the seedlings are 2 to 3 inches tall, thin to 9 to 12 inches apart for chicory roots and greens, and 3 to 4 inches apart for witloof. Plant in May for greens and roots, and about 120 days before frost for production of roots for forcing.

Greens. Young, tender leaves 6 to 8 inches long can be harvested for greens in 60 to 70 days. Chicory also may be blanched by tying the outermost leaves in the same manner as endive and escarole (see page 79).

Chicory root. Chicory root is grown as a long-season annual. Most commercial production is in Michigan, but chicory root is easily grown under a variety of climatic conditions. Dig roots in the late fall before they are frozen into the ground. At that time, the crown is 5 to 7 inches in diameter, tapering into a taproot. The usable root is 9 to 10 inches long. The roots are scrubbed to remove garden soil, cubed, then roasted for grinding.

Forcing chicory. Do not plant seeds too early for forcing roots. If you do, the roots may grow too large or develop flower stalks, making then unsuitable for forcing. Roots with a diameter of 1 to 1¾ inches at the crown are preferred for forcing. When the weather becomes cold, dig the roots and cut off the tops about 2 inches above the crown (top of root). Store the roots in a cool place with high moisture, such as an outdoor vegetable pit or underground cellar.

During the winter and early spring, roots can be prepared in a new forcing box every 2 to 3 weeks for a continuous supply. Most gardeners put their forcing boxes in the basement because the absence of light produces the pale, bleached quality of the witloof heads that is desired. Some gardeners force witloof in cold frames or hotbeds, and some force it in a trench in the garden. A sheet of clear or black polyethylene film (see page 36) should be placed over the trench to increase soil temperature.

Cut off the slender tips so that the roots are a uniform length (6 to 8 inches), and place the roots close together in a box or other container. Fill with sand or fine soil sifted between the roots to the tops of the crowns. Add 6 to 8 inches of sand or sawdust over the crowns. The blanched tops grow into compact, pointed heads. The proper temperature for forcing is between 60° and 70°F. Water thoroughly after preparing the forcing box. One or two additional waterings may be necessary. Forcing requires 3 to 4 weeks to develop firm heads.

When the heads (chicons) break the surface, remove the sand or sawdust. With a knife, cut off the head at the point of attachment with the root. Prepare heads for the kitchen by removing dirty and loose outer leaves. Store the excess in a plastic bag in the refrigerator. Chicory heads keep for 2 to 4 weeks. Smaller side heads develop after the main chicon is harvested. These heads also may be used, though the shoot quality begins to deteriorate after the second flush of sprouts as the root's reserves are exhausted.

Dandelion

Dandelion, *Taraxacum officinale,* is a hardy perennial whose leaves are gathered as potherbs or greens. Dandelion may be cultivated in the home garden when wild plants are not available. The variability in plant types is great. The named varieties, Thick-Leaf and Improved Thick-Leaf, are superior in flavor and growth characteristics to the wild dandelion.

Dandelion requires a long growing season and develops best at low temperatures. Sow seeds ¼ to ½ inch deep in late spring to early summer, and thin seedlings to 8 to 12 inches apart in the row. The plants form a rosette of leaves and overwinter in the garden. They can grow in

any well-drained garden soil. A polyethylene tunnel can be placed over the row to force growth in late winter for early spring cutting.

Harvest in the fall when plants reach satisfactory size. Cut just below the crown with a sharp knife so that the leaves remain attached. Unharvested plants may be left for use the following spring. Harvest in early spring before the plants form flower stalks and go to seed. If flowering occurs, the greens become bitter and are of poor quality. The cultivated sorts become just as weedy as the wild types if allowed to reseed freely. Some gardeners blanch the inner rosette of leaves by tying the outer leaves together over the plant. Blanching makes the leaves milder and less bitter.

Garden Cress

Garden cress, *Lepidium sativum,* is a hardy, cool-season salad green. Curleycress is a named variety that grows rapidly (12 to 20 days to harvest). It is used as a garnish or spicy addition to salads. Winter cress, *Barbarea verna,* (often listed as Upland Cress in garden catalogs), requires 50 days to harvest. The familiar watercress is an aquatic plant that grows in shallow, cool, fresh, moving water (such as streams) and is not usually suited for home gardening.

Sow 10 to 15 seeds per foot of row, and cover them ¼ to ½ inch deep. Plant garden cress at 2-week intervals as soon as the ground can be worked in the spring. Garden cress grows very rapidly and usually is not thinned. Plant seeds of winter cress in late summer at the same time that you plant fall spinach. Thin seedlings of winter cress to 2 to 3 inches apart in the row. Plantings of either type made in the heat of summer usually produce disappointing results.

The cresses require relatively moist soil and cool growing conditions. They can be grown in protected cold frames during the winter months. Pick the leaves when they are 3 to 5 inches long, or cut the entire plants at any size before the seedstalks form.

Garden Huckleberry

Garden huckleberry, *Solanum melanocerasum* (also known as wonderberry or sunberry), is a tender, warm-season annual plant of the nightshade family. The seeds are listed in garden catalogs simply as "garden huckleberry." Ripe garden huckleberries are used for pies or preserves. Unlike true highbush blueberries, which grow on a woody, shrublike perennial plant, garden huckleberries are not eaten fresh.

Sow seeds, or start indoors and transplant outdoors after the soil has warmed in the spring. Plant seeds ½ inch deep, and thin to 12 inches apart. The plants grow semi-erect, widely branched, and 2 to 3 feet tall. They are related to tomatoes and peppers and should be given the same general care. Pick the berries when they are fully ripe (usually 2 weeks after they first turn black). The ripe berries are ½ to ¾ inch in diameter and grow in loose clusters. The green, immature berries are not edible.

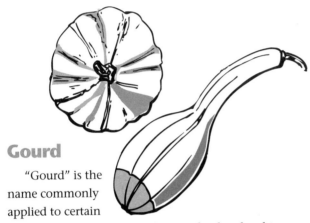

Gourd

"Gourd" is the name commonly applied to certain warm-season vining crops that are closely related to pumpkin and squash. As with other members of the family Cucurbitaceae, common nomenclature can be confusing. The term "gourd" is used to describe members of the *Cucurbita, Lagenaria, and Luffa* genera. In general, the *C. pepo* types are bitter and not eaten at any stage, being used for decoration only. Some of the *Lagenaria* and *Luffa* types are eaten when the fruits are immature, and these two genera have a wider variety of uses than the *C. pepo* gourds (See "Cucuzzi gourd" page 146, and "Chinese okra," page 145). Luffas are most notable for the "vegetable sponge," a fibrous mat of tissue that develops within the mature fruit and has a variety of scouring and cleansing uses. The Lagenarias are the most widely used gourd group. They are utilized as dippers, other utensils, storage containers, and drums and are the raw material of various styles of scrimshawlike art. Both *Lagenaria* and *Luffa* types should usually be grown on fences, trellises, or stakes for proper development of the fruit. *C. pepo* types can also be grown in this fashion if space is limited (see pages 124 and 125).

The following varieties of gourds are suitable for growing in most of the nonarid parts of the country. The *C. pepo* varieties cross-pollinate with *C. pepo* pumpkins, summer squash, or winter squash varieties (see table on pages 113 and 114). **Ornamental:** *C. pepo:* Apple; Bicolor; Large Warted; Nest Egg; Orange; Pear (bicolored, striped,

and white); Shenot (mixed-color crown of thorns); Small Warted; Spoon; and White Crown of Thorns (Bear Claw); *C. maxima* (ornamental squash): Turk's Turban. **Utility (*Lagenaria* species):** Bottle; Calabash; Cave Man's Club; Dipper; Dolphin (Maranka or Swan gourd); Drum; and Hercules' Club. **Edible (*Lagenaria* species):** Cucuzzi; Italian; New Guinea Bean (Guinea Bean); Vegetable Gourd; and Zucco. **Dishrag (*Luffa* species):** *L. acutangula, L. aegyptica,* and *L. cylindrica.* **Edible (*Luffa* species):** Chinese Okra.

Plant seeds 1 inch deep and 6 to 12 inches apart in rows 6 to 8 feet apart. Lagenarias are the most vigorous and may need to be spaced up to 12 to 15 feet between rows if the plants are not trellised. When the seedlings are well established (with one or two true leaves), thin to 2 to 3 feet apart. Plant after the danger of frost has passed and the soil has warmed thoroughly. Both *Lagenaria* and *Luffa* require a fairly long season to mature fruit. In short-season areas, you may need to start plants indoors in advance of settled warm weather to guarantee fully ripened fruit.

Control cucumber beetles (see page 40) with weekly applications of a suggested insecticide from the time that the plants emerge from the soil. Keep the rows free from weeds by shallow hoeing and cultivation until rapid vine growth covers the entire ground surface and shades out further weed competition. Some gardeners in northern locations use black polyethylene mulch (see page 36) to warm the soil for better early season growth and to control weeds.

The utility gourds (dipper, bottle, long-necked, and club varieties) develop the best-shaped fruits when the plants are grown on a fence or trellis. Direct contact with the soil may mar the surface of some sorts, too. The fruits are picked for eating when they are immature (less than 1 week after blossom). The New Guinea Bean is frequently grown on a support for easy harvesting. The pubescent fruits (covered with fine, soft, hairlike structures) hold soil if allowed to lie on the ground.

Ornamental gourds should mature on the plant until late summer or early fall, when the fruits develop hard, glossy, brightly colored shells. Utility types develop hard shells and may begin to change from green to lighter, slightly yellow shades. The stems should be quite tough, and necks on long-handled types should be stiff, not limber. Harvest with 1 to 2 inches of stem attached.

Handle gourds carefully. Bruises, scratches, or punctures result in rapid discoloration and deterioration. Cure gourds for a few days in the shade under warm, dry conditions. Wash dirty fruits, and rinse in a weak bleach solution before drying. After curing, the fruits of brightly colored ornamental varieties may be polished with a dry cloth and waxed or dipped in shellac.

Utility gourds require additional drying for extended periods in a warm, dry room. The gourds should be hung on wires until they are thoroughly dry. Even under the best drying conditions, some surface molds may develop. These usually do not affect the usefulness of the gourds and may enhance the surface with interesting patterns. Once dry, gourds may be made into dippers, plant containers, pipes, birdhouses, wastepaper baskets, works of art, or whatever the shape and size suggest.

Zucco gourds are harvested before killing frosts and stored for fall use. Some cooks use the thick flesh in soups and stews. Harvest mature dishrag gourds only after they have fully developed on the plant and have begun to develop a lighter, yellowish tinge. They may be gathered before frost and allowed to ripen slowly or may be allowed to freeze before harvest. Those harvested after a hard frost should dry quickly, with the skin loosening. When they are dry, the outer surface can be easily removed. Cut off both ends, shake out the seeds, and free the center "sponge core" by cutting lengthwise halfway through the gourd. The resulting rectangular sponge may be used as a scouring pad, bathing sponge, or innersole for shoes, and for other purposes. The American Gourd Society, P.O. Box 274, Mt. Gilead, Ohio 43338, publishes a newsletter on varieties and uses of gourds.

Horseradish

Horseradish, *Armoracia rusticana,* is a very hardy, perennial. As a condiment, it is savored for its hotness when ground or grated and mixed in sauces for seafood, pork, and beef dishes. Most home gardeners do not grow horseradish today because the prepared product is readily available in grocery stores. The connoisseur, however, continues to grow horseradish for its fresh pungency. A few plants should provide ample roots.

Maliner Kren or Bohemian are the varieties offered in most garden catalogs, but they may not be true to the original type. Maliner Kren, also called "common" horseradish by commercial growers, has crinkled, rounded leaves. The Bohemian types usually grow taller and have smooth, more pointed leaves. Either variety makes a suitably hot preparation.

Horseradish is started from crown divisions or root cuttings. Plant as soon as the soil can be worked in early spring. Place the roots 18 to 24 inches apart in shallow trenches, with the top end slightly elevated, and cover with a ridge or mound of soil to a depth of 4 to 5 inches. Crowns should be planted even with the soil level.

Horseradish grows best in deep, loose, fertile soil with dependable moisture. The plants grow 2 to 2½ feet tall, and the roots make their greatest increase in size during the cooling weather of fall. Most gardeners allow horseradish to grow as a perennial along one end of the garden and keep it weeded by shallow cultivation or heavy organic mulch. Production is better if horseradish is divided and replanted yearly, but plants survive indefinitely without any care. Apply water if the plants wilt during hot weather, especially in the late summer and early fall. The roots may be dug anytime from late fall (after a hard frost) until growth starts in the spring. Some gardeners save small pencil-sized roots to produce next year's harvest, and plant them in another row.

Use roots to prepare your favorite sauce soon after digging. Surplus sauce can be frozen in small containers for year-round use. Although the roots store best left in the garden, they can be cleaned, stored in cold (32°F), moist storage, and used as needed (see pages 167 and 168). The prepared product must be kept in a closed container and refrigerated between servings. Even under ideal conditions, ground horseradish turns brown and develops an off-flavor in 4 to 6 weeks. For this reason, gardeners like to prepare fresh horseradish in small batches to meet their immediate needs.

Horseradish is grown commercially as an annual crop. The set roots, which are 10 to 12 inches long and the diameter of a pencil, are planted in early spring; and the plants are dug in the fall. "Lifting" the roots is a practice that removes the side roots from the upper portion of the set root, forcing the plant to develop one large main root. These 1- to 2-pound roots are sold to commercial horseradish processors. The sets, which grow from the bottom of the main root, are stored to plant the following year. Illinois is the leading state in U.S. commercial production of horseradish.

Husk Tomato

Husk tomato, *Physalis pruinosa* (also known as ground cherry, strawberry tomato, Poha berry, and Physalis), is a tender, warm-season annual plant grown for the sweet honeylike flavor of the fruits. It is used in jam, preserves, or pies. The plants also are grown as pot plants or for other ornamental uses.

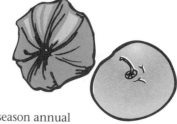

The varieties offered in garden catalogs have either a yellow, purplish, or red fruit when mature. Most varieties are listed simply as "ground cherry" or "husk tomato," but named varieties may be listed under Physalis.

Plant seeds or transplants after the soil has warmed in the spring. Sow seeds $1/4$ to $1/2$ inch deep, and thin or transplant to 18 inches apart in the row. Although lower-growing, the plants should be given the same general care as tomatoes. The berrylike fruits are smooth, about 1 inch in diameter, and completely enclosed by a papery husk. When the husks turn brown, the fruits are ripe and can be harvested. They may drop off the plant when fully mature, and plants readily reseed themselves.

Tomatillo, *Physalis ixocarpa*, is a very large, green-fruited *Physalis* that has recently come to prominence in the United States as a main ingredient of the authentic Mexican green salsa. Culture is the same as for ground cherry, except the plants are larger and need wider spacing to develop fully.

Peanut

Peanut, *Arachis hypogaea* (also known as goober pea or earth nut), is a warm-season annual plant that resembles clover. Although usually considered a crop of the Deep South, peanuts also can be grown successfully in most of the country and, with special care, even in most of the northern states.

Peanuts develop best in loose, sandy soil and require a minimum of 120 frost-free days to reach maturity. Varieties of peanuts suitable for growing in shorter-season areas are Early Northern, Early Spanish, Jumbo Virginia, Red Tennessee, and Valencia.

Plant two or three individual seeds (or the entire husk containing the seeds) 1 to $1^1/2$ inches deep in hills 10 to 12 inches apart. Allow 36 inches between rows. The seedlings emerge with three cloverlike leaflets that rapidly grow into plants 18 to 20 inches tall. In extreme northern areas, peanuts can be started indoors in peat pots in late March or early April and transplanted to the garden, after danger of frost is past, without disturbing the roots.

Keep the soil loose and hilled toward the row of plants. After the bright yellow flowers are pollinated, the flowering shoots elongate and send a "peg" into the soil. These pegs, which form the peanuts, readily enter loose soils and do not require that you cover by hand; but they cannot penetrate hard, baked soil. A light covering (1 to 2 inches) of loose organic mulch material around the plants helps to keep the soil loose and the peanuts near the surface of the ground. Do not disturb the soil after the flower pegs have buried themselves. Usually 50 to 75 peanuts are formed in each hill, usually 2 to 3 seeds per pod. Hand pull weeds in the row.

Dig the plants after they have matured (begun to turn yellow) in the fall. Harvest in early to midOctober before a hard freeze. The soil should be dry so that it can be shaken off the peanuts. Cure the peanuts by stacking the plants in an open shelter where they will not freeze, or by hanging them in a warm, dry shed or garage for a week. After the plants have dried, shake off any remaining soil, and pull the peanuts from the vines. Continue to air dry the peanuts in mesh bags or shallow pans for another week or two.

When the peanuts are dry, they are ready to shell or roast. Peanuts should be roasted in a shallow pan in a 350°F oven for 20 minutes. Roasted peanuts are favorite snacks and are also made into peanut butter. Raw peanuts are used in baking and candy. Peanut plants are sometimes grown for their ornamental value as patio or pot plants, but they usually do not yield any harvest under these conditions.

Popcorn

Popcorn, *Zea mays* var. *praecox*, can be grown in large gardens for food and in most gardens as an ornamental. With proper care, harvesting, and storage, homegrown popcorn achieves superior flavor and maximal popping size (30 to 40 times the volume of the unpopped kernels).

There are two basic types of popping corns: round "pearl" kernels (usually produced on large ears) and sharp-pointed "rice" kernels (usually produced on smaller ears). Pearl-type kernaels are smooth and rounded and produce large, whole hulls when popped. The rice-type hulless hybrids, which leave little or no hull after popping, are especially tender and are prized by home gardeners. Color varies from the standard yellow and white to red, brown, black, and even multicolored ornamental kernels. In the following, OP refers to the open-pollinated varieties. Recommended varieties include:

White varieties (hybrid unless indicated): Japanese Hulless (OP–105 days to harvest, rice kernels); Peppy (90 days, rice kernels); Purdue 307 (102 days, top white producer); Snow Puff (100 days, rice kernels); White

Cloud Hulless (85 days, rice kernels); and White Dynamite (95 days, rice kernels).

Yellow varieties (hybrid unless indicated): Creme Puff (100 days, good popping quality); Iopop 12 (94 days, pearl kernels); Purdue 410 (105 days, pearl kernels, high yield); Purdue 608 (105 days, pearl kernels, top yielder); Robust 20-70 (85 days, pearl kernels, early yellow); Tiny Tim (100 days, 6-inch ears, light yellow); and Tom Thumb (OP–heirloom with tiny, light yellow ears).

Red varieties: Robust Red S-100 (hybrid–105 days, large ears, high yield, deep red) and Strawberry (OP–105 days; rice kernels; short, round ears; both ornamental and tasty popped).

Ornamental colored popcorns: Carousel (110 days, 4- to 5-inch ears, calico or mixed colors on each ear); Cutie Blues (100 days, 4-inch ears, solid dark blue); Cutie Pops (100 days, 4-inch ears, calico); Indian Finger (110 days, 2½- to 4½-inch ears, calico); Papoose (85 days, 4- to 6-inch ears, calico); and Seneca Mini Indian (103 days, 3- to 5-inch ears, calico).

Popcorn may be grown in any good, fertile, well-drained garden soil that can produce good sweet corn. Plant at the same time as early or midseason sweet corn. Select early maturing varieties for northern areas so that the corn has sufficient time to mature before frost. If at all possible, you should physically separate sweet corn and popcorn plantings. If that cannot be done, planting and maturity dates should be planned so that sweet corn and popcorn do not pollinate at the same time. Cross-pollination ruins the sweet corn (making it starchy, tough, and tasteless) and reduces the popping efficiency of the popcorn.

Space rows 30 to 40 inches apart. Plant kernels ½ to 1 inch deep (two to three kernels per foot of row). Thin the plants to 6 to 8 inches apart. Some gardeners check-plant four kernels per hill, with the hills spaced 40 inches apart in two directions. This planting method permits cross-cultivation to help keep down weeds. In most gardens, the first method is preferred.

Side-dress nitrogen fertilizer (see page 20) when the plants are 12 to 18 inches tall. Cultivate or hoe shallowly, close to the plants. Irrigate if an extended dry period occurs, especially during pollination and ear development. Popcorn planted near sweet corn or field corn may be pollinated by these crops. Cross-pollinated popcorn still pops, but do not save cross-pollinated ears for seed the following year. (Never save seed produced from hybrid varieties.) The resulting cross may have little or no popping ability.

The popcorn should mature in the garden, and the plants should dry. As the ears mature and dry, the stalks of some varieties, particularly the rice types, may become weakened and fall over from the weight of the ears. If this happens, the ears should be harvested immediately and should finish drying off the plant, to avoid moisture damage or sprouting caused by contact with the soil. Popcorn can usually be harvested when both the husks and leaves have turned brown. Popcorn normally dries to less than 20 percent kernel moisture on the stalk in the garden before the first frost. A light frost does not damage popcorn unless the plants are still green or the kernel moisture is above 35 percent; and freezing does not damage popcorn unless the kernel moisture is above 20 percent.

Harvest by hand, shuck the ears, and place them where they can continue to dry. If shucks are pulled back, but not removed, they help wick moisture from the ears and speed drying. These ears can be strung in bunches with twine or string and hung to dry in a dry area with good air circulation. To prevent rodents from eating the popcorn, store in coarse-mesh sacks or wire baskets and hang from a beam. Popcorn dries naturally in an outdoor shelter to about 13 to 14 percent kernel moisture—ideal for popping. If stored in a heated room during the winter, popcorn dries to 7 percent kernel moisture. This moisture content is too low for good popping. Avoid using heat above 100°F to dry popcorn, as kernel damage may occur.

As ears reach proper dryness, the kernels shell from the ears much more easily than from damper ones. When the ears have dried, the kernels are tightly pressed together, the ear has a very solid feel, and some kernels may even start to be forced from the ear by the shrinking cob. Popcorn dried on the cob as fully as possible is of the highest quality because it absorbs as much of the sugars stored in the cob as possible before being removed; during shelling, it sustains less seed coat and kernel damage that might hamper proper popping. Many gardeners prefer to air dry the ears for a week or two until they are nearly dried (longer if necessary), shell them, further air dry the kernels in shallow pans, and place the kernels in moistureproof jars or cans for storage. Kernels around the tip of the ears, especially, may be damaged in some way or greatly undersized. These and any other damaged kernels elsewhere on the ear should be removed before the entire ear is shelled; this helps eliminate many unpopped kernels from the stored product later. Popcorn can be conveniently stored almost indefinitely in the home freezer. Package in 1-pound or 2-pound containers, and use as needed.

The popcorn should be "fanned" before storage to remove the papery cob dust that is mixed with the kernels. Simply drop kernels from one container to another in the outside air and allow the breeze to separate the dry, light chaff from the heavy grain. Two or three passes back and forth between containers should be enough. Judge by when chaff stops coming off the corn.

If the corn becomes too dry for some reason, you can increase the moisture content by adding 1 tablespoon of water to a 1-quart container of popcorn. Seal the container, shake several times, and leave at room temperature for a few days. The moisture content of the shelled popcorn increases about 2 percent. Do not overdo this procedure, or mold or other damage could happen.

Radicchio

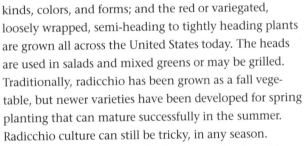

Radicchio, *Cichorium intybus* (leaf chicory), is a unique, tangy-flavored vegetable that has long been grown in Italy and only recently has been introduced into this country. There are many kinds, colors, and forms; and the red or variegated, loosely wrapped, semi-heading to tightly heading plants are grown all across the United States today. The heads are used in salads and mixed greens or may be grilled. Traditionally, radicchio has been grown as a fall vegetable, but newer varieties have been developed for spring planting that can mature successfully in the summer. Radicchio culture can still be tricky, in any season.

The Giulio variety was the first strain developed for spring planting, and it is vigorous and resistant to bolting. It produces small heads months before other varieties. Caesar, another early heading variety that may be planted in early summer, consistently produces wine-colored, uniform heads with white midribs. Red Treviso and Early Treviso are planted in midsummer and form slender, spear-shaped heads resembling belgian endive or small Cos lettuce. If heads have not formed by Labor Day, cut off the leafy top to an inch above the crown, taking care not to injure the growing point; and in the cool weather of fall, tight, attractive heads form. Milano and Red Verona (Rossa Di Verona) are the best known Italian varieties. In the summer, they form loose, green rosettes that turn into brilliant little red heads in the cool weather of fall. Some people prefer to cut them back in late fall, 1 inch above the crown, and let small heads quickly form. Rubello and Firebird (both hybrids) are two of the newest introductions, and both are tolerant to summer heat.

Radicchio is very tolerant to cool weather and continues to produce even after frosts. It can be grown on a variety of soil types, but avoid acidic soils and overfertilization, especially with nitrogen. Ideally, plant seed in deep, well-drained soils in rows 24 to 28 inches apart, with seed about ³/₄ inch deep. When seedlings are established in the row, thin to about 4 to 6 inches between plants. Maintain the planting bed free of weeds throughout the growing season.

Shallot

Shallot, *Allium cepa* var. *aggregatum,* is a hardy member of the onion family that is prized for its delicate, meaty, onionlike flavor. Many gourmet chefs use shallots for sauces, stews, gravies, and roasts. Shallots are planted and cared for in much the same manner as onions.

Although there are several varieties of shallots, they are usually listed in garden catalogs simply as "shallots." Bulbs for planting may be obtained from seed houses, another gardener, or the gourmet section of a food store. Varieties available by name include Dutch Yellow, French Epicurean, Frog Legs, Pink, and Prince de Bretagne. Varieties with a pink tinge are generally more highly regarded.

Shallots produce a cluster of bulbs from each single bulb planted. To plant, divide the clump of shallots into individual bulbs, which resemble large, fat onion sets. Plant these individual bulbs 1 to 1¹/₂ inches deep and 3 to 4 inches apart. Allow 12 to 24 inches between rows. Planting during late winter or early spring, as soon as the soil can be tilled, gives the best yields. In the southern half of the country, the next year's crop can be planted in late October to sprout and overwinter in the garden. The bulbs should be planted 2 to 3 inches deep (deeper than in the spring) to help prevent frost heaving. Shallots are very hardy and survive most winters, especially if there is good snow cover.

Shallots may be pulled as green onions when their tops are 6 to 8 inches tall. Each bulb produces 8 to 10 sprouts, ³/₈ inch or larger in diameter, depending on the variety. For dry bulbs, allow the tops of the plants to die down naturally in summer. Harvest and handle in the same manner as dry onions (see page 90). The dry bulbs may be placed in a mesh bag and stored under cool, dry conditions. If harvested while the tops remain strong, the shallots may be braided into garlands, which are attractive hanging in the kitchen until the bulbs are used. Shallots keep well and are stored much more easily than onions until planting time in the spring. Some varieties may remain useful into the second winter after harvest.

Onion yellows is a viral disease that affects all members of the onion family, but particularly vegetatively (nonseed) propagated types like shallots and multiplier onions. The virus infects the plants as they grow, deforms the foliage, stunts their growth, and then overwinters in the bulbs. If these bulbs are planted the following year, insects can quickly infect the whole planting as well as any onions in the vicinity. For this reason, planting stock should be obtained only from reputable seed houses or others who can give you reasonable assurance of freedom from this disease.

Southern Pea

Southern Pea, *Vigna unguiculata* (also known as cowpea, black-eyed pea, and crowder pea), is an important garden vegetable in the southern part of the United States. It is not actually a pea but a member of the bean family and is adaptable to all areas of the country except the most northerly or high-altitude sites. Southern pea may be harvested as a green shellout vegetable or as a dry bean. Many people eat black-eyed peas and rice on New Year's Day for good luck. The yardlong or asparagus bean is technically classified as a southern pea but is eaten as a green bean, pod and all, rather than as a shellout vegetable or dry bean.

Varieties of southern pea suitable for growing in most of the country include Big Boy, Brown Crowder, California Blackeye, Colossus, Crowder, Mississippi Silver, Purple Hull, and White Crowder.

Southern peas are grown in a manner similar to green beans. Plant seeds 1 inch deep and 4 to 6 inches apart after the danger of frost has passed. Allow 24 to 36 inches between rows. The bushy plants grow 24 to 30 inches tall.

The peas are ready to harvest as shellouts when the pods appear firm and plump, with swellings around each individual seed inside (about 60 to 70 days after planting). Pick twice a week. The pods range from 3 to 8 inches long; and the "peas" are colored or speckled or have an eye pattern, depending upon the variety. Pods develop in the order they are pollinated, so that the pods mature first on the lower portion of the plant. Many gardeners harvest all of the seeds that they want for fresh use and then allow the remaining beans to mature and dry on the plants. The vines then may be pulled and dried at the end of the season and the beans shelled for winter use or as seed for next year.

Asparagus beans, *Vigna unguiculata* subspecies *sesquipedalis* (yardlong beans), usually are grown in a single row, the same as cowpeas, and then trained on strings or wires as pole beans because the plants are vining. All members of this group are sensitive to cold weather. Seed is usually planted 2 weeks later than green beans, when the soil is thoroughly warm. The first pods are ready to harvest in 60 to 90 days. Although the name implies long fruits, they should be harvested when young, 8 to 10 inches long, about $3/8$ inch in diameter, and still tender enough to snap when bent sharply.

Asparagus beans are often used as oriental vegetables. They are cut or snapped and then stir-fried or steamed. It is best to keep them picked regularly, maybe freezing the excess, rather than allowing the pods to get tough and the seeds to develop, which slows down or stops additional pods from setting. Most gardeners pick beans daily during the peak of the season. Two varieties are offered, one red- and the other black-seeded. If allowed to mature, the beans may grow up to 3 feet long. When they reach this length, however, they are past the best stage for cooking as snap beans. Mature asparagus beans may be shelled and used in the same manner as southern peas or dry beans. The plants continue to produce for several weeks if beans are kept picked when immature.

Spaghetti Squash

Spaghetti squash (also known as vegetable spaghetti) is a *C. pepo* variety that is oval, yellowish, and 8 to 10 inches long. It may be planted and cared for in much the same manner as other squash (see "Winter Squash," page 116). When cooked by baking or boiling, the flesh separates into spaghetti-like strands that taste like squash. These strands, which are low in calories, can be served with cheese, meat sauce, or sour cream. Spaghetti squash can also be eaten as a salad by chilling the precooked filaments and serving with seasoning or salad dressing.

Sunflower

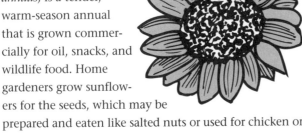

Sunflower, *Helianthus annuus,* is a tender, warm-season annual that is grown commercially for oil, snacks, and wildlife food. Home gardeners grow sunflowers for the seeds, which may be prepared and eaten like salted nuts or used for chicken or wild bird feed.

The plants have ornamental value as background screens. Some varieties of sunflowers grow extremely tall; others have been developed for their multiple, attractive yellow, red, or white flower heads. Most varieties of sunflower require 100 to 120 days to develop mature seed heads. Mammoth Russian and Grey Stripe are tall varieties (6 to 12 feet) that bear large (12- to 24-inch) single heads. Other widely adapted varieties are Manchurian and Royal Hybrid 2141. Ornamental or dwarf sunflowers (1½ to 6 feet tall) may be multiflowered and of various colors (including white), bear single or double flowers, and have many branches and smaller flower heads.

Plant seeds 1 inch deep. Thin seedlings of the ornamental varieties to 12 inches apart, and seedlings of the taller varieties to 24 to 36 inches apart. Sunflowers need full sun and can grow in most garden soils with good drainage. Side-dress nitrogen fertilizer twice during the season to promote growth. Sunflowers shade and suppress weeds, as well as surrounding crops, around their bases.

The tall, large-seeded varieties of sunflower are harvested for snack food. Allow the heads to mature in the garden. At maturity, the back of the head is brown and dry; most of the yellow petals have dried and fallen; the seeds are plump; and the seedcoats are black-and-white striped. Cut the main stem about 1 foot below the head before the seed starts to loosen and shatter. Rub the seeds loose by hand, dry, and store for future use. Sunflower seeds may be eaten without processing, dehulled and roasted, or salted in the hull.

In many areas, heads may need to be bagged (after they are pollinated) to keep birds and squirrels from stealing the harvest of seeds. Heads also may be picked when the back turns from green to rich yellow and then dried in a dry, protected location.

In the garden, sunflowers may "volunteer," that is, come up the next year, where seeds shatter from the mature heads. A few of these plants left in out-of-the-way spaces in the garden can lend a naturalistic feel to the garden. When small, they transplant fairly well. Birds also may sow a few seeds in unusual locations if sunflower seed is regularly fed at a bird feeder. Incidentally, care must be taken when feeding sunflower seed because an accumulation of hulls under the feeder kills grass and other herbaceous vegetation. Clean the hulls up regularly or site the feeder where there is no danger of damage to lawns or other desirable vegetation.

Vine Crops

The vine crops family (Cucurbitaceae) is a large group of plants, including all the gourds, melons, pumpkins, squashes, and cucumbers with which we are familiar. There are a number of plants from this family that are grown mainly in other parts of the world. Most members of this family require large amounts of space in the garden. These ethnic types may have fruits of different shape, color, and size than more familiar varieties of vine crops grown in the United States.

Bitter melon, *Momordica charantia,*(foo gwa) is grown for its attractive foliage and fruit. The fruit has a definite bitter taste from the presence of quinine. Acceptance of this flavor is rapidly acquired by both adults and children in areas where bitter melon is commonly grown and consumed.

Bitter melon is usually trained on a trellis to display its beauty and conserve space. Being a warm-weather crop, it is not seeded until after frost danger is past in the spring and the ground is thoroughly warm. The seed is slow to germinate, requiring up to 2 weeks. Bitter melon requires high fertility and plenty of water. When vines are 8 to 12 inches long, they need support and can be started up a trellis or fence. You can harvest both young buds and green fruit, as they are less bitter. Mature yellow fruits are not eaten but may be used to harvest next year's seed crop.

Calabaza, *Cucurbita moschata,* is a common name that identifies several strains of pumpkins and squashes grown in the tropics. Calabaza grows on a vine similar to other winter-type squashes but which is usually longer. The leaves are mottled and grayish green in color. Fruit size, shape, and color vary greatly between growing areas due to outcrossing and local strain selection. The most common form of the fruit weighs about 6 to 10 pounds and has a round shape, which is flattened a bit on the top and bottom. Its color is usually either green or yellow mottled with buff-cream. The firm, meaty flesh is light yellow, with a comparatively large central cavity. The seeds are rather small, which is typical for *C. moschata* pumpkin and squash varieties.

Calabaza tolerates hot weather conditions, much like other members of the cucurbit family. A tender crop, acclimated to the tropics, it is easily injured by frost and freezes. It should be planted in the spring as soon as the danger of frost is past and the ground has warmed to at least 60°F. Because calabaza requires a somewhat longer growing season than some other common varieties of squash, planting should not be delayed much past this early opportunity, especially in northern areas. In subtropical areas of the United States, fall crops may be sown. Calabaza can be grown as far north as 40 degrees north latitude. Other than planting earlier, cultural practices are similar to those for the common kinds of squashes. The plant requires about four warm months from seeding to harvest.

Because seed is not readily available through regular channels, some searching may be necessary to find a seed source. Once you have seed of calabaza, it must be isolated from all other *C. moschata* varieties or be hand-pollinated if you want to keep seed to plant in upcoming years. Other members of this group that cannot be grown near calabaza intended for seed production include Golden Cushaw, processing pumpkins, and all butternut-type squashes.

Chinese cucumber,

Cucumis sativus (kee chi), has been in existence for hundreds of years. Unlike many so-called ethnic vegetables, there are several recognized and readily available varieties. Chinese cucumbers are forerunners of the "burpless" varieties, which are usually thinner in diameter and longer than conventional cucumber fruit. Some of the more common varieties include Early Occhai, Green Knight, Green Prolific, Kyoto, Serpentine, Sooyou Long, Tokyo Slicer, Yamato Extra Long, and Yard Long.

Rules for planting oriental cucumber are the same as for conventional cucumbers. Plant after frost danger is past and when the soil is warm. They may be grown on the ground or on fences or trellises to conserve space. Fruit grown on supports are longer and straighter. Plant seeds 1 inch deep, in rows at the base of the support. After seedlings are established, thin to 10 to 12 inches apart. In short-season growing areas, they may be started

inside in peat pots and transplanted. Unless cucumbers have a continuous, ample supply of water, they may develop a bitter taste. If you keep mature fruits harvested, more continuously develop.

Armenian cucumbers, also called syrian, turkish, or yard-long cucumbers, have lighter-colored fruits but are also members of the chinese cucumber group, with all cultural and handling suggestions the same.

Chinese okra (cee gwa), *Luffa acutangula* or *aegyptica (L. cylindrica)*, is the immature fruit of the plant grown as vegetable sponge, dishcloth gourd, running okra, and loofah. Both species are sometimes grown in this country. Angled luffa is *L. acutangula,* and the smooth-fruited version is *L. cylindrica* or *L. aegyptica.*

Both luffas have value as food items, but most gardeners grow them for their fibrous interior, which is useful as a rough cloth or sponge for cleaning and scouring. (See "Gourd," page 138). The two species are somewhat similar in appearance. Both are vigorous, climbing, annual vines with several-lobed cucumberlike leaves. When crushed, the leaves have a rank odor.

Both male and female flowers are yellow and occur on the same plants, with males greatly outnumbering females. The male flower, which occurs in clusters, is rather large and bright yellow. The female flower is solitary, with the tiny, slender ovary attached.

Mature *Luffa* fruits are shaped like cucumbers but are larger, 1 to 2 feet in length and 4 to 5 inches thick. The exterior is green. The interiors of both are cucumberlike when immature but quickly develop a network of fibers surrounding a large number of flat, blackish seeds. Small (less than 6 inches long), young luffa gourds are desired and are prepared like squash or eaten raw like cucumbers. Some varieties, particularly the smooth type, are sweeter than others.

Because chinese okra requires much growing space, plant seeds in hills spaced 6 feet apart, or space plants about 3 to 4 feet apart in a single row. Plant along a fence or provide a trellis. Prepare the soil and fertilize as you would for squash or cucumbers. Because fruits touching the soil may develop decay, mulch is helpful.

Chinese pumpkin, *Cucurbita pepo* (nung gwa); see "Pumpkin," page 103.

Cucuzzi gourd, *Lagenaria siceraria,* is a vining, musky-scented annual plant of the same species as dipper, birdhouse, and other utility gourds. It has large, hairy, shallow-lobed leaves on long petioles. Like the *Lagenaria* utility gourds, both male and female flowers are white, with the male flowers borne on long slender stems that raise them above the foliage. Fruits are edible only in the young, immature stage, usually up to about 10 inches in length, before the hard fibrous shell begins to form. They are light green in color, with a very smooth surface. As their name might imply, cucuzzi is a popular Italian vegetable, often served in a tomato sauce.

Shape varies, especially if fruit is not trellised to keep it off the ground; but most fruits are long and cylindrical, routinely up to 3 feet long and 3 inches in diameter at maturity, with record lengths exceeding 8 feet. If grown flat on the ground, the fruits are coiled and twisted; when grown on supports, most are very straight and club-shaped, due to the influence of gravity.

The interior is white and pulpy and contains many seeds, which at maturity are $\frac{1}{2}$ inch long, white, and uniquely shaped. One end of the seed is pointed, while the other has three lobes.

Like other members of this species, the plant grows vigorously, climbing on anything within reach. Plant and grow cucuzzi as you would pole beans, but give it much more room. A structure like a grape arbor can be used to advantage. Vines may stretch to 25 feet or more in agreeable weather. The snake gourd, *Trichosanthes anguina,* also called the club, viper, or serpent gourd, is very similar in appearance to the cucuzzi.

Fuzzy gourd, *Benincasa hispida* var. *chieh-gua* (mao gwa), is a small-sized cousin of the winter melon, in the same species. Fuzzy gourds are grown in the same manner, but the fruits may be used like summer squash in bread, soup, casseroles, and stir-fries or may be cut in half and stuffed. The outside of the fruits has a distinctive fuzzy coat that is removed by first rubbing and then peeling.

Plant seed an inch deep and 3 to 4 inches apart next to a fence or trellis, and train up the supports to keep the fruits off the ground. Harvest when fruits are 4 to 6 inches in length. Allow a few gourds on the best-looking plants to mature for next year's supply of seed.

Pickling melon, *Cucumis conomon* (chung choy), is native to China and Japan and may be processed like sour pickles or pearl onions or by any favorite pickle recipe. Pickling melons are also good cooked and eaten as a vegetable.

Because pickling melon is another warm-weather crop, sow seed, an inch deep and 6 inches apart, after all danger of frost, allowing room for the rows to develop to 6 feet wide. Harvest when fruits have matured to the size you choose for the type of pickle you want to make, similar to the way conventional cucumber types are harvested. In all cases, harvest fruit before they start to lighten in color. There is a wide choice of varieties, from light to dark green in color.

Sweet melon, *Cucumis melo* (chung gwa), is similar to familiar melons like honeydews and cantaloupes. Size varies from a few ounces to 3 pounds. Many varieties are available, including Honey Gold, Honey Drip, Takii Honey, and Sakata's Sweet. Varieties range from white to golden rinds, with various degrees of netting. Plant four to five seeds per hill, 1 inch deep, then thin to the two best plants. Melons are best planted after danger of frost is past and the ground has thoroughly warmed.

Knowing when fruit is ripe enough to harvest is a knack that is developed by experience. Aroma is one of the best indices for ripeness of fruit, as the pleasant, sweet smell increases with maturity. The cantaloupe types "slip," that is, the stem of the ripe fruit is easily removed from the vine; the honeydew types do not slip.

West Indian gherkin, *Cucumis anguria* (also known as gherkin or burr gherkin), is a native of Africa. This plant is most commonly grown in South America. The plant's appearance is somewhat like watermelon's leaves and vines. The fruits are 1 to 2 inches in length, oval to oblong, covered with spines, and pale green in color, turning yellow when mature. They are usually processed into sweet pickles that are superior to the tiny cucumber pickles offered in the store as gherkins, which are really *Cucumis sativus.* Production is handled in the same manner as cucumbers for pickles. See page 76.

Winter melon, *Benincasa hispida* (Doan Gwa), can be grown with great success and is cultivated the same as watermelon. This plant is commonly known as wax gourd because the fruit appears gray and waxy. It is grown for soup and main dishes or to serve on a relish tray.

The seed requires warm soil outdoors or may be started in peat pots indoors. In the garden, plant two seeds 1 inch deep and a foot apart. Young stem tips and fruit may be harvested, but the mature fruit is most prized. When mature, it is the size and shape of a watermelon and has a whitish wax layer, which develops only when the melon is fully ripe. The fruit is then ready for use or may be stored for as long as several months.

Herbs

Herbs

A vegetable gardening book, like a garden, is incomplete without herbs. Herbs are easy to grow, beautiful, fun, and rewarding to use. Most of them are as easy to grow as common vegetables. Whether you use them in formal herb gardens or interplanted with your vegetables or landscaping, you can always find space in a garden for a few herbs.

Although some herbs are used for medicine, fragrance, crafts, dyeing, and cosmetics, those listed here are common and versatile culinary herbs.

While the average cook knows how to use sage when stuffing the Thanksgiving turkey, chives on a baked potato, and garlic for Caesar salad, many herbs still present a mystery to most Americans—especially herbs fresh from the garden. Today's famous chefs consider nothing less than fresh herbs for their creations; and you, too, can add a pinch of oregano or a dab of sweet basil, fresh from the garden, to prepare an outstanding, nutritious low-salt dish. Herbs are user-friendly: Once you begin to use them, you soon come to appreciate the pure pleasure of herbs.

Although herbs have long been ignored in American gardens, there is no "mystery" about them. Over the last 5 to 10 years, herbs have made a breakthrough in popularity throughout the country. Whereas herbs were previously in demand only in trendy spots like California and some East Coast locations, they have now "arrived." Herb books and recipes are abundant today. Among the hundreds of plants used over the centuries as "herbs," however, there are dangerous plants that can cause illness or even death if misused. Therefore, always purchase herb plants from a reputable source to know exactly what you are buying. Do some reading to understand each herb's uses. Unless you become an expert in field botany, foraging for wild herb plants usually is not recommended.

Herb gardens may be formal, informal, limited to individual specimen plants, or integrated into other, larger garden plans. Small herb gardens of 5 to 10 square feet may be located near doorways or along walkways, may be incorporated around the patio or terrace, and also may be worked into a rock garden. Some herb plants can be grown successfully indoors for use throughout the year. Tender perennial varieties need to winter indoors, either in a sunny location or in a home greenhouse.

Herbs usually do well in any soil that is suitable for vegetables. The soil should be moderately fertile and well supplied with organic matter. Good soil drainage is essential for most herbs. If your soil drainage is poor, it is preferable to grow herbs in raised beds, containers, or pots. Even if you are blessed with excellent soil, raised beds may be a good idea (see "Raised Beds," page 5).

It is not always best to grow herbs from seed. Although rosemary, thyme, and mint can be started from seed, they are grown most successfully from plants or rooted cuttings. All the annual herbs come easily from seed. For early plantings, starting seedlings in greenhouses or cold frames can lengthen the harvest season. Direct sowing also can be used successfully later in the season. Because basil prefers germinating with some light, cover seeds minimally, if at all.

Most of the perennials can be started from seed, with the exception of french tarragon, which does not form viable seed and must be started from some form of cuttings or division. The finest-flavored varieties of most perennials must be vegetatively propagated as well. In some instances, a large crop of seedlings can be started and the best-flavored plants selected to propagate for future crops.

Herb gardeners experience relatively few problems from insects or diseases. Many of the strong odors and tastes of herbs have evolved to ward off or discourage insects. Good soil and air drainage are essential elements of disease control.

Culinary experts classify herbs into two groups: robust herbs and fine herbs. Herbs added while food is being prepared or cooked are classified as robust; herbs that may be eaten uncooked in salads or sprinkled over a cooked dish are classified as fine herbs. Fine herbs are also often used before or during cooking. Parsley is used both raw and in cooking. This herb is unique because it serves as a "blender" of other herbs and flavors.

Fresh herbs are always preferable to dried when they are available. Drying, even under ideal conditions, causes loss of essential oils and flavors. While some herbs maintain good quality dried, others are almost worthless. Although the fresh product includes water, the flavors may actually be more intense. Use less dried product by weight or volume, but experiment with fresh herbs to adjust quantities.

Plant dealers sometimes offer combination packs or "herb gardens" that contain four to six different herb plants. For many varieties of herbs, a very few plants produce enough harvest to season a family's cooking needs. Fresh flavors are very intense, and only small amounts are required. As your tastes become more sophisticated, some types may be needed in somewhat larger quantities. To start, though, a nice assortment usually does the trick.

An idea for assortments might be ethnic groupings. Italian seasonings usually include such herbs as basil, oregano, fennel, flat-leaf parsley, and garlic (or garlic chives). A Mexican assortment would contain cilantro (coriander), basil, chile peppers, and tomatillo. Because you usually will not buy large numbers of plants, you should look for high-quality, single-plant packs. A few good plants are a better investment than several of lesser quality.

The following are the most widely used culinary herbs in U.S. gardens.

Angelica

Angelica, *Angelica archangelica,* is a biennial of the Umbelliferae family. Leaves may be used in salads, stems may be candied, roots may be cooked like a vegetable, and seeds may be used in cooking. All plant parts are aromatic and useful. Angelica produces rounded umbels of white flowers, followed by seeds. If the flower stems are removed before flowering, the plant remains vegetative for several years.

Beginners should buy started plants, which self-sow to some degree in future years if seeds are allowed to mature on the plants. If plants cannot be found, sow very fresh seed 1/4 inch deep in moist, partly shaded locations. Seeds lose viability soon after ripening (within 2 weeks). Space plants at least 2 feet apart. As with other biennial plants, sow seed yearly to have flowering plants each year. Stems are bitter when raw; but, when cooked, they taste like parsley. Leaves may be dried for out-of-season use. The essential oil is used for flavoring liqueurs like Benedictine, chartreuse, and vermouth.

Angelica prefers a cool climate and moist conditions. It once was believed to cure or prevent the plague, so was called angelica "the guardian angel."

Anise

Anise, *Pimpinella anisum,* is an annual, grown commercially in Europe, that is easily adapted to conditions in much of the United States. Like most members of the Umbelliferae family, the plant grows a rosette of foliage, stores energy, and then bolts up to a height of 24 to 30 inches, producing seed. The seed heads resemble those of wild carrot or caraway.

Seeds should be planted early in the spring at the rate of 10 to 15 per foot in rows 2 to 3 feet apart. Germination of anise seed is sometimes poor or very spotty. The surface of the soil should be made smooth and the seeds covered to a depth of 1/2 inch. The stand should be thinned to 3 to 6 inches apart. Only light cultivation is needed for weed control.

Green leaves may be harvested as soon as plants become established. The fruiting umbels (seed-bearing stalks) should be harvested when seeds begin to turn brown in the summer. Clip the umbels from the plants and thoroughly dry them in bags to catch the shattering seeds. When thoroughly dry, the seeds should be separated from the stems, cleaned, and stored for later use.

The fresh leaves have a flavor similar to that of the seeds and may be added to fruit salads. They blend especially well with apple salads. The seeds are used in cookies and candy.

Anise Hyssop

Anise hyssop, *Agastache foeniculum* (also called licorice mint), is a fragrant 3- to 4-foot perennial plant in the mint family. The showy, short purple flower spikes are irresistible to bees and butterflies. The fragrance is a blend of anise and mint, with anise predominating (hence the name). Clumps of this herb commonly grow 3 to 4 feet tall and 1 to 2 feet across.

Seeds should be sown in flats in late winter or early spring to be set out after the last frost, or they may be direct-seeded 1/4 to 1/2 inch deep in the garden when the soil has warmed and mellowed in midspring. Plants ultimately should be spaced 18 to 24 inches apart. Although the plant is a perennial, it will grow and make a good floral showing the first year, especially if started early indoors. Plants survive most winters in Zone 5, especially under good snow cover and with good winter drainage.

Mature leaves may be harvested fresh for tea or may be dried. The flowers make attractive edible garnishes and dry easily for use in winter everlasting bouquets. In the garden, anise hyssop makes an especially attractive midbackground or accent planting. If flowers are regularly picked or if the spent flowers are regularly removed, the plants rebloom until frost. Gourmet honey producers often plant large ares with this herb because bees turn the abundant nectar into anise-flavored honey. While long-term winter survival is not dependable in northern areas, it readily self-seeds if some of the flower heads are left on the plant to mature. Also, because it flowers abundantly the first year, it can be treated as an annual in areas where it winterkills.

While anise hyssop is still not one of the most easy-to-find herbs today, it has recently increased in popularity. You may still have to scour several specialty seed catalogs or visit several herb plant sales to find your original planting stock. This handsome and useful plant will more than reward the search.

Basil

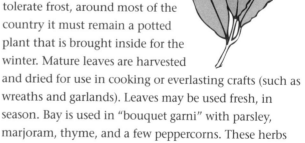

Basil, *Ocimum basilicum* and other *Ocimum* species, is an aromatic, tender annual plant with a spicy odor and flavor. Basil plants may be either green or purple. Basil is known for its attractive foliage and growth habits and often is used as a border plant. Dark Opal basil won an All-American Selections award because it offers wide adaptability and attractiveness in ornamental gardens. Its flavor, however, is a bit strong for most palates.

The plants usually grow from 12 to 18 inches tall. There are many basil species and countless variations in plant habit, leaf shape, stiffness, and featheriness. To keep the plants actively growing, remove all flowers in the bud stage. Flowers that escape make attractive edible garnishes. To harvest, cut back the growing terminals, leaving one or two pairs of leaves on the main stem to produce new shoots for the next picking. Plants can easily produce numerous harvests throughout the warm parts of the growing season, when they grow rampantly.

Basil plants should be thinned or transplanted 8 to 10 inches apart so that they develop into strong plants.

Basil may be used both as a green leaf and dried for winter. Because basil is extremely sensitive to frost, it must be harvested before the first freeze. Many gardeners cut back a plant or two and put them in containers or pots in the house for winter use.

Basil is one of the most popular seasonings in various ethnic styles of cooking. It is also one of the easiest to grow once its needs are understood. Heat is the key. In the spring, basil seedlings need warm greenhouse conditions to develop well. Temperatures below 50°F cause damage to basil resembling frost injury in other crops. Fortunately, basil plants develop quickly from seed and need not be started very early in the spring to be ready when outdoor conditions are suitable.

For field production, black plastic mulch helps warm the soil and keeps down weeds. Although basil stands some amount of dry soil, trickle irrigation with black plastic works very well. If there is a need for basil early in the season, row covers with some sort of support to keep the cover from damaging the succulent basil plants could be used to advantage. Sweet basil is the generic green-leaved variety available. Other types that find market acceptance include Lettuce-Leaf, Mammoth, Dark Opal, and Cinnamon basil. For ornamental edgings and for garnishing, both Purple Ruffles and Green Ruffles are hard to beat. Spicy Globe is a dependable producer of fine-textured, low-mounded plants that make an ideal low border for beds.

Excess basil production that flowers and produces seed makes a very attractive dried material for everlasting arrangements.

Bay Laurel

Bay laurel or bay tree, *Laurus nobilis,* is a tender perennial tree native to Mediterranean climates. Because it does not tolerate frost, around most of the country it must remain a potted plant that is brought inside for the winter. Mature leaves are harvested and dried for use in cooking or everlasting crafts (such as wreaths and garlands). Leaves may be used fresh, in season. Bay is used in "bouquet garni" with parsley, marjoram, thyme, and a few peppercorns. These herbs act as a unit, imparting a subtle and unusual flavor.

Plants may be started from cuttings or seeds. Because only one or two plants are needed, it may be easier to buy started plants from your favorite herb source. Although cuttings do not root very well, or very fast, seeds germinate poorly and slowly, too.

As long as plants are protected from the cold, they should thrive for years in their pots or tubs. When pruning to shape plants, you can hang whole branches to dry. Single leaves may be tray dried.

Bergamot

Bergamot or bee balm, *Monarda didyma,* is a popular ornamental perennial plant with a range of blossom colors. Bergamot is native to North America, and the leaves have been used to make an infusion called "Oswego tea." The leaves contain thymol. Oil of Bergamot comes not from this plant but from a *Citrus* tree.

In the early spring, plants may be started indoors from seed, in flats for transplanting into the garden when the temperature warms. The choicest ornamental varieties are vegetatively propagated by divisions. Plant 12 to 18 inches apart in rows 3 feet apart, or plant on 18-inch centers in mixed beds or borders. Like their mint relatives, they tend to spread vigorously in the garden from underground stems.

Harvest the foliage and flowers in full bloom and dry quickly. Store in airtight containers. Fresh bergamot may be chopped, mixed with water, frozen in ice cubes, and used as needed. Flowers may be frozen whole by putting them in ice cube trays, gently covering with water, and freezing. Leaves may be made into a tea or used to replace mint leaves as a flavoring.

Borage

Borage, *Borago officinalis,* is a self-sowing annual with thick, coarse stems; large, coarse, hairy leaves; and vivid, sky blue, star-shaped flowers. An occasional plant has pink flowers.

Seed should be sown ½ to 1 inch deep, in midspring when the weather has begun to settle. Thin seedlings to 1 to 2 feet apart. Plant in locations sheltered from the wind, or stake the plants, as the flower stalks are very brittle and easily broken over.

Young leaves have a cucumberlike flavor and are used in salads, drinks, soups, or stews. The colorful blossoms make lovely edible garnishes and can be added to drinks, desserts, and salads or candied for cake decorations.

Caraway

Caraway, *Carum carvi,* is a biennial plant grown for its seeds. Caraway seeds are used in baking and with many vegetables. Caraway is particularly popular for use with cabbage or cole slaw, carrots, cheese, potatoes, and breads. Some cooks crush the seed with oil and onion juice to make a mixture used in roasting pork.

Roots may be used when young and tender. They are prepared like parsnips, then served with butter or white sauce. Young leaves may be used in spring soups or spicy green salads. They also flavor vegetables like spinach or summer squash.

Plant seeds ½ inch apart in the spring in rows 2 feet apart, and thin to 6 to 8 inches apart in the row. Through the first season, the plants grow a rosette of finely cut foliage resembling a carrot and then they die down with freezes during the winter. They regrow in the spring to send up seedstalks (umbels) during the second summer. When the seeds begin to turn from green to brown, cut them from the plant before they shatter. A few plants usually produce enough seed for a family. Bag dry the umbels thoroughly, either in the shade or sun, and separate the seed by rubbing the heads over screens or papers. When the seed has become thoroughly dry, place in sealed containers for storage.

Where winters are mild, caraway may be sown in autumn as well (grown as a winter annual). A limited number of sources now offer an annual variety that bolts to seed the same year it is planted.

Catnip

Catnip, *Nepeta cataria,* is a coarse-leaved, gray-green, hardy perennial with square stems. Soft white fuzz covers the stems and leaves. Catnip was brought to America as a cash crop by early European settlers and has escaped to become naturalized over most of North America. It is found almost universally around old farmsteads.

Plants may be started in flats in late winter, indoors or in the greenhouse, to be transplanted into the garden. Mature plants may be increased by division of the clumps or by stem-tip cuttings in the early season. Protect newly set plants from possible cat attacks, which can quickly ruin small plants.

Best fragrance requires abundant sunlight, though some shade can be tolerated. Gather leaves and stem tips in summer when the plant is in full bloom. Dry carefully and quickly, then strip the leaves from the tough stalks. Store in closed containers. For tea, steep in hot water a little more dried leaf than you would use of regular tea. Steep covered, as the flavor and aroma are very volatile. Dried leaves may be used to stuff cat toys, which are very popular with cats and cat lovers.

Celery

Celery, *Apium graveolens* (see "Celery," page 66).

Chamomile

Chamomile, the famous tea herb, is actually two different plants possessing the same flavor. One plant is a tall, erect annual reaching 2 to 3 feet in height, *Matricaria recutita,* commonly known as german chamomile. The other, *Chamaemelum nobile (Anthemis nobilis),* roman chamomile, is a low-growing (3- to 6-inch) perennial. Both have daisylike flowers, feathery foliage, and a sweet applelike fragrance and flavor. Chamomile in Greek means "ground apple."

Either type can be started from seeds, though it is easier to propagate roman (perennial) chamomile from offshoots or divisions. Sow tiny seeds in spring. For the german (annual) chamomile, seeds should be sown in fall or early spring. Freezing and thawing seem to enhance germination. Once established, chamomile usually reseeds if a few blossoms are allowed to mature and shatter seed. Both types like well-drained soil and sunny locations.

Harvest the blossoms for drying when the petals begin to curve back from the disk florets. Separate the flowers from the stems, as the stems have a bitter off-flavor that spoils the flavor of the sweet blossom. Tray dry the flowers and store in closed containers. Steep in hot water for traditional chamomile tea.

Chervil

Chervil, *Anthriscus cerefolium,* is a hardy annual plant of the Umbelliferae family. Like parsley, there are curled- and plain-leaf types. The flavor of both is between anise and parsley—a warm, subtle taste in the background. The delicate fernlike leaves are borne in a basal rosette, before it bolts up to flower and set seed. Both leaves and stems are used in cooking, and whole sprigs are used as a garnish. Chervil accompanies parsley, thyme, and tarragon in the "fines herbes" of French cooking, which are added at the last minute to soups, stews, and sautes. Lengthy cooking makes chervil bitter.

As chervil transplants poorly, direct seeding is best. It prefers light to germinate. Sow in a trench without soil covering, and mist regularly to keep moist or cover the row with cheesecloth or other porous cover to keep seeds moist until they germinate. When seedlings are 2 inches tall, thin to 6 to 12 inches apart. Sow successive plantings to assure a continuous supply, as they quickly bolt to seed, especially in hot weather. Seeds may be sown in late fall to germinate the following spring. Harvest leaves when they are fully expanded but still tender.

Chives

Chives, *Allium schoenoprasum,* is a perennial plant belonging to the onion family. It is grown throughout most of North America. The small, bulbous plants grow in clumps 8 to 12 inches tall. The attractive violet-colored flowers appear in May.

The plants are usually propagated by dividing the clumps, keeping four to six bulblets per clump. They are planted in the same manner as onion transplants (see page 91). They can be divided in the fall or early spring. It is necessary to divide clumps every 2 to 3 years to prevent overcrowding. Chives may also be started from seed planted in the early spring. Seedings vary in height, thickness of the leaves, and number of leaves per plant. If extremely uniform plants are needed, selections for type can be made when old plantings are divided after 2 to 3 years. Single clumps of the plants can be separated into individual plants and then form identical clumps of their own.

The tender leaves and the stem may be harvested whenever desired during the season. Chives are normally harvested by snipping off the amount of leaves you need, then chopping them into or onto whatever dish is being prepared. The flavor is similar to onion but more subtle. The bulbs are not used. Some gardeners dry the leaves; others chop them fresh and freeze them for winter use. Many gardeners dig a clump of chives in late January, place them in a pot, and bring them in the house for fresh use during the winter.

Chives are used with many foods and frequently blended with other herbs to make excellent combinations for salads and omelets. The green leaves add a delicate onionlike flavor to soups, salads, and sauces. The flowers should be removed to ensure greater growth of the green edible portion. The flower heads are very popular edible garnishes on dishes that have the chopped leaves as an ingredient. Chives are a pretty, dependable perennial that needs division only every 2 to 4 years to keep growth vigorous.

Garlic chives, *Allium tuberosum,* is another member of the onion family that has flat leaves like leek and garlic.

The flavor is very much like garlic, and the tops are harvested like the regular chives. Garlic chive has white flowers and grows taller than regular chives. Flower heads are edible. Remove seedheads before they mature to prevent excessive production of weedy seedlings.

Cilantro and Coriander

Cilantro and coriander, *Coriandrum sativum,* are two products derived from different stages of the same plant. In fact, coriander is generally considered a spice and cilantro an herb. Cilantro is the green rosette of foliage that forms when the plants are immature. When a combination of day length and temperature reaches a certain level, the plant is induced to flower. Coriander is the seed that forms when plants are allowed to flower and mature.

Both Asian and Latin cuisines use large quantities of cilantro, which is called either chinese or mexican parsley, depending on who is using the cilantro. Mexican salsa is the number-one use of cilantro in the United States today.

With some varieties, bolting can be a problem, especially in summer. Other varieties, like Long-Standing and Santos, have been selected to hold longer without bolting. These types may give an extra week or two of leafy production before the inevitable flowering. Successive plantings are necessary to maintain a supply of cilantro. Even then, in the heat of summer it may be difficult to keep it picked before flowering starts. Cilantro plantings that get away and flower then can be harvested as coriander seed. Resume planting in late summer for abundant crops in the cooler, shorter days of fall.

By contrast, if you want coriander seed, then a variety that quickly bolts is desired. Coriander is an annual plant that is found in all parts of the world. It has long been cultivated for the flavor and odor of its dried seeds.

The seeds should be planted in early spring in rows 20 to 30 inches apart. Plant one seed every inch, and do not thin. Whole cilantro rosettes should be harvested by cutting at the base when the plants have made abundant leaf growth, but before seedstalks appear. Leaves may be harvested from the plants even after seedstalk formation begins. The flowers are borne in flat umbels resembling queen anne's lace (wild carrot).

For coriander, the seed heads should be cut when they are starting to turn brown and before shattering of the seed begins (about 90 days from planting). Another method is to harvest the entire plant when most of the seeds are mature, and tie the plants in bundles or spread them on screens to dry. As soon as the plants are dry, separate the fruit by rubbing the plants together. Clean the fruit by winnowing in a light breeze before storing it in containers. Cleaning is necessary to ensure the pleasing flavor of the coriander fruit because both the foliage and green seed may have an off-taste.

The seeds are used in desserts (particularly cookies) in dressings, with meat dishes, and in combination with many other spices and herbs.

Dill

Dill, *Anethum graveolens,* is a common herb that has become very much associated with cucumber pickles. The plant is a tall-growing, self-reseeding annual with feathery leaves and open, umbrella-shaped seedheads. The plants are similar to wild carrot in appearance. Dill is easily grown from seed. It can usually grow in all types of soil; but it prefers well-drained, fertile conditions. To prevent dill from becoming a weed in your garden, remove the heads before the seed shatters so that the plants do not reseed.

After the seeds have germinated and the seedlings have established themselves (1 to 2 inches tall), thin them to 6 to 9 inches apart. The ultimate height of the plants should be 3 to 3½ feet.

The method of harvesting depends upon how you intend to use the herb—as dill weed, flower heads, or seed. The most common use is in pickles, for which the flower heads are preferred. Cut the stems with the flowers in full bloom. Tie the stems in bunches and dry in the open or bag dry as described on page 163. For seed, allow the flowers to mature (usually 2 to 3 weeks after the blossoms appear), then cut and tie the plants. Hang the plants in bunches with papers spread beneath them to collect the seed.

"Dill weed," the immature rosette of foliage that grows before the plant bolts to seed, is at its best when used fresh from the garden. The flavor of the foliage is similar to the seed, but more subtle and more useful for cooking. Successive plantings are the only way to keep dill weed available through the season. A recently introduced variety, Fernleaf, keeps producing bushy side shoots through the season and is an especially good variety for home gardeners who want a steady but not overwhelming supply. For out-of-season use, dill weed may be prepared by bag drying or tray drying the young plant foliage before the flower heads appear. After drying, remove the stems, and place the foliage in a container that is stored in the dark. Many gardeners dry the self-seeded dill that appears in their gardens in the fall. It normally winterkills anyway and makes the dill weed of the highest quality. Dill weed is used as a fine herb in salads, omelets, and herb blends.

Fennel

Fennel, *Foeniculum vulgare,* is a licorice- or anise-flavored annual with leaves resembling dill; it usually is one of two distinct types. The first grows tall and stemmy and produces seeds, and the other forms a flattened rosette of thickened petioles (often referred to as a "bulb") and is called finocchio or florence fennel. This second type is becoming more common on vegetable markets, and once in a great while it can be found in upscale restaurants, where its mild sweet flavor is a real treat steamed. The aniselike flavor of fennel is used widely with fish. Fennel seeds are the ingredient that gives italian sausage its characteristic taste. Fennel seed is also said to act as an appetite suppressant when chewed, though sources differ on this point. The bulbing type may bolt to seed in the heat of summer without forming acceptable rosettes. A red- or bronze-leaved form is also available.

Fennel is grown from seed, which germinates easily. Seedlings do not transplant well because they have a taproot, but they transplant acceptably if started in cell packs or peat pellets so that the roots can be moved undisturbed. Seeds may be sown outdoors as soon as frost danger is past. Thin seedlings to stand 8 to 10 inches apart as soon as they are well established. Bulbs of florence fennel should be covered with soil, when they are as large as a good-sized egg, to blanch them. Harvest the bulbs, tie the tops, and hang them in a dry, cool place. They store acceptably in this manner for a limited time.

When hot summer days come too soon after the last frost, seedlings started ahead of time may be the only way to get good bulbs to form on finocchio before the plants bolt to seed. Again in late summer, seedlings may be set out to mature in cool fall weather. Fennel grown for seed may be seeded directly and allowed to bolt,

flower, and set seed. Plants should be staked, as they rapidly become top-heavy. Plants in flower grow 3 to 5 feet tall, with thick, hollow stems, and fine, feathery foliage. Golden yellow flowers appear in flat-topped clusters (umbels) atop the plants. Harvest seed when it begins to turn brown. Stems and leaves may be harvested as needed throughout the season, whenever they are green, succulent, and the proper size. If seed is desired, do not harvest the entire plant when it is small. Like dill, if seeds are allowed to shatter from mature plants, they reseed themselves plentifully.

Garlic

Garlic, *Allium sativum,* a member of the onion family, may be grown successfully throughout the temperate United States in home gardens. Garlic is started by planting small cloves that are divisions of the large bulb. Each bulb may contain a dozen or more cloves, depending on variety; each clove is planted separately. The larger the clove, the larger the size of the mature bulb at harvest. Do not divide the bulb until you are ready to plant—early separation of the cloves results in decreased yields. Select "seed bulbs" that are large, smooth, fresh, and free of disease.

Garlic is a member of the onion family that is commonly sold as a vegetable, though its use is more like an herb. Its health benefits are becoming so well-known that it might as well be considered here as an herb. Garlic is used both cooked and raw in a wide variety of dishes.

Although garlic is a perennial, it needs annual division and replanting to produce the bulbs that are common on the market. Several types are available, both with and without topsets. Elephant garlic is not really a garlic at all, but a type of leek that forms a pungent bulb that tastes like and resembles the garlic bulb.

Garlic grows best on friable loam soils that are fertile and high in organic matter. Gardeners that grow good onion crops can grow good garlic. Garlic does well at high fertility levels. Apply 3 pounds of 10-10-10 fertilizer per 100 square feet. The bulb is small if the soil is excessively dry, and it is irregular in shape if the soil becomes compacted.

Throughout all but the hottest and coldest areas of the country, fall planting is preferable. Dry bulbs are normally divided into cloves and planted in the fall. Plants root and begin to sprout before cold weather. Planting should be late enough to allow roots to develop well and top growth to begin before the soil freezes. In most areas, this planting date is sometime in October. In the first thaw of spring, the plants are off and growing luxuriantly.

If planting must be delayed until spring, garlic should be planted very early (March or April) to permit full development. Fall preparation of the soil is desirable so that the soil can be fertilized and planted with minimal tillage whenever it first can be worked. Plant the cloves 3 to 5 inches apart in an upright position (with points up) to assure a straight neck, and cover them to a depth of 1 to 2 inches. Allow 18 to 30 inches between rows, or plant 5 inches apart in all directions on raised beds.

Bulbing occurs in June, and bulbs can be dug when the tops start to yellow, usually in July or August. Tops normally cannot be allowed to dry completely in the field because the unpredictable moisture in the soil may begin to rot the delicate papery wrapper scales. Do not wait until all leaves have browned, but harvest when about five green leaves remain: This assures good wrappers on the dried bulbs. Place the bulbs on trays with screens or slatted bottoms, and remove the tops when dry. Bulbs can be braided or bunched with twine and hung in a dry, dark, airy place to complete drying. The mature bulbs are best stored under cool, dry conditions. They then usually keep for months.

An interesting recent development is the culture of garlic in the form of scallions. Topsets or small cloves are planted fairly thickly in a row and the green plants dug, cleaned, and bunched like green onions. The whole plant, tops and all, is then chopped into dishes for flavor.

Geranium, Scented

Scented geraniums are actually *Pelargonium* species selected for their flavors and fragrances, which mimic a wide variety of other plants. Flowers are often secondary to the scent and shape of the foliage, but some types have colorful and attractive inflorescenses. The pungent, spicy foliage is used for potpourri, perfumes, or sachets. As a flavoring, some are used in desserts, punch, vinegar, and tea. Leaves may be used fresh when they reach full size or may be harvested, tray dried, and stored in sealed containers until needed.

Pelargoniums are very tender perennials (Zone 10) and must be grown as house plants throughout winter in most of the United States. They are normally propagated from stem-tip cuttings, which root fairly readily for most types. Some of the flowering types actually come rather true from seed. Plant outside in containers or in ground beds only after all danger of frost has passed. Harvest leaves as needed. Some of the most popular types include lemon-, rose-, apple-, and peppermint-scented. If you become bitten by the novelty bug, there are hundreds of types available.

Horehound

Horehound, *Marrubium vulgare,* is a hardy, bushy perennial with woolly leaves and stems, growing up to 2 feet tall. The best-known use of this herb is as a soothing agent for sore throats, usually in the form of candies, cough drops, and syrups. It also makes an attractive ornamental plant in the garden.

Sow seeds $1/2$ inch deep in light, sandy soil. Thin seedlings to stand 1 foot apart, or plant flat-started seedlings at 1-foot spacing. Horehound also may be divided to produce new plants. Unless you remove seed heads before seed is shed, horehound can become a weed in the garden.

Harvest by cutting one-third of the top growth, removing the leaves, and quickly tray drying. Because horehound loses flavor quickly, drying should be fast and the dried product stored in airtight containers. In the second year, for the highest flavor, harvest as plants are just budding to flower.

Horseradish

Horseradish, *Armoracia rusticana,* is an herb commonly grown as a vegetable. (See page 139).

Hyssop

Hyssop, *Hyssopus officinalis,* is a compact, fine-textured, perennial plant with a strong, slightly medicinal smell. Plants make a nice edging for beds, especially if kept sheared to about 6 inches. Hyssop makes a good flower show between June and August.

Leaves and flowers are used to flavor salads, soup, liqueurs, stews, and stuffings (with sage). Hyssop also can be dried for tea. Oil of hyssop is occasionally used in perfumery.

Hyssop starts fairly easily from seeds, cuttings, or division. Divide mature plants in spring or fall, when plants are fairly dormant. Cuttings should be taken from young, actively growing stem tips. Seeds should be sown in early spring, ¼ inch deep in rows 1 to 2 feet apart. Thin to stand 1 foot apart. The quality of mature plants tends to decline after 4 or 5 years; they should be severely divided for rejuvenation or be replaced.

Lavender

Lavender, *Lavendula species,* is a very highly perfumed plant. Both the flowers and foliage have been used in sachets, potpourri, and perfumes. Lavender is sometimes used culinarily to flavor cakes, icings, and vinegars.

There are several species and cultivars of lavender. Some of these, mostly English types, are hardy, with protection, into Zone 5 gardens. Some of the others are much more tender and may not survive much beyond Zone 7. In northern locations, plants may require being planted pot and all in the summer garden and then being brought back indoors each winter.

Many types do not flower well until at least the second year. A new seed-propagated variety called Lavender Lady apparently flowers abundantly from seeds sown in late winter and set out as transplants in late spring.

While all species of lavender can be propagated by seed, most of the choice varieties are selections that must be maintained by asexual reproduction. Munstead and Hidcote, as well as Lavender Lady, are all fairly hardy varieties to try.

Lavender does not tolerate damp or shady conditions in the garden. Give it good drainage and full sun. Harvest flower heads before the last flowers open. The aromatic oil content is highest at this time.

Lemon Balm

Lemon balm, *Melissa officinalis,* is a loosely branched, upright perennial that is a member of the mint family. The aroma and flavor are strongly like lemon, with a subtle undertone of mint. In the garden, bees literally cover the blossoms of lemon balm. Dried, it is used to prepare a mild, lemony tea. It can also be used in salads, vegetables, and fish dishes. The essential oils reputedly possess some bacteriocidal quality. If you rub fresh lemon balm on wood surfaces, the wax polishes the wood and the lemony scent perfumes it.

Lemon balm germinates easily from seeds, provided the seeds are not covered, but exposed to light. Keep them moist until they sprout. It also propagates easily from division or stem-tip cuttings. Space plants 2 feet apart. They appreciate full sun but tolerate some shade. They are less likely to become invasive and weedy if they are held back by some shade.

For peak flavor, harvest before flowering. Balm may be used fresh (chopped and frozen into ice cubes) or dried for winter use. For tea, stems can be included in the dried product. After the first year, three or more harvests may be made annually, cutting 2 to 3 inches above ground level. Plants harvested this heavily may need a fertility boost at least once a year. Dry quickly and store in airtight containers.

Lemon Verbena

Lemon verbena, *Aloysia triphylla,* is a tender, deciduous woody tree, hardy outdoors only into Zone 9. It is most commonly grown in pots or tubs and moved into greenhouses or light rooms for the winter. All parts have the distinctive lemony fragrance. The long leaves are narrow and pointed. Although lemon verbena may be started from seed, few plants are produced that way. Cuttings taken in midsummer root fairly readily. Because the mother plant may wilt after cuttings are taken, pamper it with adequate water and a bit of shade until it recovers.

Harvest leaves and tips as needed. Because the plant is a fairly fast grower, making one heavy harvest at midsummer and another in the fall before returning it indoors helps to keep the plant in bounds. The plant is a fairly heavy feeder and should be fertilized regularly. Keep the soil moist, but never allow the roots to remain soggy. Place pots of lemon verbena on stone surfaces to keep them from rooting into the ground over the summer. Breaking these roots might severely affect the health of the plant.

Lemon verbena is used as a lemony tea, to flavor other beverages, and in any dish that calls for a lemon flavor. Fresh leaves are tough, so strain them from beverages, marinades, and dressings before serving. For an unexpected touch, add finely crushed dried leaves to banana, zucchini, or carrot breads or to cooked rice.

Lovage

Lovage, *Levisticum officinale,* is a perennial herb that resembles both celery and angelica. Hardy throughout North America, it grows to 4 to 5 feet in height. Yellow florets are borne in umbels. Lovage has a long history of medicinal use. Not as widely grown as in past years, lovage has been staging a minicomeback. It tastes like celery but with an extra-peppery bite, which makes it a good addition to health-conscious cooking. Leaves should be chopped finely as they are a bit tough. Stems are hollow and may be used as "straws" in drinks like tomato juice or bloody marys.

Plants are usually grown from fresh seed sown either in the fall or early spring. Thin or transplant seedlings at least 1½ to 2 feet apart. Lovage likes rich, moist soil and some shade and makes a good background plant in mass plantings. Harvest leaves and stems anytime desired. Seeds should be harvested by picking whole heads as they start to brown but before they shatter. Dry, rub the seeds free, then separate them from stems and chaff. Store in closed containers. Stems may be candied like angelica. Roots may be dug, washed, and stored until needed. Leaves may be dried and stored for making tea.

Mint

Mint, *Mentha* species, comes in a wide range of varieties. The most common are spearmint and peppermint. Spearmint is used principally for flavoring iced tea, other beverages, and chewing gum; peppermint is used in medicines, candy, and gum.

Mint is propagated from roots, rooted cuttings, or entire plants. Because plants produce spreading lateral stems, mint is an invasive plant that should be planted in enclosed areas or where its spread can be controlled. If mint is not contained, the underground stems spread rapidly and become a garden weed. A large tile or chimney flue set on end may be used for individual mint plants to contain their growth. Half barrels may also be used to advantage.

In most of the United States, mint lives as a perennial. Because mint thrives under continuously moist conditions, to ensure high-quality production, you should mulch the area. In the late fall, commercial mint growers turn the top 6 inches of soil (which contain the rhizomes or underground stems) to form a soil mulch. This practice also is recommended for home gardeners where it is practical.

No special care is necessary for mint, other than removing the weeds, keeping the soil moist, and making sure it does not invade nearby areas. Because the plants grow rapidly in the spring, the leaves are available for use throughout the growing season, with best-quality foliage in July and August, when essential oils in the leaves peak.

Many gardeners harvest their mint when the flower buds first appear. Dry the mint thoroughly, remove the leaves, and store them in a sealed container. Commercial mint is grown for the plant oil, which is removed by a distilling process that is not practicable for the home gardener.

Some gardeners are especially interested in various flavors of mint, such as peppermint, spearmint, orange mint, apple mint, curly mint, and a host of other types. All are popular in teas and for flavoring. All mints are propagated and grown in much the same way. The vigor and hardiness varies, but most mints prosper in American gardens.

While many mints can be started from seed, the best and truest flavors come from vegetatively propagated plants. Peppermint, however, is a sterile hybrid, so beware "peppermint" seed. Care should be taken to get propagating material from sources clean of *Verticillium*, the number-one disease pest of mints. Mints tolerate some slight shade.

Oregano

True greek oregano, *Origanum heracleoticum*, is a hardy perennial that survives outdoors, at least into the mild areas of Zone 5. If hardiness is in doubt, use a generous application of mulch in November or December, and uncover the plants in April.

The oregano seeds commonly sold (*Origanum vulgare*) produce plants that are useless in the kitchen. They form rank, rather tasteless plants that produce purplish pink flower heads, which are attractive in dried arrangements and in the garden but are culinary disasters. True greek oregano seeds can be obtained, but care must be exercised because the common variety is sometimes sold as "greek." Even given the right strain, there is variability between plants sufficient to make it necessary to propagate the most desirable plants by stem-tip cuttings, root cuttings, or crown divisions. Unfortunately, the poor-quality oregano is more dependably hardy than the really tasty one. As with other herbs, cutting to slow or reduce flowering keeps production moving through the season.

Harvest of oregano is handled the same as harvest of sweet marjoram, a close relative. Oregano dries easily when cut and hung as described for other herbs (see pages 163). The leaves are dried, removed from the stems, and placed in a closed container until needed. The dried leaves are used in many Spanish, Italian, and Mexican dishes, as well as in stuffings for fish and game.

Parsley

Parsley, *Petroselium crispum,* is an herb commonly grown as a vegetable. (See page 93).

Rosemary

Rosemary, *Rosmarinus officinalis,* is a small, tender, perennial, evergreen shrub that is not winter hardy much beyond mild Zone 6 areas. Some gardeners mulch the rosemary plant, protect it with rose cones, or use a combination of rose cones and mulch during the winter months. In areas where it is dependably hardy, rosemary grows into an impressive shrub, hedge, or trailing ground cover.

The narrow leaves have a spicy odor, making rosemary valuable for flavoring and as a scenting agent. Rosemary is used sparingly, as an accent in numerous dishes. The flavor is vaguely pinelike. There are various types, from upright to prostrate, with flower colors from the standard blue to white or pink. The varieties Arp and Hill's Hardy are more winter hardy than standard varieties.

The plants propagate fairly easily from stem-tip cuttings and make very acceptable plants in one season. Starter rosemary plants may be purchased from greenhouses, garden centers, or mail-order herb nurseries. Some gardeners pot a rosemary plant from the garden in the fall and bring it into the house for use over the winter and stem propagation in the spring. If the plants can be overwintered in a bright house or greenhouse, they quickly grow into magnificent specimens that flower more profusely. Some varieties of rosemary can be started from seed in a cold frame or indoors.

When transplanting rosemary to the garden in the spring, allow 1 foot or more between plants so that the individual plants maintain their beauty. The growth can be pruned back several times during the season for drying. When the stems are thoroughly dry, strip the leaves and store them in closed containers.

Fresh or dried leaves are used sparingly—as an accent in soups, leafy greens, poultry, stews, and sauces. One of the fine herbs, rosemary also may be added without cooking as an excellent ingredient in mixed herbs.

Rue

Rue, *Ruta graveolens,* is a semi-evergreen perennial nonwoody plant that grows to 3 feet in height. The blue-green foliage and bright yellow flowers, which appear from summer through fall, make it an attractive plant. Its upright, uniform habit makes it a good hedge for herb gardens. It can be eaten in small amounts, though it has a somewhat bitter taste. Overexposure to rue can cause redness, swelling, and even blistering of the skin in some people, almost like poison ivy. After ingesting rue, a person may find the skin more sensitive to sunlight.

Rue may be started from seeds, cuttings, or divisions. Start seeds in late winter in flats for transplanting to the garden in late spring. Seedlings prefer full sun and well-drained soil. Space them about 18 inches apart. Plants can be grown in pots, either indoors or on the patio. Rue can be harvested several times each season. After harvest, feed the plants to stimulate regrowth. Harvest seed pods when they are dry but before they open. Prune back to healthy buds in the spring.

Sage

Sage, *Salvia officinalis* (and other species), is a shrubby perennial plant of the mint family. It is one of the most widely cultivated herbs. Plants may grow to a height of 18 inches and begin to bloom the second season. Common garden sage is the one perennial herb that comes readily from large, easy-to-handle seeds and produces a very acceptable herb product. The flavor so associated with poultry stuffings has other uses as well.

Once established, the plants live a long time, needing only an annual spring pruning and regular harvesting. Sage makes beautiful flowers, which can be of use in the landscape. For best herb production, however, severe spring pruning discourages most flower production, which occurs at the expense of vigorous vegetative growth.

Plants may be propagated from seeds, stem cuttings, or crown divisions. Seeds can be planted in cold frames, in window boxes, or inside the house. Transplant the young seedlings when they are 2 to 3 inches tall. Space seedlings 15 to 18 inches apart so that they become large, attractive plants.

Harvest can begin when leaves begin to mature in late spring and can continue into the fall. Cut 6 to 8 inches of top growth from the plants at least twice during the growing season. After drying these stem tips, strip the leaves from them and place in closed containers for winter storage. Many herb growers use the bag-drying method (see page 163) and do not remove the sage until they are ready to use it. Plants should not be cut back too severely in late fall, as this weakens their winter-survival ability.

Use the leaves sparingly with onion for stuffing pork, turkey, duck, or goose. Rubbing the powdered leaves on the outside of fresh pork, ham, and loin results in a flavor resembling that of stuffed turkey. Some people steep the dried leaves for tea.

Sage makes attractive silvery gray plants that can be fairly easily worked into landscapes. There are also several varieties of vegetatively propagated sages available. Tricolor is striped green, red, and white. Golden has green leaves edged in attractive yellow. Purple has leaves with an overall purple glow. None of these colored varieties is as hardy as the common green sort, unfortunately, but they survive most Zone 5b winters.

Salad Burnet

Salad burnet, *Poterium sanguisorba,* is a very hardy, bushy, perennial herb. The 12-inch tall, loose clump of compound leaves arching outward resembles a fern. The flowers are small and pinkish, borne in rounded heads. Seeds should be removed to encourage continued leafy regrowth through the season. Left to mature, they freely reseed and possibly become weedy.

Leaves taste and smell like cucumber and are used in salads, salad dressings, drinks, sandwiches, and a variety of other dishes. Once very popular, burnet is considerably tastier than some of today's trendier greens. Use only new tender leaves, as older ones become a bit bitter.

Plants may be divided in spring before growth begins. If seeds are left to mature, burnet readily reseeds itself. Sow seeds in late fall or early spring, and thin to 12 to 15 inches apart. Plants like full sun and slightly alkaline (high-pH) soils. Once established, the plants need little attention.

Savory, Summer

Summer savory, *Satureja hortensis,* is an annual plant belonging to the mint family. It is well-adapted throughout most of the country and grows under a wide range of climatic conditions but prefers a dry, fertile loam. Not well-known, summer savory is a very tasty and adaptable herb. There is also a winter, perennial type of savory, hardy into Zone 5. The flavor of the summer variety usually is thought to be better.

Summer savory is easily grown from seeds in the spring. The seeds may be started in a cold frame or seeded directly in the row. Plants grow quickly from seed but have some tendency to become leggy when grown in flats. This tendency usually corrects itself if the plants are kept in flats for as short a time as possible. In the garden, seeds should be planted ¼ to ½ inch deep, with 10 to 12 seeds per foot. The seedlings should be thinned to 6 inches apart. The plants grow to a height of 12 to 15 inches and require little cultivation other than weeding.

The tender leaves and stems may be used anytime during the growing season. The plants may be cut when blooming begins and are usually dried when the top growth is 6 to 8 inches tall. Two, three, or more crops may be harvested if enough of the plant is left to regrow after cutting. Two or three nodes left on the plant should be sufficient to permit regrowth. In fact, the plant keeps producing through the season if tips are continually harvested to keep it from flowering. Once full flowering starts, the plant most likely matures and dies.

The cut top growth may be tied into small bundles and hung or spread on papers or screens to dry in a fairly dark, well-ventilated place. When the cut herb is thoroughly dry, strip the leaves from the stems and store them in a closed container. Woody stem pieces, which interfere with the flavoring of foods, should be removed and discarded.

Summer savory is a fine herb and may be used both fresh and cooked. It is excellent in herb blends. Fresh or dried summer savory leaves may be added to the water for cooking green beans or used in soups, stuffings, sauces, and many egg dishes, and with veal and poultry. Like parsley, it mixes well with other herbs and spices, and it probably should be used more often. Along with parsley, summer savory is considered one of the mixer herbs, which help blend various flavors.

Savory, Winter

Winter savory, *Satureja montana,* is a short-lived perennial, semi-evergreen plant, forming a fine-textured, compact bush 6 to 12 inches tall and 12 to 24 inches across. The plant is dependably hardy in Zone 5b, or farther north where winter snow cover is adequate. Excess winter moisture leads to premature death of this herb, so plant where good drainage can be provided. Even under ideal conditions, plants should be divided every 2 or 3 years. Replant vigorous, healthy outer portions of the clumps, and discard the woody middles.

Seeds of winter savory germinate more slowly than summer savory and should be started in flats indoors or in a greenhouse and transplanted into the garden. Established plants may be propagated by division or by stem-tip cuttings, which root fairly easily.

The plants may be sheared to form low, mounded edgings for planting beds. Cutting back overwintered plants heavily in the spring before new growth begins reinvigorates the plants and helps to keep them in bounds, as older clumps keep expanding if left unchecked. There is a low, creeping form of the plant that can be used as a ground cover or hanging-basket herb.

Summer savory has a sweet, peppery flavor, while winter savory has a stronger, piney flavor. Although the summer variety has the more popular flavor, winter savory is often used with stronger-flavored game meats. Winter savory has the advantage of staying green and usuable well into the fall, or even beyond, in milder climates and and greening again early in the spring, giving a much longer fresh-harvest season than the front-tender summer variety.

Sorrel, French

French sorrel, *Rumex scutatus,* is a perennial with shield-shaped leaf blades on long sturdy petioles that grow in a rosette from a large taproot, which reaches 1½ to 2 feet in length. Seedstalks arise that greatly resemble the related wild dock species. In the garden, it is grown for the leaves, which have an acidic, "lemony" flavor. Classic use is in a french sorrel soup. It is also eaten raw in salads or cooked like spinach. Also like spinach, the leaves contain oxalic acid, which can aggravate gout, kidney stones, and arthritis. Leaves should be used sparingly if oxalic acid in the diet is a problem for individuals. Use sorrel to spice up other dishes rather than as the main item.

Seed may be started in flats or sown in the garden as soon as soil can be worked in the spring. Plant 1 inch deep, and thin or transplant seedlings to 1 foot apart in full sun in fairly rich soil. Cut back seedstalks to keep plants producing fresh greens. Divide every 3 to 4 years. A nonseeding variety, Profusion, is available (plants only) that produces no seedstalks, only leaves, not wasting any energy on flowering and seed production.

Sweet Cicely

Sweet cicely, *Myrrhis odorata,* is a hardy perennial of the Umbelliferae family, growing to 3 feet in height. The taste is a combination of anise and lovage. The leaves are triply compound, with deeply toothed leaflets borne in basal rosettes resembling ferns. Flowers are 2-inch white umbels followed by shiny, dark brown, sharply ridged seeds that grow as long as 1 inch and have a spicy, anise-like flavor. The leaves are used fresh as garnishes and in salads, anywhere sweetness is needed. The roots are steamed and used like parsnip. The seeds are used like anise or caraway seed in candy, syrup, cakes, and liqueurs.

Buying started plants or moving self-sown plants seems to work best as a source of sweet cicely. Seeds require a complicated and poorly understood series of stratifications to germinate. Use fresh seed, and sow in the fall in a well-marked row to let natural freezing and thawing help germinate the seeds. Space plants 12 to 18 inches apart in the garden. Leaves may be harvested whenever they are young and fresh, seeds as they ripen. Other than the seeds, sweet cicely is seldom dried.

Sweet Marjoram

Sweet marjoram, *Origanum majorana,* is an example of how common names within the oregano-marjoram group sometimes become confusing. Although sweet marjoram is a tender perennial, it frequently winterkills in much of the United States and is usually cultivated as an annual. Planting in favorable locations, mulching, and using other forms of protection make overwintering possible in areas with mild winters.

Sweet marjoram may be started from seed, by cuttings with the aid of a rooting hormone, or by division of crowns. It grows easily from seed, though the seed and seedlings are fairly fine. Care should be taken to thin the seedlings while they are small. Once established, sweet marjoram is a hardy little plant. Transplant to a permanent location in the spring when plants are 2 to 3 inches tall and the weather has dependably warmed. They respond best to rich, moist soil and full sunlight. Space the plants 6 to 8 inches apart. The plant may be dug up in the fall to overwinter as a houseplant and be redivided for use the following spring where winters are harsh, or marjoram can be allowed to overwinter outdoors in areas where it is hardy.

Like so many of the other herbs, marjoram should be harvested regularly to keep flowering and seeding to a minimum. As soon as the first blooms appear, cut back the plants several inches. The plants can be cut back three or more times each season. The leaves and flower tops should be dried rapidly, the stems removed, and the clean, dry leaves stored for winter. Fresh leaves, of course, may be used whenever available.

The flavor of sweet marjoram is especially good with veal and liver, in herb butter, on cold roast beef sandwiches, in egg and meat dishes, and in poultry stuffings and soups. It also adds flavor to potato salad, creamed potatoes, and green beans. Chopped sweet marjoram leaves in melted butter may be added to cooked spinach before serving. If there is a sweet, almost perfumelike tastiness to a dish, sweet marjoram is often the mystery ingredient.

Sweet Woodruff

Sweet woodruff, *Galium odoratum (Asperula odorata)*, is a hardy, low-growing perennial ground cover plant that thrives best in moist, shaded, woodsy settings. Thin, lance-shaped leaves grow in whorls around the stem. Clusters of white, star-shaped flowers appear at the stem tips in early summer. Sweet woodruff has traditionally been crushed and used to flavor May wine in Germany. Oddly, the foliage displays its sweet odor only when crushed or dried.

The genus name may be either *Galium* or *Asperula*, depending on which school of botanical thought one follows These genera are so closely related that this is probably of concern only to plant biologists, not gardeners. Like sweet cicely, seeds require freezing and thawing to germinate, a process that may take 200 days. If plants are once started, they obediently self-sow future generations for an adequate supply in subsequent years. Cuttings or divisions are also good propagation techniques for sweet woodruff. In favorable locations, the plant may become weedy and invasive.

The sweet, haylike aroma is developed by cutting and drying the herb. Foliage may be harvested as needed by cutting near the base. Either tie and air dry, or chop and tray dry. Store in closed containers. Overconsumption of sweet woodruff may have serious side effects, so use it in moderation.

Tarragon

French tarragon, *Artemisia dracunculus,* is the queen of all herbs. Most famous in French cuisine, in fact, it is used throughout the world for its licoricelike flavor with a mild bite. It is often used to negate the "fishy" character of seafood dishes. French tarragon does not form viable seeds, rarely even blooming in temperate regions. Seeds of "tarragon" are always a disappointment, as they produce rank, tasteless plants of russian tarragon. Due to the widespread use of french tarragon and its relatively difficult propagation, it always sells at a premium.

Plants can be divided or stem-tip cuttings rooted to form new plants. The plant forms numerous rhizomes in the fall, which can be separated and used to create an abundance of new plants the next spring. Tarragon is a vigorous perennial plant. French tarragon plants or crown divisions are usually planted 1 foot apart in the row and need to be subdivided every 3 to 4 years.

After a plant has become established, the leaves of the tender top can be harvested throughout the growing season and used fresh. Repeated harvest of this herb over the season keeps the plants branching out, producing new tender shoots. Although it is preferable to use tarragon fresh, some gardeners use it dried, despite the loss of much of its characteristic flavor in the drying process. Some sources describe dried tarragon as "little better than hay." If you are going to preserve tarragon for use in winter, the leaves and tops should be dried rapidly without light and stored in a dark brown, sealed glass jar to prevent rapid deterioration.

Tarragon leaves are used in salads, dressings, vinegars, fish sauces, tartar sauces, and certain egg dishes. They are also blended with other herbs to make an excellent addition to the mixture. Tarragon can easily overpower in a mixture, so blend with caution. Tarragon vinegar can be made by putting a fresh stem or two of washed tarragon in a pint of apple or wine vinegar. Allow a few weeks for the flavor balance to develop.

It is normal for the plants to go into a dormancy in the fall. Potted plants on balconies actually may appear to die. Many of them get thrown out, although they are only resting. Although tarragon is sometimes listed as winter tender, it should withstand –30°F if the crowns are given excellent drainage. What causes winterkill most often are soggy conditions. Once established in the ground, tarragon produces very well, asking only to be divided regularly to avoid overcrowding.

Thyme

Thyme, *Thymus vulgaris* and other *Thymus* species, is a small, low, mound-forming, shrublike perennial that grows to a height of 3 to 10 inches, depending on variety. Common thyme may be used fresh or as a dried herb. There are literally hundreds of varieties of thyme, some culinary, others decorative. For culinary purposes, either french or english is the most agreeable with common recipes. Seed-grown varieties of thyme also may make acceptable plants, but individual seed sources should be evaluated. For the classic varieties, cuttings are preferable, and they root with surprising ease. Several related varieties of thyme are often used as ornamentals in rock gardens and along walks.

Thyme is best propagated from seed started indoors, by dividing clumps, or by making stem cuttings. When the plants are 2 to 3 inches tall, set them 1 foot apart in a row. Most thyme growers start new plants every 3 or 4 years. Old plants should be divided; otherwise, they become excessively woody and do not produce the tender leaves desired in culinary use. Most varieties of thyme survive U.S. winters pretty well, especially with good snow cover. Most spread out and form dense mats that benefit from annual spring mowings to stimulate lush new growth. New plantings should be started every few years to avoid encroachment from perennial weeds. A well-drained, sunny location is essential for growing thyme successfully.

Harvest when the plants begin to bloom, by cutting off 5 to 6 inches of the flowering tops with clippers or a sharp knife. Often two or more crops can be harvested during one season. The plants should be spread on a fine screen or newspaper in a dark, well-ventilated room to dry. After the plants are thoroughly dry, strip the leaves and flowering tops from the stems and store them in a closed container.

The leaves, usually blended with other herbs, may be used in meat dishes, poultry stuffings, gravies, soups, egg dishes, cheese dishes, and clam chowder. Thyme's creeping form makes it a rock garden and edging favorite. In the spring, most varieties have a stunning floral display.

Drying Herbs

The herbs should be gathered at the proper stage of maturity after morning dew has dried from the plants (usually about 10 a.m.). Herbs harvested for drying should be washed only if they are splattered with dirt or otherwise soiled, and then as carefully as possible with clear water only. Clean herb leaves should not be washed, as washing may remove some of the soluble flavor components.

The clean herbs should be dried rapidly in the shade to retain color and flavor. A dark, well-ventilated room such as an attic is ideal if it is not too hot. No herb should be dried at temperatures exceeding 100°F. Higher temperatures cause loss of the plant oils and may be responsible for flavor changes. Two common methods of drying are bag drying and tray drying.

Bag drying. Collect 8 to 12 stem tips about 4 to 8 inches long. Rinse the herbs with cold running water (only if they are dirty). Shake off excess water, and wrap with absorbent toweling. When the water has dried from the surface, place the herbs in a paper bag and tie loosely. Leave 1 or 2 inches of the stems exposed. Place the bag in a warm, dry location. When the leaves become brittle, snap them free of the stems and package them in an airtight container away from the light. When you are ready to use the leaves, pulverize by rubbing them between your hands. Leaving herbs whole preserves more of the flavor and aroma until they are used.

Tray drying. The preparation is the same for tray drying as for bag drying, except that the heavy stalks can be discarded before drying. Spread the leaves and tender stem tips one layer deep on drying trays. Put the trays in a dark, ventilated room. Turn the herbs every day to ensure uniform drying. When the leaves are dry and the stems tough, remove the leaves. Generally, the stem portions are discarded. Leaves are best packaged as nearly whole as possible. Allow the leaves to become very dry, and package in an airtight container away from the light.

The quality of herbs declines rapidly, especially in hot or brightly lighted conditions. Under proper conditions, the total shelf life of many herbs is only 1 or 2 years. When exposed to light, heat, and open air, the quality declines even more rapidly.

Microwave drying of most culinary herbs drives off too much of their flavor components to be successful. Decorative types for which flavor and aroma are not critical can be successfully dried in the microwave.

Here is an example of a small kitchen herb garden, only 36 square feet, that could supply most of the fresh herbs needed by an average household during the garden season, with enough left over to dry for winter use. If possible, the garden should be sited in a sunny spot near the kitchen door for easy, last-minute access. What a simple way to enliven and enhance your summer meals!

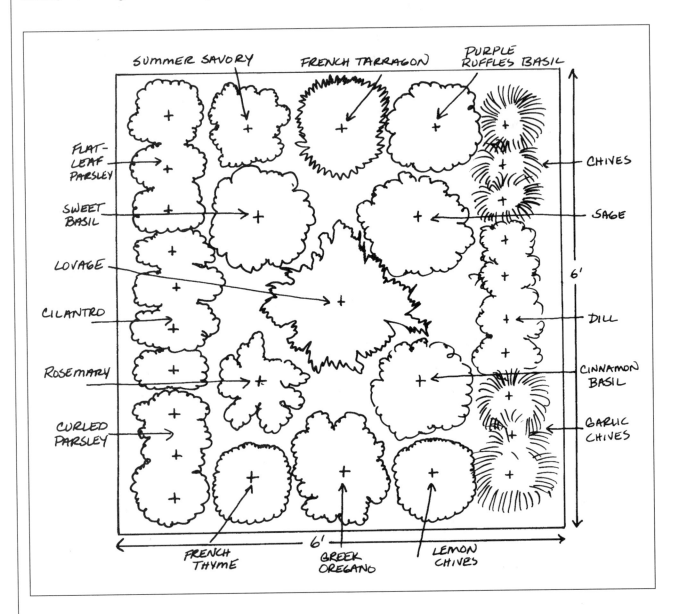

Additional Information

Appendix A: Storing Vegetables

When storing vegetables for later use, follow the recommendations given in the table below. Vegetables in the cold-moist and cool-moist groups may be stored in an old-fashioned outdoor pit, an underground cellar, or a specially designed interior storage area in the basement. Vegetables in the cold-dry and cool-dry groups may be stored in a cool area in a heated basement. Avoid water that may condense and drop from pipes of ceilings. Do not allow the vegetables to freeze.

Your vegetables will not improve in quality after they are harvested. For this reason, it is important to harvest them when they are at the proper stage of maturity. See "Major Vegetables," pages 51 to 130, for information about harvesting specific crops.

Vegetable	Storage temperature	Relative humidity	Storage period
Cold-moist group			
Asparagus	32°F	95%	2 weeks
Beet, topped	32°F	95%	1–3 months
Broccoli	32°F	95%	3 weeks
Brussels sprouts	32°F	95%	1 month
Cabbage, early	32°F	95%	3–6 weeks
Cabbage, late	32°F	95%	3–4 months
Carrot, topped	32°F	95%	4–6 months
Cauliflower	32°F	95%	2–3 weeks
Collard	32°F	95%	2–3 weeks
Corn, sweet	32°F	95%	4–8 days
Horseradish	32°F	95%	10–12 months
Kale	32°F	95%	2–3 weeks
Leek, green	32°F	95%	1–3 months
Lettuce	32°F	95%	2 weeks
Onion, green	32°F	95%	2–3 weeks
Parsnip	32°F	95%	2–6 months
Radish	32°F	95%	2–3 weeks
Turnip, greens	32°F	95%	2–3 weeks
Turnip, root	32°F	95%	4–5 months
Cool-moist group			
Bean, snap and wax	40°–45°F	90–95%	1 week
Bean, lima	40°–45°F	90–95%	1 week
Cucumber	45°–50°F	90–95%	10–14 days
Eggplant	45°–50°F	90%	1 week
Pepper, sweet	45°–50°F	90–95%	2–3 weeks
Potato, irish (late crop)	40°F	85–90%	4–6 months
Potato, sweet (after curing at 80° to 90°F for 10 days)	55°–60°F	85–90%	4–6 months
Squash, summer	45°–50°F	90%	7–10 days
Tomato (firm, colored)	60°–65°F	85–90%	4–7 days
Tomato (mature, green)	60°–65°F	85–90%	1–4 weeks
Watermelon	40°–50°F	80–85%	2–3 weeks
Cold-dry group			
Onion, dry	32°–35°F	60–70%	2-8 months
Onion, sets	32°–35°	60–70%	6 months
Shallot	32°–35°	60–70%	6–8 months
Cool-dry group			
Pumpkin	50°–55°F	60–70%	2 months
Squash, winter	50°–55°F	60–70%	2–4 months

To maintain quality after harvest, handle your vegetables carefully. Bruised or damaged vegetables decay easily. If not eaten immediately, asparagus, peas, sweet corn, and leafy crops should be cooled to below 40°F as soon as possible after harvest. Root crops (beets, carrots, parsnips, potatoes, salsify, and turnips) should not be washed if they are to be stored for extended periods. Washing may result in the development of soft rot.

Home Storage Facilities for Vegetables

Underground cellar (top) Vegetables in the cold-moist and cool-moist groups (cabbage, carrots, potatoes, and other root crops) can be stored in an underground cellar. This cellar also can be used as a storm shelter.

Outdoor pit (middle). Cross-section of an outdoor storage pit used for vegetables in the cold-moist and cool-moist groups. Place straw on the ground, and mound the vegetables on the straw. Cover with 6 inches of straw and at least 6 inches of soil. Leave an air vent to prevent overheating and place a 1-inch board on top of the pit.

Basement storage (bottom). The interior storage area (A) is used for storing vegetables in the cold-moist and cool-moist groups. This area, which is partitioned off from the central heated area, must be insulated and made vaporproof. Vegetables in the cold-dry and cool-dry groups (onion, pumpkins, shallots, and squash) may be stored on shelves outside the interior storage area (B).

Appendix B: Sprouting Seeds

Many different seeds can be sprouted and eaten. It is extremely important, however, to make sure you use only untreated seed for sprouting. Most seed intended for planting has been treated with fungicide, insecticide, or both to aid in successful germination in garden soil. None of these chemicals is particularly desirable in sprouts destined to be eaten. Adzuki, alfalfa, fenugreek, lentils, mung beans, wheat, and radish are among the seeds more commonly used for sprouting. They add variety and interest to winter and spring cooking and salads, each with a distinctive flavor.

Sprouting is a relatively easily accomplished operation. After all, it is what seeds are designed to do. Mung bean is one of the easier choices for beginners. Wash the seeds by placing them in a colander (with holes smaller than the seeds) and running water over the seeds. Any foreign matter and broken seeds should be removed. When seeds have been washed, put several spoonfuls in a widemouthed glass jar, and add cool water to fill the jar about half way. Allow the seeds to stand overnight in the upright jar, then drain, wash, and redrain. Cover the mouth of the jar with cheesecloth, fine plastic, or nylon screening, securing the netting with screw-on metal bands or rubber bands attached around the jar mouth. Set the jar on its side in a dark, relatively warm location. The seeds should be washed regularly, 2 to 3 times daily, each time draining the seeds and returning them to the jar. Light greens the sprouts, making them tough and strong in flavor. Sprouts of most seeds appear the third day at normal room temperature. When the sprouts have reached the desired size, they may be used immediately or stored in the refrigerator for several days in a closed plastic bag or box. Sprouts should be raised in fairly small batches for use rather quickly after sprouting is completed. As the skill of the sprouter increases, a wide variety of seeds lend nutritious and flavorful interest to salads, cooking, and other culinary delights.

Appendix C: Days from Flowering to Harvest for Selected Vegetables

Beans, lima (pod)	10–14
Beans, snap	6–8
Corn, pop-	75–80
Corn, sweet (after 10% of the silks appear)	18–21
Cucumber, slicing	8–10
Cucumber, pickling (varies with size desired)	3–10
Eggplant	40–50
Muskmelon	40–50
Peanut	80–90
Pea, shelling	8–10
Pea, sugar pod	5–7
Pea, snap	8–10
Pepper, green bell	40–45
Pepper, ripe (such as red, yellow, orange)	50–55
Pepper, sweet banana	30–35
Potato*	- - -
Pumpkin	40–60
Soybean, edible, green-shell stage	20–25
Squash, summer (zucchini and crookneck)	4–5
Squash, winter (note varietal differences)	40–60
Tomato	45–50
Watermelon	45–60

Factors that influence days to harvest:
Size preference
Temperature
Season
Pollination

*There is no relationship between flowering of potatoes or sweet potatoes and underground tuber or root development, as these are a function of day length.

List of Publications

Available from Information Services

1995 Illinois Urban Pest Management Handbook

Addresses concerns of people in the horticulture profession—lawn-care professionals, arborists, landscapers, nursery owners, and garden-supply store owners. Discusses pest and plant disease control in turfgrass, trees, shrubs, other ornamentals, home, and garden. Also, up-do-date information on pesticides. Revised annually. Order IPCU-95, $10, 256 pages.

Alternatives in Insect Management: Beneficial Insects and Mites

Describes biological control as an alternative to synthetic insecticides. 1990. Order C1298, $2, 25 pages.

Alternatives in Insect Management: Botanical Insecticides and Insecticidal Soaps

Discusses the origin of these insecticides and summarizes their most effective uses. Also examines the toxicity of botanical insecticides and commonly used synthetic pesticides. 1989. Order C1296, $2, 20 pages.

Alternatives in Insect Management: Insect Attractants and Traps

Explains how to use insect attractants and traps safely for determining the need for chemical control, timing control, or pest management directly through mass trapping or mating disruption. 1990. Order C1297, $2, 24 pages.

Biological Control of Insect Pests of Cabbage and Other Crucifers

Provides information on several natural enemies and offers practical advice on how to use beneficial organisms for pest management. 1993. Order NCR471, $8, 54 pages.

Controlling Weeds in the Home Garden

Describes various methods for controlling weeds, including cultivation, mechanical removal, mulching, and herbicide use. 1987. Order C1051, free (additional copies 50 cents), 11 pages.

Home Fruit Pest Control

Helps home gardeners keep pests from ruining their fruit. Discusses sprays and spraying schedules, and the prevention of mouse, rabbit, and bird damage. 1993. Order C1145-93, $1, 8 pages.

Hydroponics as a Hobby: Growing Plants without Soil

Discusses various systems, seed germination, nutrient solutions, and symptoms of nutrient deficiencies. Suggests experiments using soilless cultures. 1983. Order C844, free (additional copies $1), 18 pages.

Illinois Fruit and Vegetable Garden Schedule

Calendar format, can be used as a handy reference. Tells what tasks to perform in your garden during a particular week or month to help you achieve a bountiful harvest. 1986. Order C1262, $2, 40 pages.

Insect Traps for Home Fruit Insect Control

Addresses nonchemical insect control. Describes insect traps available and how to use them, their effectiveness in controlling specific insects, and where to obtain the traps. 1989. Order NCR359, $1.25, 8 pages.

Weeds of the North Central States

Describes and illustrates weeds commonly found in the north central region of the United States. Also discusses ways to identify weeds. Contains a glossary and index. 1988. Order B772, $5, 303 pages.

For a current catalog or to place an order, contact
University of Illinois
Information Services
67-BK Mumford Hall
1301 W. Gregory Dr.
Urbana, IL 61801
(217)333-2007
(217)244-7503 fax

Available from UI Department of Horticulture

Vegetable Crops

VC-1-80   1986 Commercial Vegetable Varieties for Plant Growers, revised January 1986, 4 pages.

VC-2-81   Garden Values for Vegetables and Small Fruits, revised October 1985, 2 pages.

VC-5-80   Organic Gardening and Soil Fertility, 2 pages.

VC-6-80   Making Compost for the Garden, revised October 1985, 4 pages.

VC-7-80   Fertilizer Guide for Market Gardeners in Illinois, revised February 1982, 4 pages.

VC-8-80   Conversion Tables for Fertilizer Calculations, revised February 1982, 4 pages.

VC-9-80   Fertilizing Your Vegetable Garden, revised September 1981, 4 pages.

VC-11-80   Harvesting Vegetables, 4 pages.

VC-14-82   Vegetable Planting Guide, 4 pages.

VC-15-81   Testing For and Deactivating Herbicide Residues, revised February 1983, 4 pages.

VC-16-82   Planting Vegetable Seeds, 4 pages.

VC-17-81   Micronutrient Applications for Vegetable Crops, 4 pages.

VC-18-82   Liming Vegetable Crops, 4 pages.

VC-19-82   Hydroponics, revised April 1985, 4 pages.

VC-21-82   Producing and Setting Out Vegetable Transplants, 4 pages.

VC-22-82   Training Tomato Plants, 4 pages.

VC-23-82   The Basics of Trickle Irrigation, 4 pages.

VC-24-82   Exhibiting Vegetables, revised May 1986, 4 pages.

VC-26-82   Fresh Market Mushroom Production, 4 pages.

VC-27-83   Storing Vegetables, 4 pages.

VC-28-83   The Fall Vegetable Garden, 2 pages.

VC-29-83   Ginseng, 4 pages.

VC-30-83   Commercial Muskmelon Production in Illinois, 4 pages.

VC-31-83   Harvesting and Drying Herbs, 4 pages.

VC-32-83   Sources of Herbs, 2 pages.

VC-34-86   Commercial Popcorn Production in Illinois, 4 pages.

VC-36-85   Selected Herbs for Illinois Gardens, 4 pages.

VC-37-85   Some Worthy Herbs for Illinois Gardens, 4 pages.

VC-38-85   Examining the Economics of Home Vegetable Gardening, 4 pages.

VC-39-85   Coldframes and Hotbeds, 4 pages.

VC-40-85   Asparagus and Rhubarb: Two Important Perennial Crops for the Home Vegetable Garden, 4 pages.

VC-41-85   Onions and Related Crops, 4 pages.

VC-42-86   Irish and Sweet Potatoes, 4 pages.

VC-43-85   Organic Gardening: Some Pros and Cons, 4 pages.

VC-44-93   Growing Herbs in the Home Garden, 5 pages.

Horticulture Marketing

HM-1-79   Pick-Your-Own Marketing of Fruits and Vegetables, 4 pages.

HM-2-79   Liability and Insurance for U-Pick Operations, 4 pages.

HM-3-79   Net Weights and Processed Yields of Fruits and Vegetables in Common Retail Units, 4 pages.

HM-4-80   Establishing a Community Farmers' Market, revised June 1987, 4 pages.

HM-5-82   Yields of Commercial Food Crops in Illinois, revised June 1987, 4 pages.

HM-6-82   Estimating the Trade Area and Potential Sales for a Pick-Your-Own Strawberry Farm, 2 pages.

A single fact sheet is free. Each additional one is 25 cents. The minimum order is $1, and orders must be prepaid. For a complete list of fact sheets or to order, write

Horticulture Facts
Department of Horticulture
University of Illinois
1105 Plant Sciences Laboratory
1201 S. Dorner Dr.
Urbana, IL 61801

Other Suggested Reading

Gardening

The Cook's Garden, Shepherd and Ellen Ogden; Rodale Press, Emmaus, PA, 1989, 230 pages.

Crockett's Victory Garden, James Underwood Crockett; Little, Brown, and Company, Boston, MA, 1977, 326 pages.

The New Organic Grower, Eliot Coleman; Chelsea Green, Chelsea, VT, 1989, 284 pages.

Square Foot Gardening, Mel Bartholomew; Rodale Press, Emmaus, PA, 1981, 347 pages.

Vegetable Gardening, David Chambers and Lucinda Mays; Pantheon Books, Knopf Publishing Group, New York, NY, 1994, 223 pages.

Heirloom Varieties

The Field and Garden Vegetables of America, Fearing Burr, Jr.; The American Botanist, Chillicothe, IL, 1994, 667 pages. (a 19th-century reprint)

The Heirloom Gardener, Carolyn Jabs; Sierra Club Books, San Francisco, CA, 1984, 310 pages.

Seed to Seed, Suzanne Ashworth (edited by Kent Whealy, photography by David Cavagnaro); Seed Savers Exchange, Decorah, IA, 1991, 222 pages.

Herbs

Growing Great Garlic, Ron L. Engeland; Filaree Productions, Okanogan, WA, 1991, 213 pages.

Herb Gardening in Five Seasons, Adelma Grenier Simmons; Viking-Penguin Books, New York, NY, 1983, 353 pages.

It's About Thyme, Marge Clark; Thyme Cookbooks, West Lebanon, IN, 1988, 318 pages.

Rodale's Illustrated Encyclopedia of Herbs, Claire Kowalchik and William H. Hylton, editors; Rodale Press, Emmaus, PA, 1987, 545 pages.

Spring and Summer Herbal Sampler, Pete Louquet, Tom Hamlin, and Don Haynie; MidValley Press, Raphine, VA, 1993, 80 pages.

Marketing

Backyard Market Gardening, Andrew W. Lee; Good Earth Publications, Burlington, VT, 1993, 351 pages.

Gardening for Profit, Peter Henderson; The American Botanist, Chillicothe, IL, 1991, 496 pages. (another 19th-century classic reprint)

Sell What You Sow, Eric L. Gibson; New World Publishing, Carmichael, CA, 1994, 302 pages.

Minor Vegetables

Manual of Minor Vegetables, James M. Stephens; Florida Cooperative Extension Service Bulletin SP-40, Gainesville, FL, 1988, 123 pages.

Oriental Vegetables, Joy Larkcom; Kodansha International, New York City, NY, 1991, 232 pages.

Unusual Vegetables, Anne Moyer Halpin; Rodale Press, Emmaus, PA, 1978, 443 pages.

Pests

Destructive and Useful Insects, C.L. Metcalf, W.P. Flint, and R. L. Metcalf; McGraw-Hill Book Company, New York, NY, 1962, 1,087 pages.

The Gardener's Bug Book, Cynthia Westcott; Doubleday & Company, Inc., Garden City, NY, 1956, 879 pages.

Plant Disease Handbook, Cynthia Westcott; Van Nostrand Reinhold Company, New York City, NY, 1971, 843 pages.

Starting Plants

The Seed-Starter's Handbook, Nancy Bubel; Rodale Press, Emmaus, PA, 1978, 363 pages.

The Solar Greenhouse Book, edited by James C. McCullagh; Rodale Press, Emmaus, PA, 1978, 328 pages.

Index of Common Names

acorn squash, 116

adzuki bean, 133

amaranth greens, 133

angelica, 150

anise, 150

anise hyssop, 150

apple, "love," 120

armenian cucumber, 145

artichoke, globe or jerusalem, 80

arugula, 133

asparagus, 51

asparagus bean, 135, 143

asparagus lettuce, 84

aubergine, 77

basil, 151

bay laurel or tree, 151

bean, 53, 133;
    adzuki, 133; asparagus, 135, 143; broad, 133;
    bush, 53; chestnut, 134; chinese, 134; chinese
    flowering, 134: dry, 53; fava, 133; four-angled, 135;
    garbanzo, 134; goa, 135; horse, 133; horticultural, 54;
    hyacinth, 134; indian, 134; italian, 53; lablab, 134;
    lima, 53; mung, 134; pharaoh, 134; pole, 53;
    romano, 53; runner, 53; shellout, 53; snap, 53; soy(-),
    134; soya, 134; string, 53; wax, 53; wild field, 134;
    windsor, 133; winged, 135; yard-long, 135, 143

bee balm, 152

beet, 56

belgium endive, 136

bell pepper, 97

bergamot, 151

berry, poha, 139

bitter melon, 144

black salsify, 110

black-eyed pea, 143

blood turnip, 56

bok choy chinese cabbage, 68

borage, 151

borecole, 81

broad bean, 133

"broccoflower," 64

broccoli, 57

brussels sprouts, 59

burdock, 135

burr gherkin, 148

burnet, salad, 160

"burr" cucumber, 77

bush bean, 53

butterhead lettuce, 84

cabbage, 60;
    celery, 68; chinese, 68; flowering, 62; napa, 68;
    nonheading, 69; tree-, 69; white mustard, 68

calabaza, 144

calabrese, 57

cantaloupe, 86

caraway, 152

carrot, 63

catnip, 152

cauliflower, 64

cee gwa, 145

celeriac, 136

celery, 66;
    german, knob, or turnip-rooted, 136

celery cabbage, 68

celery root, 136

chamomile, 153

chard, 67;
    swiss, 56, 67

cherry, ground, 139

chervil, 153

chestnut bean, 134

chickpea, 134

chicory, 136;
    leaf, 142; witloof, 136

chile, 97

chinese bean, 134

chinese cabbage, 68

chinese cucumber, 145

chinese flowering bean, 134

chinese okra, 145

chinese parsley, 154

chinese pumpkin, 104, 145

chinese radish, 108

chinese spinach, 133

chives, 153

choke, sun, 80

chung choy, 146

chung gwa, 146

cicely, sweet, 161

cilantro, 154

collard, 69

corn, sweet, 70

coriander, 154

Cos lettuce, 84

cowpea, 95

cress, 137

crisphead lettuce, 84

crowder pea, 143

cucumber, 75;
    armenian, 145; "burr," 77; chinese, 145; syrian, 145;
    turkish, 145; yard-long, 145

cucuzzi gourd, 145

dandelion, 137;
    italian, 136

dill, 154

doan gwa, 146

dry bean, 53

earth nut, 140

eggplant, 77

egyptian onion, 93

egyptian pea, 134

elephant garlic, 155

endive, 79;
    belgium or french, 136

english pea, 95

escarole, 79

fava bean, 133

fennel, 155

field bean, wild, 134

finocchio, 155

flat-leaf parsley, 93

florence fennel, 155

flowering cabbage, 62

foo gwa, 144

four-angled bean, 135

french endive, 136

french sorrel, 161

french tarragon, 162

fuzzy gourd, 146

garbanzo bean, 134

garden beet, 56

garden cress, 137

garden huckleberry, 137

garden pea, 95

garlic, 155

garlic chives, 153

geranium, scented, 156

german celery, 136

german chamomile, 153

gherkin, 146;
    burr, 146; West Indian, 77, 146

globe artichoke, 80

goa bean, 135

gobu, 135

goober pea, 140

gourd, 113, 138;
    cucuzzi, 145; fuzzy, 146

greek oregano, 158

greens, amaranth, 133

greens, mustard, 88

ground cherry, 139

guinea squash, 77

gumbo, 88

hon-toi-moi, 133

horehound, 156

horse bean, 133

horseradish, 139, 156

horticultural bean, 54

hot pepper, 97

huckleberry, garden, 137

husk tomato, 139

hyacinth bean, 134

hyssop, 156

hyssop, anise, 150

indian bean, 134

irish potato, 101

italian bean, 53

italian broccoli, 57

italian dandelion, 136

italian marrow, 112

jerusalem artichoke, 80

kale, 81

kee chi, 145

kohlrabi, 82

knob celery, 136

lablab bean, 134

laurel, bay, 151

lavender, 157

leaf chicory, 142

leaf lettuce, 84

leaf mustard, 88

leek, 83

lemon balm, 157

lemon verbena, 157

lettuce, 84

lima bean, 53

loose-leaf lettuce, 84

lovage, 157

"love apple," 120

mangel, 56

mango, 97

mao gwa, 146

marjoram, sweet, 161

marrow, 112

melon,
bitter, 144; pickling, 146; sweet, 146; water(-), 129;
winter, 146; "winter," 86
mexican parsley, 154
michihli chinese cabbage, 68
mint, 158
moss-curled parsley, 93
multiplier onion, 93, 143
mung bean, 134
muskmelon, 86
mustard cabbage, white, 68
mustard, (greens), 88
napa chinese cabbage, 68
New Zealand spinach, 112
ngau pong, 135
nonheading cabbage, 69
nung gwa, 145
nut, earth, 140
okra, 88;
chinese, 145
onion, 89;
egyptian, 93; multiplier, 93, 143; "potato," 93;
walking, 93; winter, 93
oregano, 158
oyster plant, 110
pak choi chinese cabbage, 68
parsley, 93;
chinese, 154; flat-leaf, 93; mexican, 154;
moss-curled, 93; root, 93; triple-curled, 93
parsnip, 94
pe tsai chinese cabbage, 68
pea, 95;
black-eyed, 143; cow(-), 143; crowder, 143;
egyptian, 134; english, 95; garden, 95; goober, 140;
snap, 95; snow, 95; southern, 95, 143; sugar, 95
peanut, 140
pepper, 97
pepper, white, 133
peppermint, 157
pharaoh bean, 134
Physalis, 139
pickling melon, 146
pie plant, 108
pigweed, 133
pimento pepper, 98
poha berry, 139
pole bean, 53
popcorn, 140
potato, (irish), 101

"potato onion," 93
potato, "straw," 102
"potomato," 127
pumpkin, 103, 113;
chinese, 104, 145
radicchio, 142
radish, 107
red beet, 56
rhubarb, 108
rocket salad, 133
romaine lettuce, 84
roman chamomile, 152
romano bean, 53
root parsley, 93
roquette, 133
rosemary, 159
rue, 159
runner bean, 53
russian tarragon, 162
rutabaga, 127
sage, 159
salad burnet, 160
salsify, 110
savory, 160
scorzonera, 110
shallot, 142
shellout bean, 53
snap bean, 53
snap pea, 95
snow pea, 95
sorrel, french, 161
southern pea, 95, 143
soya bean or soybean, 134
spaghetti squash, 116, 143
spaghetti, vegetable 143
spearmint, 158
spinach, 110;
chinese, 133; mustard, 88; New Zealand, 112
sprouting broccoli, 57
sprouts, brussels, 59
squash,
acorn, 116; guinea, 77; spaghetti, 116, 143;
summer, 112; sweet-potato, 116; winter, 113, 116
stem lettuce, 84
stem turnip, 82
stock beet, 56
"straw potato," 102
strawberry tomato, 139
string bean, 53

sugar beet, 56
sugar pea, 95
summer savory, 160
summer squash, 112
sun choke, 80
sunberry, 137
sunflower, 144
sunroot, 80
swede turnip, 127
sweet cicely, 161
sweet corn, 70
sweet marjoram, 161
sweet melon, 146
sweet potato, 118
sweet-potato squash, 116
sweet woodruff, 162
swiss chard, 56, 67
syrian cucumber, 145
table beet, 56
tampala, 133
tarragon, 162
thyme, 163
tomatillo, 140
tomato, 120;
    husk or strawberry, 139
topato, 127
tree, bay, 151
tree tomato, 126
tree-cabbage, 69
triple-curled parsley, 93
turkish cucumber, 145
turnip, 127;
    blood, 56; stem, 82; swede, 127
turnip-rooted celery, 136
vegetable marrow, 112
vegetable oyster, 110
vegetable spaghetti, 143
vine crops, 75, 86, 103, 112, 116, 138, 143, 144
walking onion, 93
watercress, 137
watermelon, 129
wax bean, 53
West Indian gherkin, 77, 146
white mustard, 88
white mustard cabbage, 68
white pepper, 133
wild field bean, 134
windsor bean, 133
winged bean, 135

winter cress, 137
"winter melon," 86
winter melon, (true), 146
winter onion, 93
winter savory, 160
winter squash, 113, 116
witloof chicory, 136
wonderberry, 137
wong bok chinese cabbage, 68
woodruff, sweet, 162
yam, 118
yard-long bean, 135, 143
yard-long cucumber, 145
zucchini, 115

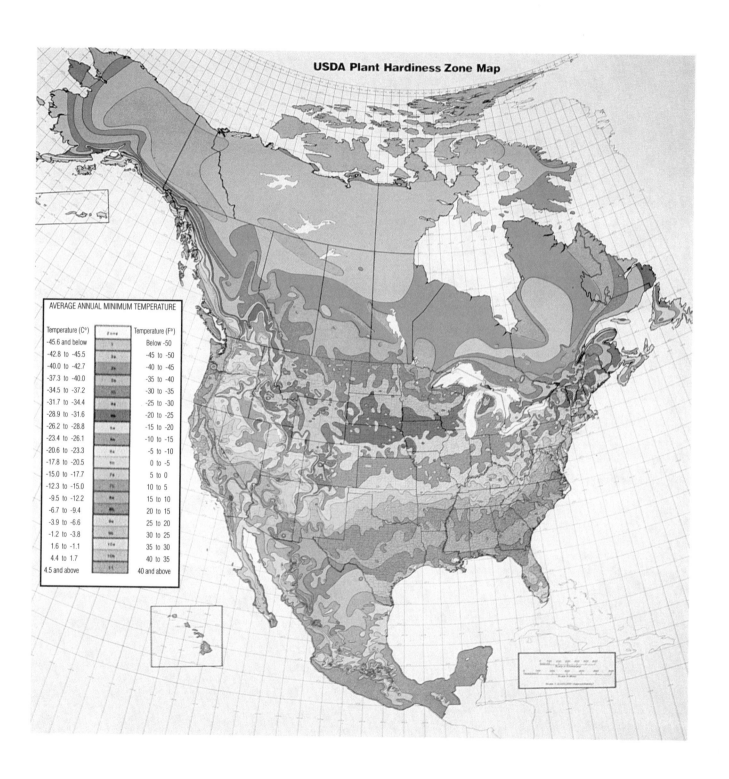

USDA Plant Hardiness Zone Map

AVERAGE ANNUAL MINIMUM TEMPERATURE

Temperature (C°)	Zone	Temperature (F°)
-45.6 and below		Below -50
-42.8 to -45.5		-45 to -50
-40.0 to -42.7		-40 to -45
-37.3 to -40.0		-35 to -40
-34.5 to -37.2		-30 to -35
-31.7 to -34.4		-25 to -30
-28.9 to -31.6		-20 to -25
-26.2 to -28.8		-15 to -20
-23.4 to -26.1		-10 to -15
-20.6 to -23.3		-5 to -10
-17.8 to -20.5		0 to -5
-15.0 to -17.7		5 to 0
-12.3 to -15.0		10 to 5
-9.5 to -12.2		15 to 10
-6.7 to -9.4		20 to 15
-3.9 to -6.6		25 to 20
-1.2 to -3.8		30 to 25
1.6 to -1.1		35 to 30
4.4 to 1.7		40 to 35
4.5 and above		40 and above